David Chappell's *Understanding .NET, Second Edition*

"David Chapp [...] *ding .NET, Second Edition,* contains excellent coverage
of the CLR, cl [...] NET, ADO.NET, and distributed applications. It is still the
best technical [...] ET to date, and I recommend it to anyone making the
transition to .

—Dave Corun
Director of Microsoft Technologies
Catalyst IT Services

"David's coverage of all things .NET is extensive and thorough. Even regular users of
Visual Studio will learn something about .NET that they didn't know."

—Harry Pierson
Architecture Strategy Team
Microsoft Corporation

"*Understanding .NET, Second Edition,* will give managers the knowledge and vocabu-
lary they need to communicate with their developers. Developers looking to obtain a
high-level view of the .NET Framework before going into each topic in depth will also
benefit from this book. This book helps developers get a bird's-eye view of .NET
Framework before they engage in the long learning curve required. This book is very
well organized and technically accurate."

—Cesar Bermudez
MCAD, MCSD, MCDBA, MCSA, MCSE, MCTS, MCT, A+, i-Net+, CIW
President
DotNet Architects, Inc.

"David Chappell has an astute understanding of Microsoft technology and an ability
to explain complex systems in a way that is both enticing and thoroughly educational.
The second edition of his book, *Understanding .NET,* shows that he remains one of
the best technology authors in the business."

—Richard Monson-Haefel
Author and Senior Industry Analyst
Burton Group

Understanding .NET
Second Edition

Independent Technology Guides

David Chappell, Series Editor

The **Independent Technology Guides** offer serious technical descriptions of important new software technologies of interest to enterprise developers and technical managers. These books focus on how that technology works and what it can be used for, taking an independent perspective rather than reflecting the position of any particular vendor. These are ideal first books for developers with a wide range of backgrounds, the perfect place to begin mastering a new area and laying a solid foundation for further study. They also go into enough depth to enable technical managers to make good decisions without delving too deeply into implementation details.

The books in this series cover a broad range of topics, from networking protocols to development platforms, and are written by experts in the field. They have a fresh design created to make learning a new technology easier. All titles in the series are guided by the principle that, in order to use a technology well, you must first understand how and why that technology works.

Titles in the Series

Brian Arkills, *LDAP Directories Explained: An Introduction and Analysis*, 0-201-78792-X

David Chappell, *Understanding .NET: A Tutorial and Analysis*, 0-201-74162-8

Eric Newcomer, *Understanding Web Services: XML, WSDL, SOAP, and UDDI*, 0-201-75081-3

For more information check out www.awprofessional.com

Understanding .NET

Second Edition

David Chappell

✦Addison-Wesley

Upper Saddle River, NJ ■ Boston ■ Indianapolis ■ San Francisco
New York ■ Toronto ■ Montreal ■ London ■ Munich ■ Paris ■ Madrid
Capetown ■ Sydney ■ Tokyo ■ Singapore ■ Mexico City

Many of the designations used by manufacturers and sellers to distinguish their products are claimed as trademarks. Where those designations appear in this book, and the publisher was aware of a trademark claim, the designations have been printed with initial capital letters or in all capitals.

The author and publisher have taken care in the preparation of this book, but make no expressed or implied warranty of any kind and assume no responsibility for errors or omissions. No liability is assumed for incidental or consequential damages in connection with or arising out of the use of the information or programs contained herein.

The publisher offers excellent discounts on this book when ordered in quantity for bulk purchases or special sales, which may include electronic versions and/or custom covers and content particular to your business, training goals, marketing focus, and branding interests. For more information, please contact:

> U.S. Corporate and Government Sales
> (800) 382-3419
> corpsales@pearsontechgroup.com

For sales outside the United States please contact:

> International Sales
> international@pearsoned.com

This Book Is Safari Enabled

Safari BOOKS ONLINE ENABLED
The Safari® Enabled icon on the cover of your favorite technology book means the book is available through Safari Bookshelf. When you buy this book, you get free access to the online edition for 45 days.

Safari Bookshelf is an electronic reference library that lets you easily search thousands of technical books, find code samples, download chapters, and access technical information whenever and wherever you need it.

To gain 45-day Safari Enabled access to this book:

- Go to http://www.awprofessional.com/safarienabled
- Complete the brief registration form
- Enter the coupon code MPIY-UJDH-HGP7-SUHT-TYYN

If you have difficulty registering on Safari Bookshelf or accessing the online edition, please e-mail customer-service@safaribooksonline.com.

Visit us on the Web: www.awprofessional.com

Library of Congress Cataloging-in-Publication Data
Chappell, David (David Wayne)
    Understanding .NET / David Chappell. — 2nd ed.
        p. cm.
    Includes bibliographical references and index.
    ISBN 0-321-19404-7 (pbk. : alk. paper)
1.   Microsoft .NET Framework. 2.   Internet programming. 3.   Computer software Development. I.   Title.

    QA76.76.M52C48 2006
    005.2'768—dc22   2006009715

ISBN 0-321-19404-7

Text printed in the United States on recycled paper at RR Donnelley in Crawfordsville, Indiana.

First printing, May 2006

To Ava and Lauren, jewels in the night.

Contents

Preface

Writing the preface for a book's second edition is fun—it means that people thought the first edition was useful enough to warrant an update. .NET has changed in significant ways since this book first appeared in 2002, changes that are reflected in this new edition. Since its original release, the .NET Framework has become the foundation for a new generation of Windows applications. Developers and the people who pay their salaries stepped up to the challenge of adopting this new environment, and the result has been better software.

Still, new people come to .NET every day. Like the first edition, the goal of this book is to help developers and their managers understand this big new world.

Who This Book Is For

.NET is huge. There are plenty of books that provide detailed examinations of each facet of this enormous technology crystal, plenty of books with hardcore, hands-on information. This isn't one of those books. I believe strongly that understanding .NET as a whole is essential before delving more deeply into any single part of the technology. Accordingly, my goal here is to provide a broad overview of the .NET technologies.

If you're looking for a big-picture introduction to the whole of .NET, this book is for you. Whether you're a developer just getting started with .NET, a technical manager who needs to make decisions about these technologies, or a student seeing some of these ideas for the first time, this book should be a useful guide. There is enough detail here to satisfy many people completely, while others will use this book as a stepping-stone to more specific knowledge. In any case, I hope the book's organization and content make it easier for you to come to grips with this mass of technology.

Fact and Opinion

Grasping a new technology requires learning the fundamentals. What are its main parts? How do they work? How do they fit together? But really understanding a technology requires more than this. You need to know not just how things work but also why they're important, how they compare to what's gone before, and what might happen next.

This book aims at providing all of these things. In the text itself, I've tried hard to remain strictly tutorial, focusing solely on describing what .NET is. In the perspective boxes, I give some broader views on various aspects of the technology. In every case, the perspective expresses my view of why things are the way they are or what the future is likely to hold. By separating the objective from the subjective, I hope to make it easier for you to distinguish between the two. By providing opinion as well as fact, I hope to make this book both more interesting and more enlightening.

Acknowledgments

I'm once again humbled by the willingness of people to help with projects like this. For this second edition, thanks go especially to my reviewers: Harry Pierson at Microsoft, Richard Monson-Haefel of the Burton Group, and Dave Corun at Catalyst IT Services. They all read every chapter and made many useful suggestions. Thanks also to Ralph Squillace and Ted Pattison, who answered key questions at important moments. Everybody who helped with the first edition once again has my heartfelt thanks: Bob Beauchemin, Keith Brown, Cori Day, Ted Demopoulos, Bill Estrem, Jeannine Gailey, Kit George, Greg Hack, Rob Howard, Maxim Loukianov, Juval Löwy, Peter McKiernan, Yahya H. Mirza, John D. Mitchell, Christophe Nassare, Eric Newcomer, David Sceppa, Aaron Skonnard, and Mike Woodring.

At Addison-Wesley I'm grateful to Elizabeth Peterson, Stephane Nakib, Jana Jones, and Karen Gettman for all they've done for me and for the Independent Technology Guides series. I'm also thankful for the efforts of Kristin Weinberger, first my editor, now my friend and (remarkably) neighbor, who originally brought me to Addison-Wesley, and for the hard work of Nancy Hendryx, the copy editor for this edition.

The list of acknowledgements in this book's first edition ended with Diana Catignani, pointing out how much poorer my life would be without her. She's now Diana Chappell, mother of our two beautiful daughters. Words cannot express the poverty that would ensue were she not my wife.

David Chappell
San Francisco
March 2006

1

Introducing .NET

What's required to create good software? While it's possible to write first-rate code in almost any environment, creating good software is much easier when the right platform and tools are available. For most Windows developers today, that platform is defined by .NET. While defining .NET clearly was once a challenge, it's now clear that the .NET label refers primarily to two things. They are:

The .NET Framework and Visual Studio are the main components of .NET

- *The .NET Framework,* which consists of the *Common Language Runtime (CLR)* and the *.NET Framework class library.* The CLR provides a standard foundation for building applications, while the .NET Framework class library offers a large set of standard classes and other types that can be used by any .NET Framework application written in any language.

- *Visual Studio,* an integrated development environment (IDE) for creating Windows applications. While this tool can be used to build software that runs directly on

1

▦ Perspective: .NET's Naming Journey

It makes sense today to think of the name ".NET" as primarily referring to the .NET Framework and Visual Studio. Things weren't always so simple, however. When .NET was first announced in the summer of 2000, Microsoft applied the term to a broad range of things. Today's .NET technologies were included, of course, but so were several other things. Many of Microsoft's server products, including SQL Server and BizTalk Server, were grouped together as the *.NET Enterprise Servers*, for example, and a wholly separate effort eventually known as *.NET My Services* was launched. There was even talk about a possible Windows .NET and Office .NET sometime in the future.

But was there a common technical underpinning for all of these things? Sadly, the answer was no. When Microsoft first sprang .NET on the world, it treated the term as a broad brand, one that could be applied to pretty much anything the company was doing. The result was a good deal of confusion among Microsoft's customers.

Thankfully, the story has gotten much simpler. The .NET Enterprise Servers are now considered part of the Windows Server System, and so they've lost the .NET tag. .NET My Services faded from the scene, while the branding boffins in Redmond decided against tacking the .NET brand onto either Windows or Office. Today, when somebody says ".NET," they're referring to the .NET Framework and Visual Studio.

Windows, its main focus is helping developers create .NET Framework applications. Visual Studio supports several programming languages for creating these applications, including C#[1], Visual Basic (VB), and C++.

Various versions exist for both of these technologies. The versions described in this book are those released by Microsoft

---

1. Pronounced "C sharp," as in the musical note.

in late 2005: version 2.0 of the .NET Framework and Visual Studio 2005.

The .NET Framework

The heart of .NET is the .NET Framework. First released in 2002, it brought enormous change to the lives of those who write Windows software and the people who manage them. Figure 1-1 shows the Framework's two main parts: the CLR and the .NET Framework class library. A .NET application always uses the CLR, and it can also use whatever parts of the class library it requires.

The .NET Framework is a foundation for creating Windows applications

Every application written using the Framework depends on the CLR. Among other things, the CLR provides a common set of data types, acting as a foundation for C#, VB, and all other languages that target the .NET Framework. Because this foundation is the same no matter which language they choose, developers see a more consistent environment.

The CLR provides a common basis for all .NET languages

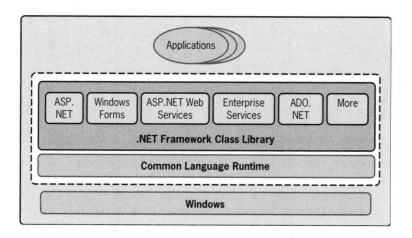

Figure 1-1   The .NET Framework consists of the Common Language Runtime (CLR) and the .NET Framework class library.

▪ Perspective: The .NET Framework vs. the Java Environment

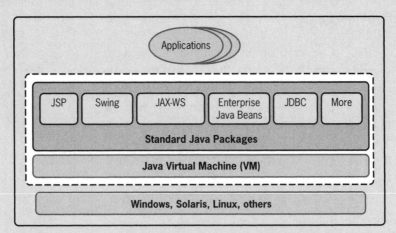

Mainstream software development today has split largely into two camps. Microsoft, promoting the .NET Framework, is in one, while most other vendors backing the Java environment are in the other. Each technology has its fans and detractors, and each has a substantial installed base today.

These competing worlds are strikingly similar. To see how similar, compare the figure above with Figure 1-1. Both environments support the same kinds of applications, and both provide a large standard library to help build those applications. The Java library, mostly known today as Java 2 Enterprise Edition (J2EE or just JEE) includes Java Server Pages (JSP) for Web scripting, Swing for building GUIs, JAX-WS (formerly JAX-RPC) for Web services–based communication, Enterprise JavaBeans (EJB) for building scalable server applications, JDBC for database access, and other classes. These technologies are analogous to the .NET Framework's ASP.NET, Windows Forms, ASP.NET Web Services, Enterprise Services, and ADO.NET, respectively. The Java virtual machine is also much like the .NET Framework's CLR, and even the semantics of the dominant languages—Microsoft's C# and VB vs. Java—are quite similar.

There are also differences, of course. One obvious distinction between the two is that the Java environment runs on diverse operating systems, while the .NET Framework focuses on Windows. The trade-off here is clear: Portability is good, but it prevents tight integration with any one system, and integration is also good. You can't have everything, at least not all at the same time. Also, Java-based products are available from multiple vendors, while only Microsoft provides the .NET Framework. Different Java vendors can provide different extensions to the core specifications, so developers can get somewhat locked into a single vendor. Still, portability across different Java platforms is possible, while the .NET Framework unambiguously ties your application to Microsoft.

This bifurcation and the competition it engenders are ultimately a good thing. Both camps have had good ideas, and each has borrowed from the other. Having one completely dominant technology, whether the .NET Framework or Java, would produce a stultifying monopoly, while having a dozen viable choices would lead to anarchy. Two strong competitors, each working to outdo the other, is just right.

Applications written in any .NET language can use the code in the .NET Framework class library. Among the most important technologies provided in this library are the following:

The .NET Framework class library provides standard code for common functions

- **ASP.NET:** Classes focused on building browser-accessible applications.

- **Windows Forms:** Classes for building Windows graphical user interfaces (GUIs) in any CLR-based programming language.

- **ASP.NET Web Services (also called ASMX):** Classes for creating applications that communicate with other applications using Web services.

- **Enterprise Services:** Classes that provide distributed transactions, object instance control, and other services useful for building reliable, scalable applications.

- **ADO.NET:** Classes focused on accessing data stored in relational database management systems (DBMS).

The .NET Framework class library contains much more than this short list indicates. Among the other services it provides are support for creating and working with XML documents, a variety of security services, and mechanisms for interoperating with applications built using older Windows technologies such as the Component Object Model (COM).

The .NET Framework supports various kinds of applications

As this short description suggests, the .NET Framework class library can be used to create many different types of applications. And because all of the services in this library are built on the CLR, applications can combine them as needed. A browser application built using ASP.NET, for example, might use ADO.NET to access stored data and Enterprise Services to perform distributed transactions.

A .NET Framework application consists of managed code

Software that uses the .NET Framework (and thus relies on the CLR) is referred to as *managed code*. As Figure 1-2 shows, an application can be built solely from managed code, relying entirely on the CLR and the relevant parts of the .NET Framework class library. An application can also be built from a combination of managed code and ordinary unmanaged code, with the two interacting as necessary. This second option, shown on the

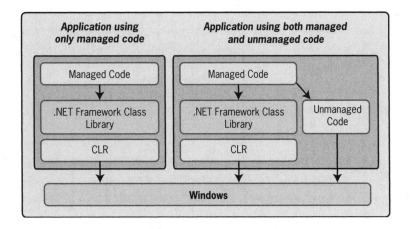

Figure 1-2   An application can be built entirely from managed code or from a combination of managed and unmanaged code.

right side of the figure, is especially important for existing applications. Most new Windows applications created today are built wholly in managed code, but it can also be useful to extend pre-.NET applications with managed code. And although it's not shown in the figure, it's still possible to create new Windows applications entirely in unmanaged code—using the .NET Framework isn't obligatory.

Managed code is typically object-oriented, so the objects it creates and uses are known as *managed objects.* A managed object can use and inherit from another managed object even if the two are written in different languages. This fact is a key part of what makes the .NET Framework class library an effective foundation: Objects written in any CLR-based language can inherit and use the class library's code. Given the fundamental role played by the CLR, understanding the .NET Framework begins with understanding this runtime environment.

Managed code is typically built using managed objects

The Common Language Runtime

Built from scratch to support modern applications, the CLR embodies a current view of what a programming environment should be. While it's hard to claim complete originality for any idea in computer science today, it is fair to say that this essential .NET technology takes an interesting new approach to programming languages.

What the CLR Defines

Think about how a programming language is typically defined. Each language commonly has its own unique syntax, its own set of control structures, a unique set of data types, its own notions of how classes inherit from one another, and much more. The choices a language designer makes are driven by the target applications for the language, who its users are meant to be, and the designer's own sensibilities.

There's widespread agreement on the features a modern programming language should offer

Yet most people agree on much of what a modern general-purpose programming language should provide. While opinions

Looking Backward: Windows DNA and COM

For most of the 1990s, application developers in the Microsoft environment relied on a set of technologies that became known as *Windows DNA*. Those technologies included the Component Object Model (COM) and Distributed COM (DCOM), a larger group of COM-based technologies known collectively as COM+, support for creating browser applications using Active Server Pages (ASP), data access support with ActiveX Data Objects (ADO), and others. The most commonly used languages for building Windows DNA applications were VB and C++, both supported by earlier versions of Visual Studio.

Tens of thousands of applications based on these technologies are in production today, providing solid evidence of Windows DNA's success. Yet the technologies Windows DNA includes were developed independently over a period of several years. Because of this, the integration among them wasn't as complete as it might have been. For example, while the Windows DNA environment let developers use various programming languages, each language has its own run-time libraries, its own data types, its own approach to building GUIs, and other differences. Applications written in different languages also accessed system services in different ways. C++ applications could make direct calls to the operating system through the Win32 interface, for instance, while VB applications typically accessed these services indirectly. These differences made life challenging for developers working in more than one language. COM, by defining common conventions for interfaces, data types, and other aspects of interaction among different software, was effectively the duct tape that held this complex environment together.

By providing a common foundation that can be used from all languages, the .NET Framework significantly simplified life for Windows developers. Applications built on the .NET Framework don't face many of the problems that COM addresses—.NET Framework applications all use the CLR, for example, which defines a common approach to interfaces and other data types—and so the glue between different languages that COM provides is no longer necessary. This is why COM technology isn't used in building pure .NET Framework applications. Instead, developers can build software that interacts in a more natural and substantially simpler way.

For the most part, the arrival of the .NET Framework was the death knell for Windows DNA and COM. It's taken quite a while for organizations to migrate to the new world of .NET, and many applications built with these older Windows technologies are still in production. Still, with few exceptions, serious new Windows development today uses .NET, not Windows DNA.

on syntax differ—some developers love curly braces, others abhor them—there's widespread agreement on what semantics a language should offer. Given this, why not define a standard implementation of those semantics, then allow different syntaxes to be used to express those semantics?

The CLR defines a common set of semantics that is used by multiple languages

The CLR provides this standard implementation. By providing a common set of data types such as integers, strings, classes, and interfaces, specifications for how inheritance works, and much more, it defines a common set of semantics for languages built on it. The CLR says nothing about syntax, however. How a language looks, whether it contains curly braces or semicolons or anything else, is entirely up to the language designer. While it is possible to implement languages with varying behaviors on top of the CLR, the CLR itself provides a consistent, modern set of semantics for a language designer to build on.

The CLR also provides other common services

Along with its standard types, the CLR provides other fundamental services. Those services include the following:

- Garbage collection, which automatically frees managed objects that are no longer referenced.

- A standard format for metadata, information about each type that's stored with the compiled code for that type.

- A common format, called *assemblies*, for organizing compiled code. An assembly can consist of one or more Dynamic Link Libraries (DLLs) and/or executables (EXEs), and it includes the metadata for the classes it contains.

A single application might use code from one or more assemblies, and so each assembly can specify other assemblies on which it depends.

Using the CLR

The CLR supports many different programming languages

The CLR was not defined with any particular programming language in mind. Instead, its features are derived largely from popular existing languages, such as C++, the pre-.NET version of VB, and Java. Today, Microsoft provides several CLR-based languages, including C#, the .NET version of VB, an extended

▪ Perspective: Standardizing C# and the CLR

C# and a subset of the CLR called the Common Language Infrastructure (CLI) are now official international standards. Microsoft originally submitted them to the ECMA standards organization, and they've also been approved by the International Organization for Standardization (ISO). Along with C#, the standardized technologies include the syntax and semantics for metadata, MSIL (rechristened the Common Intermediate Language, or CIL), and parts of the .NET Framework class library. For more details on exactly what has been submitted and its current status, see http://msdn.microsoft.com/net/ecma.

The biggest effect of establishing C# and the CLI as standards is to let others more easily implement these technologies. The most visible non-Microsoft implementation of .NET is surely the Mono project (http://www.mono-project .com). Mono's ambitious goal is to implement at least a large part of what Microsoft has given to ECMA, including a C# compiler and the CLI, along with other parts of the .NET Framework. Mono's creators say that they were attracted to the CLR for technical reasons, which must please Microsoft. (In fact, it's possible to view the CLI as the specification of a system, while .NET's CLR is just the Microsoft implementation of this specification.) Now led by Novell, the Mono project qualifies as a success in many ways, with implementations available for Linux and other operating systems. If nothing else, I admire the ambition and ability of the people who created it.

version of C++, and others. Third parties also provide languages built on the CLR.

No matter what language it's written in, all managed code is compiled into *Microsoft Intermediate Language (MSIL)* rather than a machine-specific binary. MSIL (also referred to as just IL) is a set of CPU-independent instructions for performing typical operations such as loading and storing information and calling methods. Each DLL and EXE in an assembly contains MSIL rather than processor-specific code. Installing a .NET Framework application on your system really means copying to your disk files that contain MSIL rather than a machine-specific binary. When the application is executed, MSIL is transformed into native code before it's executed.

Managed code is always compiled first into MSIL

Figure 1-3 illustrates the process of compiling and executing managed code. Source code written in VB, C#, or another language that targets the CLR is first transformed into MSIL by the appropriate language compiler. As the figure shows, the compiler

Each method is typically JIT compiled the first time it's invoked

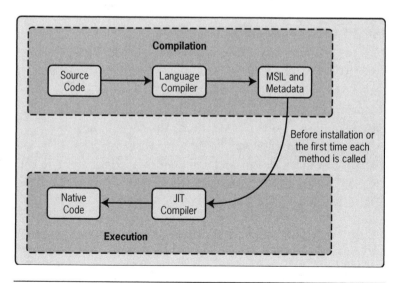

Figure 1-3   All managed code is compiled first to MSIL, then translated into native code before execution.

also produces metadata that's stored in the same file as the MSIL. Before execution, this MSIL is compiled into native code for the processor on which the code will run. By default, each method in a running application is compiled the first time that method is called. Because the method is compiled just in time to execute it, this approach is called *just in-time (JIT)* compilation.

All .NET Framework–based languages have about the same level of performance

One point worth noting is that any language built on the CLR should exhibit roughly the same performance as any other CLR-based language. Unlike the pre-.NET world, where the performance difference between VB and C++ was sometimes significant, a .NET Framework application written in C# isn't noticeably faster than the same application written in VB. While some compilers may produce better MSIL code than others, large variations in execution speed are unlikely.

The CLR is the foundation of everything else in the .NET Framework. All code in the .NET Framework class library depends on it, as do all Framework-based applications. Chapter 2 provides a more detailed look at the technology of the CLR.

The .NET Framework Class Library

The .NET Framework class library can be used from any CLR-based language

The .NET Framework class library is exactly what its name suggests: a library of classes and other types that developers can use to make their lives easier. While these classes are themselves written in C#, they can be used from any CLR-based language. Code written in C#, VB, C++, or any other language supported by the .NET Framework can create instances of these classes and call their methods. That code can also rely on the CLR's support for inheritance to inherit from the library's classes.

Surveying the Library

The .NET Framework class library is organized as a tree

The contents of the .NET Framework class library are organized into a tree of namespaces. Each namespace can contain types, such as classes and interfaces, and other namespaces. Figure 1-4

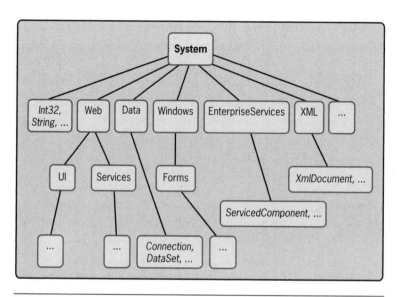

Figure 1-4   The .NET Framework class library is structured as a hierarchy of namespaces, with the System namespace at the root.

The .NET Compact Framework

While the .NET Framework is useful for writing applications on desktops and server machines, it can also be used with smaller devices, such as mobile phones, PDAs, and set-top boxes. Small devices are becoming more and more important, and they're an important piece of Microsoft's overall business strategy. These devices typically have less memory, however, so they're unable to run the complete .NET Framework. The .NET Compact Framework addresses this issue. By eliminating some parts of the .NET Framework class library, it allows use of the Framework in smaller devices.

The .NET Compact Framework targets the Windows CE operating system, but because it's built on the same foundation used in larger systems, developers can use Visual Studio as their development environment. Organizations that must create software for a range of devices can now use the same languages, the same tools, and much of the same development platform to target systems of all sizes.

shows a very small part of the .NET Framework class library's namespace tree. The namespaces shown include the following:

- **System:** The root of the tree, this namespace contains all of the other namespaces in the .NET Framework class library. System also contains the core data types used by the CLR (and thus by languages built on the CLR). These types include several varieties of integers, a string type, and many more.

- **System.Web:** This namespace contains types useful for creating Web applications, and like many namespaces, it has subordinate namespaces. Developers can use the types in System.Web.UI to build ASP.NET browser applications, for example, while those in System.Web.Services are used to build ASP.NET Web Services applications.

- **System.Data:** The types in this namespace comprise ADO.NET. For example, the Connection class is used to establish connections to a database management system (DBMS), while an instance of the DataSet class can be used to cache and examine the results of a query issued against that DBMS.

- **System.Windows.Forms:** The types in this namespace make up Windows Forms, and they're used to build Windows GUIs. Rather than relying on language-specific mechanisms, such as the older Microsoft Foundation Classes (MFC) in C++, .NET Framework applications written in any programming language use this common set of types to build graphical interfaces for Windows.

- **System.EnterpriseServices:** The types in this namespace provide services required for some kinds of enterprise applications. Implemented by COM+ in the pre-NET world, these services include distributed transactions, object instance lifetime management, and more. The most important type in this namespace, one from which classes must inherit to use Enterprise Services, is the ServicedComponent class.

- **System.XML:** Types in this namespace provide support for creating and working with XML-defined data. The XmlDocument class, for instance, allows accessing an XML document using the Document Object Model (DOM). This namespace also includes support for technologies such as the XML Schema definition language (XSD) and XPath.

Many more namespaces are defined, providing support for file access, serializing an object's state, remote access to objects, and much more. In fact, the biggest task facing developers who wish to build on the .NET Framework is learning to use the many services that the library provides. There's no requirement to learn everything, however, so a developer is free to focus on only those things relevant to his or her world. Still, some parts will be relevant to almost everybody, and so the next sections provide a quick overview of some of this large library's most important aspects.

Learning the .NET Framework class library takes time

Building Web Applications: ASP.NET

Implemented in the System.Web namespace, ASP.NET is an important piece of the .NET Framework. The successor to the very popular Active Server Pages (ASP) technology, ASP.NET applications are built from one or more pages. Each page contains HTML and/or executable code, and typically has the extension *.aspx*. As Figure 1-5 shows, a request from a browser made via HTTP causes a page to be loaded and executed. Any output the page creates is then returned to the browser that made the request.

ASP.NET applications rely on .aspx pages

Building effective Web applications requires more than just the ability to combine code with HTML. Accordingly, ASP.NET provides a range of support, including the following:

ASP.NET includes a number of things to help developers create Web applications

- Web controls, allowing a developer to create a browser GUI in a familiar way. By dragging and dropping

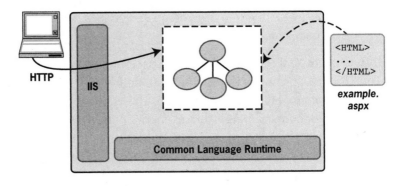

Figure 1-5   ASP.NET allows developers to create browser-accessible applications.

standard ASP.NET controls for buttons and other interface elements onto a form, it's possible to build GUIs for Web applications in much the same way as for local Windows applications.

- Mechanisms for managing an application's state information.

- Built-in support for maintaining information about an application's users, sometimes called *membership* information.

- Support for *data binding,* which allows easier access to information stored in a DBMS or some other data source.

Given the popularity of Web applications, ASP.NET probably impacts more developers than any other part of the .NET Framework class library. Chapter 5 provides more detail on this key component of the .NET Framework.

Accessing Data: ADO.NET

ADO.NET lets applications access stored data

ADO.NET lets applications work with stored data. As Figure 1-6 shows, access to a DBMS relies on a .NET Framework data provider, written as managed code. Providers that allow access to SQL Server, Oracle, and other DBMS are included with the

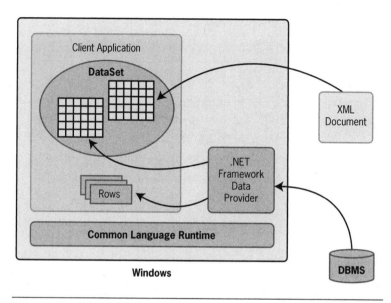

Figure 1-6   ADO.NET allows .NET Framework applications to access data stored in DBMS and XML documents.

.NET Framework. They allow a client application to issue commands against the DBMS and examine any results those commands return. The result of a Structured Query Language (SQL) query, for example, can be examined in two ways. Applications that need only read the result a row at a time can do this by using a DataReader object to march through the result one record at a time. Applications that need to do more complex things with a query result, such as send it to a browser, update information, or store that information on disk, can instead have the query's result packaged inside a DataSet object.

As Figure 1-6 illustrates, a DataSet can contain one or more tables. Each table can hold the result of a different query, so a single DataSet might potentially contain the results of two or more queries, perhaps from different DBMS. In effect, a DataSet acts as an in-memory cache for data. As the figure shows, however, DataSets can hold more than just the result of a SQL query. It's also possible to read an XML document directly into a table in a DataSet without relying on a .NET Framework data

An ADO.NET DataSet acts as an in-memory cache for data

Running the .NET Framework

The .NET Framework is meant to be the foundation for most Windows applications going forward. To make this possible, the Framework runs on many versions of Windows, including Windows 2000, Windows XP, Windows Server 2003, and Windows Vista. It's also available for the 64-bit versions of Windows XP, Windows Server 2003, and Windows Vista. The Framework doesn't run on older systems, however, such as Windows 95 or Windows NT. Given that it was released many years after these versions of Windows, this shouldn't be surprising.

The .NET Framework also supports an option called *side-by-side* execution. This allows simultaneous execution of not just multiple versions of the same application, but also multiple versions of the .NET Framework itself. For example, a single machine might have both version 1.1 and version 2.0 of the Framework installed, with each used to run applications written specifically for it. This lets organizations move forward with new versions of the .NET Framework without touching existing applications that run on earlier releases.

provider. Data defined using XML has also become much more important in the last few years, so ADO.NET allows accessing it directly. While not all .NET Framework applications will rely on ADO.NET for data access, a large percentage surely will. ADO.NET is described in more detail in Chapter 6.

Building Distributed Applications

Creating software that communicates with other software is a standard part of modern application development. Yet different applications have different communication requirements. To meet these diverse needs, the .NET Framework class library includes three distinct technologies for creating distributed applications. Figure 1-7 illustrates these choices.

ASP.NET Web Services allow communication via SOAP

ASP.NET Web Services, mostly defined in System.Web.Services, allows applications to communicate using Web services. Since it's part of ASP.NET, this technology lets developers use a similar

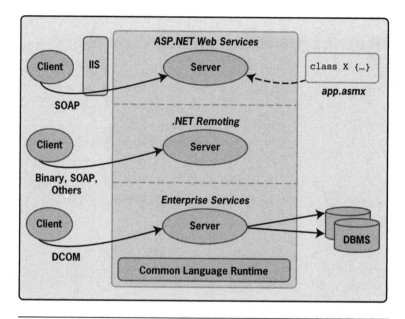

Figure 1-7   Distributed applications can use ASP.NET Web Services, .NET Remoting, or Enterprise Services.

model for creating distributed software. As Figure 1-7 shows, applications that expose methods as Web services can be built from files with the extension .asmx, each of which contains only code. Clients make requests using the standard Web services protocol SOAP[2], and the correct page is loaded and executed. Because this technology is part of ASP.NET, requests and replies also go through Internet Information Services (IIS), the standard Web server for Windows.

Communication via Web services is especially useful for interoperating with software built on platforms other than the .NET Framework, such as the Java environment. But it's not always the right solution. In some situations, the technology known as .NET

.NET Remoting focuses on communication between .NET Framework-based applications

2. "SOAP" was originally an acronym for "Simple Object Access Protocol." Today, the standards group that owns this technology has decided that SOAP no longer stands for anything—it's just a name.

■ Perspective: The .NET Framework on Non-Windows Systems

Applications written using the .NET Framework are compiled to a processor-independent form—MSIL—and shield themselves from the vagaries of a specific operating system by writing to the .NET Framework class library. This is much like the Java world, where applications are compiled to bytecode and can rely on standard Java libraries rather than making direct calls to a specific operating system. Java was expressly designed to work on multiple processors and operating systems. Is the same thing true for .NET?

To some extent, the answer is clearly yes. Microsoft itself has provided a port of the Framework's fundamentals, known as the Shared Source CLI, to the FreeBSD version of UNIX. Theoretically, the .NET Framework could become a cross-platform solution on a wide range of systems.

Yet some technical issues remain. While MSIL is clearly platform independent, some parts of the .NET Framework class library just as clearly are not. Enterprise Services, for example, providing support for scalable, transaction-oriented applications, is based on an earlier Windows technology called COM+. Accordingly, this part of the library runs only where COM+ is available. Other parts of the class library also betray their Windows origins in more or less obvious ways.

Just as important, Microsoft would face challenges in making customers believe that it's serious about long-term support of the .NET Framework on non-Windows systems. The company's laser-like focus on its own operating systems has been a hallmark of its business, as well as a primary factor in its success. If Microsoft wished to make the .NET Framework a true multiplatform rival for Java, the technical potential is there. But so far, at least, .NET is fundamentally a Windows technology.

In fact, today's most visible non-Windows implementation of .NET, the Mono project, hasn't attracted much commercial attention. Some enterprises looking to build .NET applications had hoped that Mono would provide them with a safe, non-Microsoft alternative should they need one. In practice, though, this option hasn't been appealing to many organizations. Like it or not, the great majority of people who build software on the .NET Framework should expect to run that code on some version of Windows.

Remoting, defined in the System.Runtime.Remoting namespace, is a better choice. Unlike ASP.NET Web Services, .NET Remoting focuses on direct communication between applications built on the .NET Framework. While it does support a version of SOAP, this technology also provides a binary protocol along with the ability to add extensions using any other protocol a developer needs. .NET Remoting isn't the most common choice for communication, but it can be important for some kinds of applications.

The third option for creating distributed applications using the .NET Framework is Enterprise Services. Defined in the System.EnterpriseServices namespace, it provides applications with services such as distributed transactions and more. Figure 1-7 illustrates this, showing a server application accessing two databases. If a single transaction included updates to both of these databases, Enterprise Services might well be the right choice for the application that used this transaction. Remote clients can communicate directly with an Enterprise Services application using DCOM, and it's also possible for an ASP.NET application to use Enterprise Services when necessary.

Enterprise Services provides distributed transactions and other services

All three options make sense in different situations, and having a basic understanding of all three is useful. For a more detailed look at each of them, see Chapter 7.

Visual Studio 2005

Visual Studio is by far the most popular tool for creating .NET applications today. The current version, Visual Studio 2005, is the successor to Visual Studio .NET, which was itself the first version of this tool to support creating managed code. Both tools provide a very large set of services for developers, including all of the bells and whistles of a modern IDE.

Most .NET developers today use Visual Studio

Figure 1-8 shows how Visual Studio looks to the creator of a simple .NET Framework application. Different windows show

Figure 1-8   Visual Studio provides a range of support for creators of .NET applications.

different aspects of the project, including the code itself and, in the lower right corner, any properties that may have been set. If you've never used a modern software development tool, don't be fooled by this very basic picture: Visual Studio is actually a complex and powerful IDE, one that's used by millions of developers today.

Visual Studio is a family of products

Visual Studio 2005 is actually a family of products, each aimed at a particular kind of developer. This family includes Visual Studio 2005 Express Edition, aimed at beginning developers and hobbyists, Visual Studio Standard Edition, aimed at more serious developers, and Visual Studio 2005 Professional Edition, intended for hard-core software professionals building scalable distributed applications. The product family also includes Visual Studio Tools for Office, which provides the ability to create applications in VB or C# that build on Excel, Word, Outlook, and InfoPath. Another important member of this family, one that's

What's New in Visual Studio 2005

The introduction of Visual Studio Team System and support for DSLs are probably the two biggest innovations in Visual Studio 2005. This new version of Microsoft's flagship development tool also adds several other interesting new features, including the following:

- **Refactoring support:** Refactoring allows making small modifications to software that together can lead to significant improvement. Some common refactoring changes, such as extracting code and wrapping it in its own method, or encapsulating a field inside get and set methods, can be done through a built-in Visual Studio menu.

- **Edit and continue:** In pre-.NET versions of Visual Basic, a developer could change code in a running application while it was being debugged, then continue execution from the point of the change. Known as Edit and Continue, plenty of people found this useful. Omitted from Visual Studio .NET (to the great concern of some), this feature is now available with all of the programming languages supported by Visual Studio 2005.

- **Code snippets:** Many applications include code that performs common tasks. To make implementing these easier, Visual Studio 2005 provides snippets of prewritten code for common situations. Snippets are provided for declaring standard types, such as classes, creating common constructions, such as an if statement, and other typical programming tasks. Developers can also create new snippets then store them for future use.

described in a bit more detail later in this chapter, is Visual Studio Team System, which provides a set of interrelated tools specialized for various roles in a development group.

As already described, several different programming languages can be used to create .NET Framework applications. Visual Studio 2005 ships with support for C#, VB, C++, and other languages, giving developers a range of choices. The 2005 version of the tool also adds support for using *domain-specific*

Visual Studio 2005 provides a variety of different languages

■ Perspective: The Fate of Pre-.NET Applications

Applications built using the Windows DNA technologies that preceded .NET, such as COM and Visual Basic 6 (VB6), won't generally run on the .NET Framework without at least some modification. This is a problem for the many organizations that have invested in these applications. But just how big a problem is it?

The answer depends on what kind of application we're talking about and what kind of organization is responsible for it. For example, think about a VB6 application built by a typical enterprise that solves a specific business problem. Installing the .NET Framework on the same machine that runs this app won't break the application, and since these older apps will happily run on newer versions of Windows, there's no requirement to change. If the application still meets the business need effectively, why invest the time and resources to rewrite it using .NET? True, the rewritten app would likely be better in some technical ways, but the benefits to its users—the people who ultimately pay for it—aren't likely to be large enough to justify the cost.

But suppose this VB6 application needs to be modified in some way. It's always possible to just keep on using an older version of Visual Studio, one that (unlike Visual Studio 2005) supports VB6. But Microsoft's support for these older development environments is fading away, and many organizations feel uncomfortable relying on unsupported tools. In this case, the application may need to be rewritten solely to avoid this fate.

What about applications written by independent software vendors (ISV)? For example, many ISVs (including Microsoft) have a large investment in applications written using pre-.NET versions of C++. Visual Studio 2005 allows working directly with raw C++—you don't have to use the CLR—and so there's no immediate need to change these applications. New Windows features are typically exposed via managed code, however, and so taking advantage of this new functionality will require extending the application with some CLR-based C++.

Perhaps the hardest problem is that faced by ISVs or enterprises with a substantial investment in a VB6 application that still has many years of use ahead of it. An application like this is likely to need substantial change over time, yet creating new functionality in VB6 means freezing ever more work into a legacy technology. One option is to create new code in the .NET version of VB, then connect these additions to what already exists. To make this possible, the CLR has built-in support that allows managed code to call existing DLLs, access and be accessed by COM objects, and interoperate in other ways with the previous generation of Windows software. The big challenge here is the problem just mentioned: Versions of Visual Studio that support VB6 are falling out of support (although the VB runtime itself is still supported). In this case, it might be worth the investment to rebuild the entire application on .NET, especially if significant new functionality can be added at the same time.

Yet another challenge of transitioning to a wholly new development environment is the cost of retraining developers. In the long run, avoiding the .NET Framework isn't possible for Windows-oriented organizations, so ponying up the cash for developer education is unavoidable. It's not cheap, and time will be lost as developers come up to speed on this new technology. The .NET Framework really is substantially better than its predecessors, however, so most organizations are likely to see productivity gains once developers have internalized this new environment.

languages (DSLs), an idea that's described later in this chapter. The main focus of Visual Studio, however, is helping developers create applications using general purpose CLR-based programming languages, and so the next section takes a brief look at this area.

General Purpose Languages

Although Visual Studio supports many different programming languages, the CLR defines the core semantics for most of them. Yet while the way those languages behave often has a good deal in common, a developer can still choose the language that feels most natural to her. All of these languages use at least some of the services provided by the CLR, and some expose virtually everything the CLR has to offer. Also, with the exception of C++, it's not possible to create traditional standalone binary executables in these languages. Instead, every application is compiled

Visual Studio 2005 supports CLR-based languages

into MSIL and so requires the .NET Framework to execute. This section provides a short introduction to each of the most commonly used general purpose languages built on the CLR.

C#

C# is the natural language for .NET Framework developers who prefer a C-based syntax

The two dominant languages for Windows development in the pre-.NET world were C++ and Visual Basic 6 (VB6). Both had sizable user populations (although VB6's user base was much larger), and so Microsoft needed to find a way to make both groups as happy as possible with their new environment. How, for example, could the large number of Windows developers who know (and love) C++ be brought forward to use the .NET Framework? One answer is to extend C++, an option described later. Another approach, one that has proven more appealing for most C++ developers, is to create a new language based on the CLR but with a syntax derived from C++. This is exactly what Microsoft did in creating C#.

C# looks familiar to anyone accustomed to programming in C++ or Java. Like those languages (and like the .NET version of VB), C# is object-oriented. Among the more interesting aspects of C# are the following:

- Support for implementation inheritance, allowing a new child class to inherit code from one parent class, sometimes referred to as *single inheritance*

- The ability for a child class to override one or more methods in its parent

- Support for exception handling

- Full multithreading (using the .NET Framework class library)

- The ability to define interfaces directly in C#

- Support for properties and events

- Support for attributes, allowing features such as transaction support and Web services to be implemented by inserting keywords in source code

- Garbage collection, freeing developers from the need to destroy explicitly objects they have created

- Support for generic types, a concept similar to templates in C++

- The ability to write code that directly accesses specific memory addresses, sometimes referred to as *unsafe* code

C++ or Java developers, who are accustomed to a C-like syntax, usually prefer C# for writing .NET Framework applications. VB6 developers, however, fond of their own style of syntax, often prefer the .NET version of VB, described next.

Visual Basic

From its humble beginnings at Dartmouth College in the 1960s, Basic has grown into one of the most widely used programming languages in the world today. This success was due largely to the popularity of Microsoft's Visual Basic. Yet it's likely that the original creators of Basic wouldn't recognize their child in its current form. The price of success has been adaptation—sometimes radical—to new requirements.

Visual Basic is a very widely used language

VB.NET, the first CLR-based version of this language, was a huge step in Microsoft's evolution of VB. In addition to being enormously different from the original Basic language, it was a big leap from its immediate predecessor, VB6. The primary reason for this substantial change was that VB.NET was built entirely on the CLR. The version in Visual Studio 2005, officially known as Visual Basic 2005, brings a few changes to the original VB.NET. On the whole, however, this version of the language is very much like the VB.NET incarnation that preceded it.

VB.NET was a big change from VB6

VB 2005 is much like C#, which shouldn't be surprising. Both are built on the CLR, and both expose the same core functionality.

*Visual Basic 2005
provides almost
exactly the same
features as C#*

The biggest difference between C# and VB today is in syntax; functionally, the two languages are very similar. In fact, the list of interesting features in VB mirrors C#'s list:

- Support for single implementation inheritance

- Method overriding

- Support for exception handling

- Full multithreading (using the .NET Framework class library)

- The ability to define interfaces directly in VB

- Support for properties and events

- Support for attributes

- Garbage collection

- Support for generic types

Unlike its sibling C#, VB doesn't allow creating unsafe code. The 2005 version of VB does, however, provide an addition called the My namespace, making it easier to perform some common operations. Despite these differences, it's important to realize how similar VB and C# really are. The old division between C++ and VB6, two radically different languages targeting quite different developer populations, is gone. In its place is the sleek consistency of two closely related CLR-based languages: VB and C#.

C++

*The semantics of
C++ differ from
those defined by
the CLR*

C++ presented a challenge to the creators of .NET. To be able to build .NET Framework applications, this popular language had to be modified to use the CLR. Yet some of the core semantics of C++, which allows things such as a child class inheriting directly from multiple parents (known as *multiple inheritance*), conflict with those of the CLR. And since C++ plays an important role as the dominant language for creating non-Framework-based Windows applications, modifying it to be purely Framework specific wasn't the right approach. What's the solution?

Microsoft's answer is to support standard C++ as always, leaving this powerful language able to create efficient processor-specific binaries as before. To allow the use of C++ to create .NET Framework applications, Microsoft added a set of extensions to the language. The C++ dialect provided with Visual Studio 2005 that includes these extensions is called *C++/CLI*, and it provides access to all features of the CLR. Using C++/CLI, a developer can write C++ code that takes advantage of garbage collection, defines interfaces, uses attributes, and more.

.NET Framework applications can be created using C++/CLI

Because not all applications will use the .NET Framework, Visual Studio still allows building traditional Windows applications in C++. Rather than using C++/CLI, a developer can write standard C++ code and then compile it into processor-specific binaries. Unlike VB and C#, C++ is not required to compile into MSIL.

Standard C++ can also be used to create non-Framework-based applications

Other CLR-Based Languages

It's fair to say that the great majority of .NET development is done in C#, VB .NET, and C++. Still, Visual Studio 2005 also supports two other CLR-based languages that are worth mentioning:

Visual Studio 2005 also supports JScript .NET and J#

- **JScript:** JScript is based on ECMAScript, the current standard version of the language originally christened as JavaScript. As such, JScript provides developers with a loosely typed development environment, support for regular expressions, and other aspects typical of the JavaScript language family. Yet because it's based on the CLR, the .NET version of JScript also implements CLR-style classes, which can contain methods, implement interfaces, and more. While JScript can be used for creating essentially any .NET application, the language is most commonly applied in building ASP.NET pages.

■ **J#:** Microsoft's implementation of the Java programming language, J# provides Java's syntax on top of the CLR. Don't be confused—J# isn't intended for creating applications that run on a standard Java virtual machine. Microsoft also doesn't support many of the major Java libraries, such as Enterprise JavaBeans (EJB). Instead, J# provides a way to more easily transition Java developers and existing Java code to the world of .NET.

Microsoft provides Python for the CLR

Microsoft also makes available a CLR-based version of the increasingly popular Python language. While it's not an integral part of Visual Studio, this implementation does allow access to the .NET Framework class library. It also demonstrates the ability of the CLR to support a broader range of programming languages, since Python is a *dynamic* language. Dynamic languages allow more change at runtime than more conventional approaches such as C# and VB, including things such as introducing new data types. To provide this kind of flexibility, the CLR-based version of Python relies on an interpreter rather than just a compiler.

Other vendors, such as Borland, provide CLR-based languages

Other vendors also provide tools and languages for creating .NET Framework applications. The most popular of these is probably Borland's Delphi. Widely admired as a language, Delphi has a hard-core user base around the world. The current version of this language is based on the CLR, and so it allows Delphi developers access to the services provided by the .NET Framework.

Support for multiple programming languages is one of the most interesting things about the .NET Framework. Chapter 3 takes a closer look at C#, VB, and C++/CLI, the three most popular languages for building .NET Framework applications.

Domain Specific Languages

Domain specific languages can help in moving toward model-driven development

General purpose programming languages such as C# and VB are the mainstays of modern development. Yet the idea of *model-driven development (MDD)*, where software creation depends at least in part on some kind of underlying abstract model, is a hot idea in the industry today. Visual Studio 2005 reflects this in its support for what are known as *domain specific languages* (DSLs). In general, a DSL might be expressed in text, graphically, or in some other way. For example, SQL can be thought of as a DSL designed for working with relational databases, while the graphical Orchestration Designer in Microsoft's BizTalk Server can be viewed as a DSL for defining some kinds of business logic. However it's defined, each DSL implements a set of higher-level abstractions for solving problems in a particular area.

Visual Studio 2005 supports several graphical DSLs. Each is implemented in a specific graphical tool that focuses on a particular problem domain. For example, every version of Visual Studio 2005, except the Express Editions, includes a tool called the Class Designer. As Figure 1-9 illustrates, this tool provides a graphical DSL for creating and modifying classes and class hierarchies.

Visual Studio 2005 provides a Class Designer and other DSLs

The Class Designer allows a developer to create a new class by dragging and dropping an icon from the toolbox (shown on the left in Figure 1-9) onto the design surface. Properties, methods,

The Class Designer DSL generates code from class diagrams

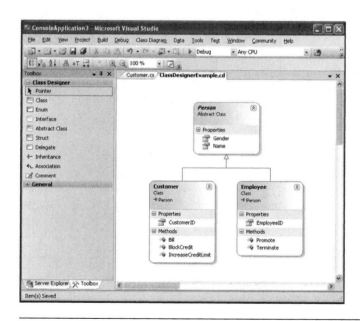

Figure 1-9   The Visual Studio 2005 Class Designer provides a DSL for defining classes and class hierarchies.

■ Perspective: Microsoft's Approach to Model-Driven Development

The dream of creating software through pictures has been with us for decades. Yet especially when they're expressed graphically, it's easy to look at DSLs and be reminded of the failure of computer-aided software engineering (CASE). Now that memories of the CASE debacle are fading, are DSLs just a repeat of this idea being foisted on a new generation?

Maybe—it's too soon to know. But increased developer productivity is a laudable goal, one that's worth taking some risks to achieve. The CASE technologies of the 1980s were far broader in scope than the relatively simple DSLs that are included in Visual Studio 2005. By avoiding the grand ambition of these earlier tools, Microsoft lessens the risk that its DSL efforts will meet the same fate. And the idea of creating at least some code graphically, especially code that targets a particular domain, is very attractive.

Microsoft is taking a small step in the DSL direction with Visual Studio 2005. The company's stated goal is to make developers perceive that modeling has value, not to move to a completely model-based development environment. Given this, starting small seems wise. Building this approach into one of the world's most widely used developer tools will certainly provide a solid test of the idea.

Microsoft isn't alone in promoting MDD, however. The Object Management Group (OMG), a multivendor consortium, has created a set of specifications for MDD. These specs define the OMG's *Model Driven Architecture (MDA)*, and they have been endorsed by a number of vendors and user organizations. Yet Microsoft has essentially ignored MDA, choosing instead to go its own way.

Microsoft and the OMG have never had an especially cordial relationship. OMG's first creation was the Common Object Request Broker Architecture (CORBA), a direct competitor to Microsoft's DCOM. Like CORBA, MDA takes an explicitly cross-platform, vendor-neutral approach. In fact, a primary MDA goal is to create models that can be implemented equally well using different technologies, such as .NET and Java. Given its diverse membership, it's not surprising that OMG starts from this perspective.

It's also not surprising that Microsoft doesn't see the value in this. Visual Studio is a tool for building Windows applications, so why complicate things by implementing an MDD approach that strives to be cross-platform? And if you're Microsoft, what value is there in working with a committee of others to define what will ultimately be a Windows technology? Unsurprisingly, Microsoft continues to believe that for Windows programming interfaces, it should be in the driver's seat. Also, like the products of many standards committees, MDA is abstract and complex. (A friend of mine who's spent a considerable amount of time in the MDA world has described it as "where the rubber meets the sky.") While ignoring MDA might make Visual Studio integration with non-Microsoft tools more challenging, Microsoft's resistance to a technology created by its competitors is entirely in line with its usual perspective on the world. And as always, competition among different approaches is likely to make this technology improve more quickly.

and other aspects of the class can also be added graphically. This is more than just a tool for drawing pictures, however. The Class Designer actually generates code that reflects the defined classes. Changes to the diagram are reflected in the code, and changes made directly to the code are also reflected in the diagram. Especially for more complex scenarios, the ability to visualize classes and their relationships can be a big help in writing good code.

Working in Groups: Visual Studio Team System

Like any development tool, the goal of Visual Studio is to help developers be more effective. Yet the majority of software today, and virtually all enterprise software, isn't created by a single individual. Software development has become a team sport, complete with specialized positions for various players.

Most software today is created by groups, not individuals

Visual Studio 2005 Team System recognizes this fact. As Figure 1-10 shows, this product suite includes components that

Visual Studio 2005 Team System includes several different tools

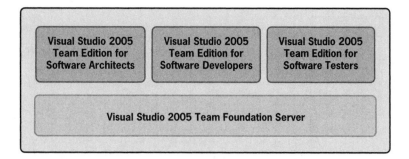

Figure 1-10   Visual Studio Team System provides different tools for
different roles in a development team.

target each member of a modern development group. Those
components include:

- **Visual Studio 2005 Team Edition for Software
  Architects:** provides a group of tools known collectively
  as the *Distributed System Designers.* Each provides a
  DSL aimed at architects designing various aspects of
  service-oriented applications. These tools include
  Application Designer for defining applications and how
  they communicate, *System Designer* for defining how
  those applications fit together for deployment, *Logical
  Datacenter Designer* for defining the structure of machines in a data center, and *Deployment Designer* for
  defining how the set of applications that comprise a
  particular system is deployed in a specific data center.
  This product also includes a version of Visio that allows
  creating Unified Modeling Language (UML) diagrams,
  entity/relationship (ER) diagrams, and other architecture-
  oriented pictures.

- **Visual Studio 2005 Team Edition for Software
  Developers:** includes tools that are useful for people
  who actually write code. These tools support static code
  analysis, exposing problems such as using an uninitial-
  ized variable, dynamic code analysis, allowing code to
  be profiled for performance improvements, and more.

- **Visual Studio 2005 Team Edition for Software Testers:** offers tools focused on the tasks performed by people who test code, such as tools for creating and running unit tests and for load testing.

- **Visual Studio 2005 Team Foundation Server:** provides the common platform for the other Team System components. Implemented as a standalone server application, Team Foundation Server keeps track of team projects, maintains a work items database, supports version control of a project's source code, and provides other common services that a software development team needs. The projects maintained by a particular Team Foundation server can also be examined using a client called the Team Explorer. Status reports and other information are available through a Team System portal built on Windows SharePoint Services.

Except for Team Foundation Server, all of the components of Visual Studio 2005 Team System are built on Visual Studio 2005 Professional Edition, which means that each one includes a complete development environment. While many .NET developers are happy with just a standalone version of Visual Studio, larger teams or those working on more complex projects can sometimes make good use of the extra tools provided by Visual Studio 2005 Team Edition.

Conclusion

Since its original release in 2002, the .NET Framework has become the foundation for a majority of new Windows applications. Judging from the evidence so far, it has surely been a success for Microsoft and for its customers. While the move to the .NET environment forces developers to climb a long learning curve, the benefits appear to be worth the effort. For the people who use it, this technology qualifies as one more step toward the ultimate goal: producing the best possible software in the least amount of time.

.NET has been a success

The Pain of Change

During a .NET seminar I gave in Moscow a few years ago, one of the participants raised his hand with a concerned expression. "I'm an experienced Windows DNA developer," he said. "If I learn this .NET stuff, can you promise me that this is the last new Microsoft technology I'll ever have to learn?"

I couldn't, of course. What I could promise him was that he was in the wrong profession. Even if my worried questioner sticks with the Microsoft platform for the rest of his career, it's all but certain that new technologies will appear that he'll need to understand. As long as the hardware we depend on keeps getting better, and as long as creative people work in this field, new software technologies will continue to appear.

Fortunately, changes as large as .NET aren't common. Bringing out new languages, a large new library, and significant revisions to other core technologies all at once, as Microsoft did with .NET, was almost too much to swallow. Yet bringing out those same changes piecemeal would likely have been worse, if only because the integration among them would certainly have suffered. To make progress, vendors are sometimes forced to make their customers swallow a large amount of change all at once.

The .NET environment is now a standard part of the software world. Still, don't think it's the last word in software technology—it's not. If you don't like change, get out of the software business.

2

The Common Language Runtime

The Common Language Runtime (CLR) is the foundation for everything else in the .NET Framework. To understand .NET languages such as C# and Visual Basic (VB), you must understand the CLR. To understand the .NET Framework class library—ASP.NET, ADO.NET, and the rest—you must understand the CLR. And since the .NET Framework has become the default foundation for new Windows software, anybody who plans to work in the Microsoft environment needs to come to grips with the CLR.

Everything in the .NET Framework depends on the CLR

Software built on the CLR is referred to as *managed code*, and the CLR provides a range of things that support creating and running this code. Perhaps the most fundamental is a standard set of types that are used by languages built on the CLR, along with a standard format for metadata, which is information about software built using those types. The CLR also provides technologies for packaging managed code and a runtime environment for executing managed code. As the most elemental part of

The CLR supports the creation and execution of managed code

the .NET Framework, the CLR is unquestionably the place to start in understanding what the Framework offers.

Building Managed Code: The Common Type System

A programming language usually defines both syntax and semantics

What is a programming language? One way to think about it is as a specific syntax with a set of keywords that can be used to define data and express operations on that data. While language syntaxes differ, the underlying abstractions of most popular languages today are very similar. All of them support various data types such as integers and strings, all allow packaging code into methods, and all provide a way to group data and methods into classes. When a new programming language is defined, the usual approach is to define underlying abstractions such as these—key aspects of the language's semantics—concomitantly with the language's syntax.

The Common Type System defines core semantics but not syntax

Yet there are other possibilities. Suppose you choose to define the core abstractions for a programming model without mapping them to any particular syntax. If the abstractions were general enough, they could then be used in many different programming languages. Rather than inextricably mingling syntax and semantics, these two things could be kept separate, allowing different languages to be used with the same set of underlying abstractions. This is exactly what's done in the CLR's *Common Type System (CTS)*. The CTS specifies no particular syntax or keywords, but instead defines a common set of types that can be used with many different language syntaxes. Each language has its own syntax, but if that language is built on the CLR, it will use at least some of the types defined by the CTS.

Types are an important part of a programming language

Types are fundamental to any programming language. One simple but concrete way to think of a type is as a set of rules for interpreting the value stored in some memory location, such as the value of a variable. If that variable has an integer type, for example, the bits stored in it are interpreted as an integer. If the variable has a string type, the bits stored in it are interpreted as characters. To a compiler, of course, a type is more than this. Compilers must also understand the rules that define what kinds of values are allowed for each type and what kinds of operations are legal on these values. Among other things, this knowledge allows a compiler to determine whether a value of a particular type is being used correctly.

The set of types defined by the CTS is at the core of the CLR. Programming languages built on the CLR expose these types in a language-dependent way. (For examples of this, see the descriptions of C# and VB in the next chapter.) While the creator of a CLR-based language is free to implement only a subset of the types defined by the CTS and even to add types of his own to his language, most languages built on the CLR make extensive use of the CTS-defined types.

CLR-based languages expose CTS types in different ways

Introducing the Common Type System

A substantial subset of the types defined by the CTS is shown in Figure 2-1. The first thing to note is that every type inherits either directly or indirectly from a type called Object. (All of these types are actually contained in the System namespace, as mentioned in Chapter 1, so the complete name for this most fundamental type is System.Object.) The second thing to note is that every type defined by the CTS is either a *reference* type or a *value* type. As their names suggest, an instance of a reference type always contains a reference to a value of that type, while an instance of a value type contains the value itself. Reference types inherit directly from Object, while all value types inherit directly from a type called ValueType, which in turn inherits from Object.

The CTS defines reference and value types

Value types tend to be simple. The types in this category include Byte, Char, signed and unsigned integers of various lengths, single- and double-precision floating point, Decimal,

Value types are simpler than reference types

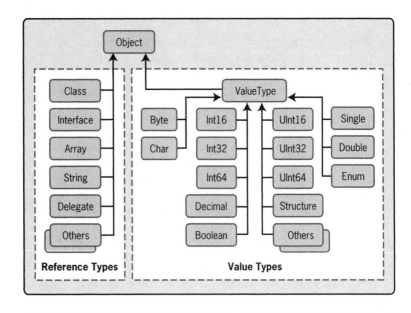

Figure 2-1   The CTS defines reference and value types, all of which inherit from a common Object type.

Boolean, and more. Reference types, by contrast, are typically more complex. As shown in the figure, for instance, Class, Interface, Array, and String are reference types. Yet to understand the difference between value types and reference types—a fundamental distinction in the CTS—you must first understand how memory is allocated for instances of each type. In managed code, values can have their memory allocated in one of two main ways, both managed by the CLR: on the *stack* or on the *heap.* Variables allocated on the managed stack are typically created when a method is called or when a running method creates them. In either case, the memory used by stack variables is automatically freed when the method in which they were created returns. Variables allocated on the managed heap, however, don't have their memory freed when the method that created them ends. Instead, the memory used by these variables is freed via a process called *garbage collection,* a topic that's described in more detail later in this chapter.

A basic difference between value types and reference types is that a standalone instance of a value type is allocated on the stack, while an instance of a reference type has only a reference to its actual value allocated on the stack. The value itself is allocated on the heap. Figure 2-2 shows an abstract picture of how this looks. In the case shown here, three instances of value types—Int16, Char, and Int32—have been created on the managed stack, while one instance of the reference type String exists on the managed heap. Note that even the reference type instance has an entry on the stack—it's a reference to the memory on the heap—but the instance's contents are stored on the heap[1]. Understanding the distinction between value types and reference types is essential in understanding the CTS type system and, ultimately, the types used by CLR-based languages.

Value types typically live on the stack, while reference types live on the heap

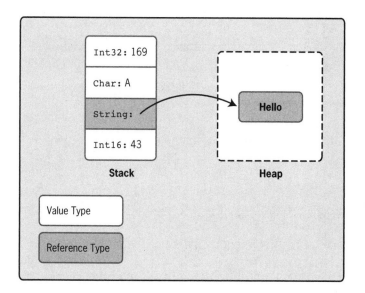

Figure 2-2   Instances of value types are allocated on the managed stack, while instances of reference types are allocated on the managed heap.

---

1. A reference type might contain a value type, which means that some value type instances exist on the heap.

A Closer Look at CTS Types

The root Object type provides methods that are inherited by every other type

The CTS defines a large set of types. As already described, the most fundamental of these is Object, from which every CTS type inherits directly or indirectly. In the object-oriented world of the CLR, having a common base for all types is useful. For one thing, since everything inherits from the same root type, an instance of this type can potentially contain any value. Object also implements several methods, and since every CTS type inherits from Object, these methods can be called on an instance of any type. Among the methods Object provides are Equals, which determines whether two objects are identical, and GetType, which returns the type of the object it's called on.

Value Types

The ValueType type provides methods that are inherited by every value type

All value types inherit from ValueType. Like Object, ValueType provides an Equals method (in fact, it overrides the method defined in Object). Value types cannot act as a parent type for inheritance, however, so it's not possible to, say, define a new type that inherits from Int32. In the jargon of the CLR, value types are said to be *sealed.*

Value types include Byte, Int32, Boolean, and more

Many of the value types defined by the CTS were shown in Figure 2-1. Defined a bit more completely, those types are as follows:

- **Byte:** An 8-bit unsigned integer.

- **Char:** A 16-bit Unicode character.

- **Int16, Int32, and Int64:** 16-, 32-, and 64-bit signed integers.

- **UInt16, UInt32, and UInt64:** 16-, 32-, and 64-bit unsigned integers.

- **Single and Double:** Single-precision (32-bit) and double-precision (64-bit) floating-point numbers.

- **Decimal:** 96-bit decimal numbers.

- **Enum:** A way to name a group of values of some integer type. Enumerated types inherit from System.Enum and are used to define types whose values have meaningful names rather than just numbers.

- **Boolean:** True or false.

Reference Types

Compared with most value types, the reference types defined by the CTS are relatively complicated. Before describing some of the more important reference types, it's useful to look first at a few elements, officially known as *type members*, that are common to several types (including both reference and value types). Those elements are as follows:

Many CTS types have common type members

- **Methods:** Executable code that carries out some kind of operation. Methods can be *overloaded*, which means that a single type can define two or more methods with the same name. To distinguish among them, each of these identically named methods must differ somehow in its parameter list. Another way to say this is to state that each method must have a unique *signature.* If a method encounters an error, it can throw an *exception*, which provides some indication of what has gone wrong.

- **Fields:** A value of some type.

- **Events:** A mechanism for communicating with other types. Each event includes methods for subscribing and unsubscribing and for sending (often referred to as *firing*) the event to subscribers.

- **Properties:** In effect, a value together with specified methods to read and/or write that value.

- **Nested types:** A type defined inside another type. A common example of this is defining a class that is nested inside another class.

Type members have characteristics

Type members can be assigned various characteristics. For example, methods, events, and properties can be labeled as *abstract*, which means that no implementation is supplied; as *final*, which means that the method, event, or property can't be overridden; or as *virtual*, which means that exactly which implementation is used can be determined at runtime rather than at compilation. Methods, events, properties, and fields can all be defined as *static*, which means they are associated with the type itself rather than with any particular instance of that type. (This allows a static method to be invoked on a class without first creating an instance of that class.) Members can also be assigned different *accessibilities*. For example, a *private* method can be accessed only from within the type in which it's defined or from another type nested in that type. A method whose accessibility is *family*, however, can be accessed from within the type in which it's defined and from types that inherit from that type. For even broader use, a method whose accessibility is *public* can be accessed from any other type.

Reference types include Class, Interface, Array, and String

Given this basic understanding of type members, we can now look at reference types themselves. Among the most important are the following:

- **Class:** A CTS class can have methods, events, and properties; it can maintain its state in one or more fields; and it can contain nested types. A class's visibility can be *public*, which means it's available to any other type, or *assembly*, which means it's available only to other classes in the same assembly. (Assemblies are described later in this chapter.) Classes have one or more *constructors*, which are initialization methods that execute when a new instance of this class is created. A class can directly inherit from at most one other class and can act as the direct parent for at most one inheriting child class. In other words, a CTS class supports single but not multiple implementation inheritance. If a class is marked as *sealed*, however, no other class can inherit from it. A class marked as *abstract,* by contrast, can't be instantiated but can serve only as the base class (that is, the parent) for another class that inherits from it. A class can also have one or more members marked as abstract, which means the class itself is abstract. If a class inherits from another class, it may *override* one or more methods, properties, and other type members in its parent by providing an implementation with the same signature. A class can also implement one or more interfaces, described next.

- **Interface:** An interface can include methods, properties, and events. Unlike classes, interfaces do support multiple inheritance, so an interface can inherit from one or more other interfaces simultaneously. An interface doesn't actually implement anything, however. Instead, it provides a way to group type definitions together, leaving the implementation to whatever type supports the interface.

- **Array:** An array is a group of values of the same type. Arrays can have one or more dimensions, and their upper and lower bounds can be set more or less arbitrarily. All arrays inherit from a common System.Array type.

- **Delegate:** A delegate is effectively a pointer to a method. All delegates inherit from a common System.Delegate type, and they're commonly used for event handling and callbacks. Each delegate has a set of associated members called an *invocation list.* When the delegate is invoked, each member on this list gets called, with each one passed the parameters that the delegate received.

As the next chapter shows, CLR-based programming languages such as C# and VB construct their own type system on top of the CTS types. Despite their different representations, however, the semantics of these types are essentially the same in C#, VB, and many other CLR-based languages. In fact, providing this foundation of common programming language types is one of the CLR's most important roles.

The core types are the same in CLR-based languages such as C# and VB

Converting Value Types to Reference Types: Boxing

Boxing transforms an instance of a value type into an instance of a reference type

There are cases when an instance of a value type needs to be treated as an instance of a reference type. For example, suppose you'd like to pass an instance of a value type as a parameter to some method, but that parameter is defined to be a reference to a value rather than the value itself. For situations like this, a value type instance can be converted into a reference type instance through a process called *boxing*.

Boxing a value type instance moves its value to the heap

When a value type instance is boxed, storage is allocated on the heap, and the instance's value is copied into that space. A reference to this storage is placed on the stack, as shown in Figure 2-3. The boxed value is an object, a reference type, that contains the contents of the value type instance. In the figure, the Int32 value 169 shown in Figure 2-2 has been converted to a value of type Object, and its contents have been placed on the heap. A boxed value type instance can also be converted back to its original form, a process called *unboxing*.

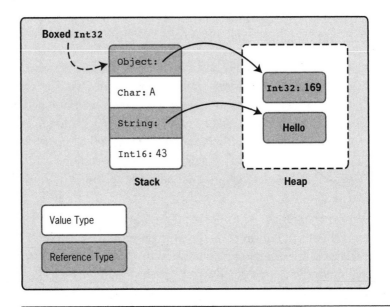

Figure 2-3   Boxing converts a value type instance into an instance of an analogous reference type.

Languages built on the CLR commonly hide the process of boxing, so developers may not need to request this transformation explicitly. Still, boxing has performance implications—doing it takes time, and references to boxed values are a bit slower than references to unboxed values—and boxed values behave somewhat differently than unboxed values. Even though the process usually happens silently, it's worth knowing what's going on.

CLR-based languages can make boxing invisible

The Common Language Specification

The CTS defines a large and fairly complex set of types. Not all of them make sense for all languages. Yet one of the key goals of the CLR is to allow creating code in one language, then calling that code from another. Unless both languages support the same types in the same way, doing this is problematic. Still, requiring every language to implement every CTS type would be burdensome to language developers.

The solution to this conundrum is a compromise called the Common Language Specification (CLS). The CLS defines a (large) subset of the CTS that a language must obey if it wishes to interoperate with other CLS-compliant languages. For example, the CLS requires support for most CTS value types, including Boolean, Byte, Char, Decimal, Int16, Int32, Int64, Single, Double, and more. It does not require support, however, for UInt16, UInt32, or UInt64. Similarly, a CTS array is allowed to have its lower bound set at an arbitrary value, while a CLS-compliant array must have a lower bound of zero. There are many more restrictions in the CLS, all of them defined with the same end in mind: allowing effective interoperability among code written in CLR-based languages.

The CLS defines a subset of the CTS to enable cross-language interoperability

One important thing to note about the rules laid down by the CLS is that they apply only to externally visible aspects of a type. A language is free to do anything it wants within its own world, but whatever it exposes to the outside world—and thus potentially to other languages—is constrained by the CLS. Given the goal of cross-language interoperability, this distinction makes perfect sense.

Compiling Managed Code

Compiling managed code generates MSIL and metadata

When source code written in a CLR-based language is compiled, two things are produced: instructions expressed in Microsoft Intermediate Language (MSIL), and *metadata,* information about those instructions and the data they manipulate. Whether this code is initially written in C#, VB, or some other CLR-based language, the compiler transforms all of the types it contains—classes, structs, integers, delegates, and all the rest—into MSIL and metadata.

MSIL and metadata are contained in a DLL or EXE

Figure 2-4 illustrates this process. In this example, the code being compiled contains three CTS types, all of them classes. When this code is compiled using whatever compiler is appropriate for the language it's written in, the result is an equivalent set of MSIL code for each class along with metadata describing those classes. Both the MSIL and the metadata are stored in a standard Windows portable executable (PE) file. This file can be either a DLL or an EXE, with the general term *module* sometimes used to mean either of these. This section takes a closer look at MSIL and metadata.

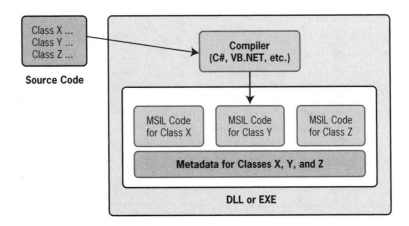

Figure 2-4   Compiling managed code written in any language produces MSIL and metadata describing that MSIL.

Microsoft Intermediate Language (MSIL)

MSIL is quite similar to a processor's native instruction set. However, no hardware that actually executes these instructions

MSIL defines a virtual instruction set

■ Perspective: Why Use MSIL?

The idea of compiling from a high-level language into a common intermediate language is a staple of modern compiler technology. Even before .NET, for instance, the compilers in Visual Studio transformed various programming languages into the same intermediate language, then used a common back end to compile this into a machine-specific binary. In this pre-.NET world, it was this binary that a user of the application would install.

For .NET Framework applications, however, what gets copied to the disk when an application is installed is not a machine-specific binary. Instead, it's the MSIL for this application, code that's analogous to the intermediate language that formerly remained hidden inside the compiler. Why make this change? What's the benefit of distributing code as MSIL?

The most obvious answer is the potential for portability. As discussed in Chapter 1, at least the core of the .NET Framework is available for systems that use non-Windows operating systems and non-Intel processors. Still, it's fair to view the .NET Framework as primarily a Windows-focused technology, and so portability isn't MSIL's primary purpose.

But portability isn't the only advantage of using an intermediate language. Unlike binary code, which can contain references to arbitrary memory addresses, MSIL code can be verified for type safety when it is loaded into memory. This allows better security and higher reliability, since some kinds of errors and a large set of possible attacks can be made impossible.

One potential drawback to using an intermediate language is that it might lead to slower code. The reality, though, is that since MSIL is always compiled before execution rather than interpreted, as described later, this turns out not to be a problem in most situations. And even if it were, hardware speeds just keep increasing. It's great working in software, isn't it? If things are too slow today, just wait a little while. They'll probably be fast enough in a year or two.

(today, at least) is available. Instead, MSIL code is always translated into native code for whatever processor this code is running on before it's executed. It's probably fair to say that a developer working in the .NET Framework environment need never fully understand MSIL. Nevertheless, it's worth knowing at least a little bit about what a compiler produces from code written in C# or VB or any other CLR-based language.

The CLR defines a stack-based virtual machine

As implied earlier in this chapter, the abstract machine defined by the CLR is stack based, which means that many MSIL operations are defined in terms of this stack. Here are a few example MSIL instructions and what they're used for:

- **add:** Adds the top two values on the stack and pushes the result back onto the stack.

- **box:** Converts a value type to a reference type; that is, it boxes the value.

- **br:** Transfers control (branches) to a specified location in memory.

- **call:** Calls a specified method.

- **ldfld:** Loads a specified field of an object onto the stack.

- **ldobj:** Copies the value of a specified value type onto the stack.

- **newobj:** Creates a new object or a new instance of a value type.

- **stfld:** Stores a value from the stack into a specified field of an object.

- **stobj:** Stores a value on the stack into a specified value type.

- **unbox:** Converts a boxed value type back to its ordinary form.

In effect, MSIL is the assembly language of the CLR. One interesting thing to notice about this tiny sample of the MSIL instruction set is how closely it maps to the abstractions of the CLR's CTS. Objects, value types, and even boxing and unboxing all have direct support. Also, some operations, such as the `newobj` used to create new instances, are analogous to operators more commonly found in high-level languages than they are to typical machine instructions.

MSIL reflects the CTS

▪ Perspective: MSIL vs. Java Bytecode

The concept of MSIL is similar to what Java calls *bytecode.* Java fans might point out, with some justification, that Microsoft has copied an approach first made popular by their technology. Microsoft sometimes responds to this claim, again with some justification, by observing that the idea of an intermediate language predates both Java bytecode and MSIL, with antecedents stretching back to UCSD Pascal's p-code and beyond.

In any case, it's interesting to compare the two technologies. The broad outlines are similar, with both the Java virtual machine and the CLR defining a stack-based virtual environment. One obvious difference is that Java bytecode was specifically designed to support the Java language, while MSIL was defined to support multiple languages. Still, a substantial amount of language semantics is embedded in MSIL, so while it is somewhat broader than Java bytecode, MSIL isn't completely general. Concepts defined by the CTS, such as the distinction between reference and value types, are fundamental to MSIL. This distinction is part of both C# and VB, and it will likely appear in most CLR-based languages. Another difference is that the Java virtual machine was designed to allow byte-code to be interpreted as well as compiled, while MSIL's designers explicitly targeted just-in-time (JIT) compilation (which is described later in this chapter). While interpreting MSIL is probably possible, it appears that it would be significantly less efficient than interpreting Java bytecode.

For a more detailed comparison of MSIL and Java bytecode, see K. John Gough's *Stacking Them Up: A Comparison of Virtual Machines*, available at various places on the Web.

For developers who wish to work directly in this low-level argot, the .NET Framework provides an MSIL assembler called *Ilasm.* Only the most masochistic developers are likely to use this tool, however, or those who need very low-level control. Why write in MSIL when you can use a simpler, more powerful language such as VB or C# and get the same result?

Metadata

Compiled managed code always has associated metadata

Compiling managed code always produces MSIL. Compiling managed code also always produces metadata describing that code. Metadata is information about the types defined in the managed code it's associated with, and it's stored in the same file as the MSIL generated from those types. Figure 2-5 shows an abstract view of a module produced by a CLR-based compiler. The file contains the MSIL code generated from the types in the original program, which once again are the three classes X, Y, and Z. Along with the code for the methods in each class, the file contains metadata describing these classes and any other types defined in this file. This information is loaded into memory when the file itself is loaded, making the metadata accessible at runtime. Metadata can also be read directly from

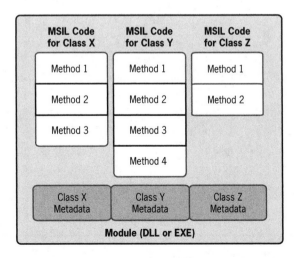

Figure 2-5   A module contains metadata for each type in the file.

the file that contains it, making information available even when code isn't loaded into memory. The process of reading metadata is known as *reflection,* and it's described in a bit more detail in Chapter 4.

What Metadata Contains

Metadata describes the types contained in a module. Among the information it stores for a type are the following things:

- The type's name

- The type's visibility, which can be *public* or *assembly*

- What type this type inherits from, if any

- Any interfaces the type implements

- Any methods the type implements

- Any properties the type exposes

- Any events the type provides

Metadata provides detailed information about each type

More detailed information is also available. For example, the description of each method includes the method's parameters and their types, along with the type of the method's return value.

Because metadata is always present, tools can rely on it always being available. Visual Studio, for example, uses metadata to provide IntelliSense, which shows a developer things like what methods are available for the class name she's just typed. A module's metadata can also be examined using the MSIL disassembler tool, commonly referred to as *Ildasm.* This tool is the reverse of the Ilasm tool mentioned earlier in this chapter— it's a disassembler for MSIL—and it can also provide a detailed display of the metadata contained in a particular module.

Tools can use metadata

Attributes

Metadata also includes *attributes.* Attributes are values that are stored in the metadata and can be read and used to control various aspects of how this code executes. Attributes can be added

Attributes contain values stored with metadata

to types, such as classes, and to fields, methods, and properties of those types. As described later in this book, the .NET Framework class library relies on attributes for many things, including specifying transaction requirements, indicating which methods should be exposed as SOAP-callable Web services, and describing security requirements. These attributes have standard names and functions defined by the various parts of the .NET Framework class library that use them.

Developers can create custom attributes

Developers can also create custom attributes used to control behavior in an application-specific way. To create a custom attribute, a developer using a CLR-based programming language such as C# or VB can define a class that inherits from System.Attribute. An instance of the resulting class will automatically have its value stored in metadata when it is compiled.

Organizing Managed Code: Assemblies

An assembly is one or more files that comprise a logical unit

A complete application often consists of many different files. Some files are modules—DLLs or EXEs—that contain code, while others might contain various kinds of resources such as image files. In .NET Framework applications, files that make up a logical unit of functionality are grouped into an *assembly*. Assemblies, described in this section, are fundamental to developing, deploying, and running .NET Framework applications.

Metadata for Assemblies: Manifests

Each assembly has a manifest

Assemblies are a logical construct; there's no single über-file that wraps all of the files in an assembly. In fact, it's not possible to tell what files belong to the same assembly just by looking at a directory listing. Instead, determining which files comprise a particular assembly requires examining that assembly's *manifest*. As just described, the metadata in a module, such as a DLL, contains information about the types in that module. An assembly's manifest, by contrast, contains information about all of the modules and other files in an assembly. In other words, a manifest is metadata about an assembly. The manifest is contained in one of the assembly's files, and it includes information about the assembly and the files that comprise it. Just as a tool such as Visual Studio generates metadata for each module it compiles, so too it generates an assembly with an appropriate manifest.

As Figure 2-6 shows, an assembly can be built from a single file or a group of files. With a single-file assembly, the manifest is stored in the file itself. With a multifile assembly, the manifest is stored in one of the files in the assembly. In either case, the manifest describes the entire assembly, while the metadata in a particular module describes the types in that module. Among the things an assembly's manifest includes are the following:

An assembly's manifest contains the assembly's name, its version number, and more

- The name of the assembly. All assemblies have a text name and can optionally have a strong name as well, as described in the next section.

- The assembly's version number. This number has the form <major version>.<minor version>.<build number>.<revision>. For example, the version number for an assembly that's part of a released application might be 1.2.1397.0. Note that versioning is per assembly, not per module.

- The assembly's culture, indicating the culture or language an assembly supports.

- A list of all files contained in this assembly, together with a hash value that's been computed from those files.

- What other assemblies this one depends on and the version number of each of those dependent assemblies.

Most assemblies consist of just a single DLL. Whether it contains one file or multiple files, however, an assembly is logically an indivisible unit. For example, assemblies define a boundary for

Assemblies define a scope for types

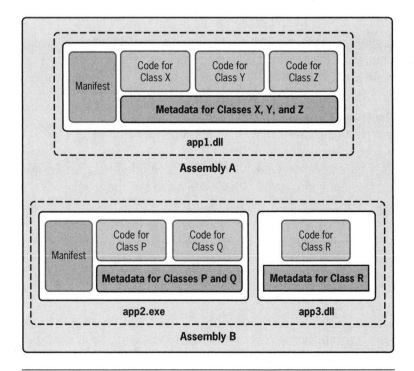

Figure 2-6   An assembly is often just a single DLL, but it can also include more than one file.

scoping types. To the CLR, a type name really consists of the name of the type together with the name of the assembly in which the type is defined.

Assemblies don't require registry entries

One important corollary of the way assemblies are structured is that, unlike COM classes, CLR classes don't have associated registry entries (unless they are also accessible as COM classes for backward compatibility, an option described in Chapter 4). When the CLR needs to find a class in some other assembly, it does not look up the class in the registry. Instead, it searches according to a well-defined (although slightly complex) algorithm that's described later in this chapter.

Requiring no registry entries also means that installing an assembly can entail simply copying its constituent files to an appropriate directory on the target machine's disk. Similarly, an assembly can often be uninstalled by simply deleting its files. Unlike older COM-based applications, software built on the .NET Framework doesn't need to modify the system registry.

Installing a .NET Framework application might require just copying its assemblies

Categorizing Assemblies

There are various ways to categorize assemblies. One distinction is between *static* and *dynamic* assemblies. Static assemblies are produced by a tool such as Visual Studio, and their contents are stored on disk. Most developers will create static assemblies, since the goal is usually to build an application that can be installed on one or more machines and then executed. It's also possible to create dynamic assemblies, however. The code (and metadata) for a dynamic assembly is created directly in memory and can be executed immediately upon creation. Once it has been created, a dynamic assembly can be saved to disk, then loaded and executed again. Probably the most common examples of dynamic assemblies are those created by ASP.NET when it processes .aspx pages, a topic covered in Chapter 5.

Both static and dynamic assemblies exist

Another way to categorize assemblies is by how they are named. Completely naming any assembly requires specifying three things: the assembly's name; its version number; and, if one is provided, the culture it supports. All assemblies have simple text names, such as "AccountAccess," but an assembly can also have a *strong name*. A strong name includes the usual three parts of an assembly name, but it also includes a digital signature computed on the assembly and the public key that corresponds to the private key used to create that signature. Strong names are unique and so can be used to identify a particular assembly unambiguously. If desired, it's also possible to embed the certificate of the entity creating an assembly's digital signature in the assembly itself. This allows anyone using the assembly to decide whether they trust this entity and so are willing to execute the assembly.

An assembly can have a strong name

Strong-named assemblies have their version numbers automatically checked by the CLR when they're loaded. Version control

The CLR performs version checking on assemblies with strong names

for assemblies without strong names, however, is the responsibility of the developer creating and using those assemblies. Because assemblies have version numbers, it's possible for multiple versions of the same assembly to be installed on the same machine at the same time. And because an assembly can specify exactly which version it requires of every other assembly it depends on, the pain that has resulted from DLL conflicts in the past can be minimized.

Assemblies can minimize DLL hell

Before .NET, installing a new version of a DLL required by one application would commonly break another application that relied on that same DLL. Poetically referred to as DLL hell, one of the goals of the .NET Framework was to address this problem. Using strong-named assemblies, a CLR-based application can insist on a particular version of each assembly it depends on without restricting other applications' use of new versions. Developers must still pay attention, however, or conflicts might arise. For example, suppose two versions of an assembly each write to the same temp file. Unless they agree on how this file should be shared, running both versions at once will lead to problems.

Executing Managed Code

Assemblies are loaded into memory only when needed

Assemblies provide a way to package modules containing MSIL and metadata into units for deployment. The goal of writing code is not to package and deploy it, however; it's to run it. The final section of this chapter looks at the most important aspects of running managed code.

Loading Assemblies

When an application built using the .NET Framework is executed, the assemblies that make up that application must be found and loaded into memory. Assemblies aren't loaded until they're needed, so if an application never calls any methods in a particular assembly, that assembly won't be loaded. (In fact, it need not even be present on the machine where the application is running.) Before any code in an assembly can be loaded, however, it must be found. How is this done?

The answer is not simple. In fact, the process the CLR uses to find assemblies is too complex to describe completely here. The broad outlines of the process are fairly straightforward, however. First, the CLR determines what version of a particular assembly it's looking for. By default, it will look only for the exact version specified for this assembly in the manifest of the assembly from which the call originated. This default can be changed by settings in various configuration files, so the CLR examines these files before it commences its search.

The CLR follows well-defined but involved rules to locate an assembly

Once it has determined exactly which version it needs, the CLR checks whether the desired assembly is already loaded. If it is, the search is over; this loaded version will be used. If the desired assembly is not already loaded, the CLR will begin searching in various places to find it. The first place the CLR looks is usually the *global assembly cache (GAC)*, a special directory intended to hold assemblies that are used by more than one application. Installing assemblies in this global assembly cache requires a process slightly more complex than just copying the assembly, and the cache can contain only assemblies with strong names.

The CLR looks first in the global assembly cache

If the assembly it's hunting for isn't in the global assembly cache, the CLR continues its search by checking for a *codebase* element in one of the configuration files for this application. If one is found, the CLR looks in the location this element specifies, such as a directory, for the desired assembly. Finding the right assembly in this location means the search is over, and this assembly will be loaded and used. Even if the location pointed to by a codebase element does not contain the desired assembly, however, the search is nevertheless over. A codebase element is meant to specify exactly where the assembly can be found. If the assembly is not at that location, something has gone wrong, the CLR gives up, and the attempt to load the new assembly fails.

The CLR can next look in the location referenced by a codebase element

If no codebase element exists, the CLR searches in other places

If there is no codebase element, however, the CLR will begin its last-ditch search for the desired assembly, a process called *probing*, in what's known as the *application base*. This can be either the root directory in which the application is installed or a URL, perhaps on some other machine. (It's worth pointing out that the CLR does not assume that all necessary assemblies for an application are installed on the same machine; they can also be located and installed across an internal network or the Internet.) If the elusive assembly isn't found here, the CLR continues searching in several other directories based on the name of the assembly, its culture, and more.

Despite the apparent complexity of this process, this description is not complete. There are other alternatives and even more options. For developers working with the .NET Framework, it's probably worth spending some time understanding this process in detail. Putting in the effort up front is likely to save time later when applications don't behave as expected.

Compiling MSIL

A compiler that produces managed code always generates MSIL. Yet MSIL can't be executed by any real processor. Before it can be run, MSIL code must be compiled yet again into native code that targets the processor on which it will execute. Two options exist for doing this: MSIL code can be compiled one method at a time during execution, or it can be compiled into native code all at once before an assembly is executed. This section describes both of these approaches.

JIT Compilation

MSIL code is typically JIT compiled before it's executed

The most common way to compile MSIL into native code is to let the CLR load an assembly and then compile each method the first time that method is invoked. Because each method is compiled only when it's first called, the process is called *just-in-time (JIT) compilation.*

Figures 2-7, 2-8, and 2-9 illustrate how the code in an assembly gets JIT compiled. This simple example shows just three classes,

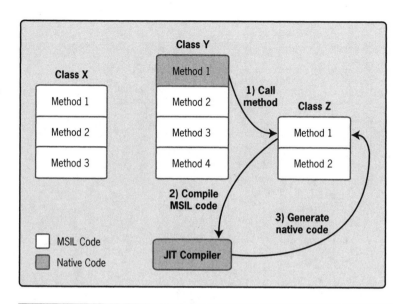

Figure 2-7   The first time class Z's method 1 is called, the JIT compiler is invoked to translate the method's MSIL into native code.

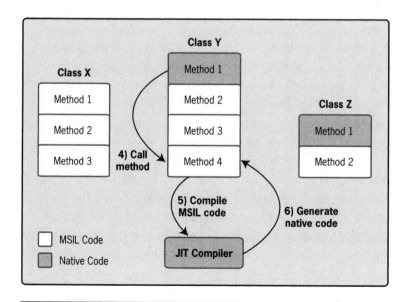

Figure 2-8   When class Y's method 4 is called, the JIT compiler is once again used to translate the method's MSIL into native code.

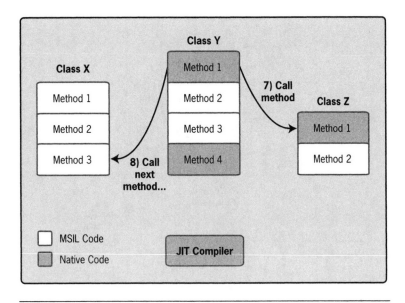

Figure 2-9   When class Z's method 1 is called again, no compilation is necessary.

A method is JIT compiled the first time it is called

once again called X, Y, and Z, each containing some number of methods. In Figure 2-7, only method 1 of class Y has been compiled. All other code in all other methods of the three classes is still in MSIL, the form in which it was loaded. When class Y's method 1 calls class Z's method 1, the CLR notices that this newly called method is not in an executable form. The CLR invokes the JIT compiler, which compiles class Z's method 1 and redirects calls made to that method to this compiled native code. The method can now execute.

A method always executes as native code

Similarly, in Figure 2-8, class Y's method 1 calls its own method 4. As before, this method is still in MSIL, so the JIT compiler is automatically invoked, and the method is compiled. Once again, a reference to the MSIL code for the method is replaced with one to the newly created native code, and the method executes.

Figure 2-9 shows what happens when class Y's method 1 again calls method 1 in class Z. This method has already been JIT compiled, so there's no need to do any more work. The native code has been saved in memory, so it just executes. The JIT compiler isn't involved. The process continues in this same way, with each method compiled the first time it is invoked.

When a method is JIT compiled, it's also checked for type safety. This process, called *verification*, examines the method's MSIL and metadata to ensure that the code makes no illegal accesses. The CLR's built-in security features, described in the next section, depend on this, as do other aspects of managed code behavior. Still, a system administrator can turn off verification—it's not required—which means that the CLR can execute managed code that is not type safe. This can be useful, since some compilers such as Visual Studio's Visual C++ can't generate type-safe code. In general, however, verification should be used whenever possible with .NET Framework applications.

Methods can be verified when they're JIT compiled

With JIT compilation, only those methods that get called will be compiled. If a method in an assembly is loaded but never used, it will stay in its MSIL form. Also, note that compiled native code is not saved back to disk. Instead, the process of JIT compilation is carried out each time an assembly is loaded. Finally, it's important to emphasize that the .NET Framework does not include an interpreter for MSIL. Executed code is either JIT compiled or compiled all at once, as described next.

Compiled code is not saved on disk

Creating a Native Image: NGEN

Instead of JIT compiling, an assembly's MSIL code can be translated into native code for a particular processor all at once using the Native Image Generator (NGEN). Contained in the file Ngen.exe, this command-line tool can be run on an assembly to produce a directly executable image. Rather than being JIT compiled one method at a time, the assembly will now be loaded as native code. This makes the initial phase of the application faster, since there's no need to pay the penalty of JIT

NGEN allows compiling an assembly into native code before the assembly is loaded

compilation on the first call to each method. Using NGEN doesn't make the overall speed of the application any better, however, since JIT compilation slows down only the first call to a method.

Deciding whether NGEN makes sense for a particular application can take some thought. Although a Windows service is available that automatically creates and updates NGEN-produced images, creating these precompiled images makes sense only for some kinds of .NET applications. It's probably fair to say that ordinary JIT compilation is the right choice in the majority of cases.

Securing Assemblies

An assembly defines a scope for types, a unit of versioning, and a logical deployment unit. An assembly also defines a security boundary. The CLR implements two different types of security for assemblies: *code access* security and *role-based* security. This section describes both.

Code Access Security

Code access security can limit what running code is allowed to do

Think about what happens when you run a pre-.NET Windows executable on your machine. You can decide whether that code is allowed to execute, but if you let it run, you can't control exactly what the code is allowed to do. This was a barely acceptable approach when all of the code loaded on your machine came from disks you or your system administrator installed. Now that most machines are connected to a global network, however, this all-or-nothing approach is no longer sufficient. It's often useful to download code from the Internet and run it locally, but the potential security risks in doing this can be huge. A malicious developer can create an application that looks useful but in fact erases your files or floods your friends with e-mail or performs some other destructive act. What's needed is some way to limit what code, especially downloaded code, is allowed to do. The code access security built into the CLR is intended to provide this.

Unlike the pre-.NET solution for controlling whether downloaded Windows code can run—asking the user—the .NET Framework's code access security doesn't rely on the user knowing what to do. Instead, what CLR-based code is allowed to do depends on the intersection of two things: what *permissions* that code requests and what permissions are granted to that code by the *security policy* in effect when the code executes. To indicate what kinds of access it needs, an assembly can specify exactly what permissions it requires from the environment in which it's running. Some examples of permissions an assembly can request are the following:

Code access security compares requested permissions with a security policy

- **UIPermission:** Allows access to the user interface

- **FileIOPermission:** Allows access to files or directories

- **FileDialogPermission:** Allows access only to files or directories that the user opens in a dialog box

- **PrintingPermission:** Allows access to printers

- **EnvironmentPermission:** Allows access to environment variables

- **RegistryPermission:** Allows access to the system registry on the machine

- **ReflectionPermission:** Allows access to an assembly's metadata

- **SecurityPermission:** Allows granting a group of permissions, including the right to call unmanaged code

- **WebPermission:** Allows establishing or receiving connections over the Web

Within these general permissions (and others—more are defined), finer-grained options can also be used. For example, FileIOPermission can specify read-only permission, write/delete/overwrite permission, append-only permission, or some combination of these. An assembly can also indicate

Fine-grained permissions are possible

◼ Perspective: The Perils of Mobile Code

Nobody knows better than Microsoft how dangerous code downloaded from the Internet can be. The company has received a huge amount of criticism in this area over the last few years.

One of the first lightning rods for attack was Microsoft's support for downloading ActiveX controls from Web servers. An ActiveX control is just a binary, so if the user allows it to run, it can do pretty much anything that user is allowed to do. Microsoft's Authenticode technology allows a publisher to sign an ActiveX control digitally, but it's still up to the user to decide whether to trust that publisher and run the control. In practice, only ActiveX controls produced by large organizations (such as Microsoft itself) have seen much use on the Internet. Most people think, quite correctly, that it's too dangerous to run even signed code from any but the most trusted sources.

Microsoft has received even more criticism and much more adverse publicity for e-mail-borne attacks. Various viruses have cost many organizations a lot of money, providing a very visible example of the dangers of running code received from a stranger. Yet educating the enormous number of nontechnical Windows users about these dangers is effectively impossible. Relying on the user not to run potentially dangerous code won't work. And even if it were possible to educate every user, there would still be unintentional bugs that could be exploited by attackers.

The Java world addressed this problem from the beginning. Because Java focused early on mobile code in the form of applets and because Java has always been built on a virtual machine, software written in Java could be downloaded with less risk. With the advent of the CLR, Microsoft was able to provide the same kind of "sandboxing" that Java offers. The latest incarnation of Microsoft's support for safely downloading and executing code, called ClickOnce deployment, is described in Chapter 4.

whether the permissions it requests are absolutely necessary for it to run, or whether they would just be nice to have but aren't essential. An assembly can even indicate that it should never be granted certain permissions or demand that its callers have a specific set.

There are two different ways for a developer to specify the permissions he'd like for an assembly. One option, called *declarative security*, lets the developer insert attributes into his code. (How attributes look in various CLR-based languages is shown in the next chapter.) Those attributes then become part of the metadata stored with that code, where they can be read by the CLR. The second approach, known as *imperative security*, allows the developer to specify permissions dynamically within his source code. This approach can't be used to request new permissions on the fly, but it can be used to demand that any callers have specific permissions.

An assembly can use declarative or imperative security

The creator of an assembly is free to request whatever permissions he wishes. The permissions actually granted to the assembly when it runs, however, depend on the security policy established for the machine on which the assembly is running. This security policy is defined by the machine's system administrator, and it specifies exactly which permissions should be granted to assemblies based on their identity and origin.

Administrators establish security policy

Each assembly provides *evidence* that the CLR can use to determine who created this assembly and where it came from. Evidence can consist of:

An assembly provides evidence of its origins

- The identity of an assembly's publisher, indicated by the publisher's digital signature on the assembly.

- The identity of the assembly itself, represented by the assembly's strong name.

- The Web site from which an assembly was downloaded, such as www.qwickbank.com.

- The exact URL from which an assembly was downloaded, such as http://www.qwickbank.com/downloads/accounts.exe.

- The zone, as defined by Microsoft Internet Explorer, from which an assembly was downloaded. Possible zones include the local intranet, the Internet, and others.

The CLR determines what an assembly is allowed to do

When an assembly is loaded, the CLR examines the evidence it provides. It also looks at the permissions this assembly requests and compares them with the security policy established for the machine on which the assembly is being loaded. The assembly is granted any requested permissions that are allowed by the security policy. For example, suppose an assembly downloaded from the Web site www.qwickbank.com carries the digital signature of QwickBank as its publisher and requests FileIOPermission and UIPermission. If the security policy on this machine is defined to allow only UIPermission to assemblies published by QwickBank and downloaded from QwickBank's Web site, the assembly will not be able to access any files. It will still be allowed to run and interact with a user, but any attempts to access files will fail.

An assembly's permissions are checked at runtime

As this simple example illustrates, permissions are checked at runtime, and an exception is generated if the code in an assembly attempts an operation for which it does not have permission. These runtime checks can also prevent an assembly with limited permissions from duping an assembly with broader permissions into performing tasks that shouldn't be allowed. An assembly can even demand that any code calling into it has a specific digital signature. Finally, note that all of the mechanisms used for code security depend on the verification process that's part of JIT compilation. If verification has been bypassed, these mechanisms can't be guaranteed to work.

While fully understanding the .NET Framework's code security takes some effort, two things should be clear. First, this mechanism is quite flexible, offering options that address a wide range of needs. Second, in a world of global networks and mobile code, providing an enforceable way to limit what code can do is essential.

Role-Based Security

Code access security allows the CLR to limit what a particular assembly is allowed to do based on the assembly's name, who published it, and where it came from. But code access security provides no way to control what an assembly is allowed to do based on the identity of the user on whose behalf the assembly is running. Providing this kind of control is the goal of role-based security.

The foundation for role-based security is a *principal* object. This object contains both the identity of a user and the roles to which she belongs. A user's identity is indicated by an *identity* object, which contains both the user's identity, expressed as a name or an account, and an indication of how that identity has been authenticated. In an all-Windows environment, for example, authentication might be done with Kerberos, while some other mechanism might be used on the Internet. The user's role typically identifies some kind of group the user belongs to that is useful for deciding what that user is allowed to access. For example, the fictitious QwickBank might have roles such as loan officer, teller, clerk, and others, each of which is likely to be allowed different levels of access.

A user can belong to one or more roles

Code in an assembly can demand that only users with a specific identity or a specific role be allowed to access it. This demand can be made for a class as a whole or for a specific method, property, or event. Whatever granularity is chosen, the demand can be made either imperatively or declaratively. For *imperative demands*, the code must make an explicit call to cause a check, while in *declarative demands*, the code contains attributes that are stored in metadata and then used by the CLR to check the user's identity automatically. In either case, the result is the

An assembly can use roles to limit what its users are allowed to do

same: The user will be granted access to this class, method, property, or event only if her identity or role matches what the assembly specifies.

Garbage Collection

Garbage collection frees unused objects

The managed heap plays an important role in the execution of a .NET Framework application. Every instance of a reference type—every class, every string, and more—is allocated on the heap. As the application runs, the memory allotted to the heap fills up. Before new instances can be created, more space must be made available. The process of doing this is called *garbage collection.*

Describing Garbage Collection

Garbage collection happens automatically

When the CLR notices that the heap is full, it will automatically run the garbage collector. (An application can also explicitly request that the garbage collector be run, but this isn't an especially common thing to do.) To understand how garbage collection works, think once again about the way reference types are allocated. As Figure 2-10 shows, each instance of a reference type has an entry on the stack that points to its actual value on the heap. In the figure, the stack contains the decimal value 32.4, a reference to the string "Hello," the integer value 14, and a reference to the boxed integer value 169. The two reference types—the string and the boxed integer—have their values stored on the heap.

Garbage objects can appear anywhere in the heap

But notice that the heap also contains information for an object of class X. The figure isn't drawn to scale—this object would likely take up much more space than either the string or the boxed integer—but it's entirely possible that the chunk of heap memory allocated for the object would be in between the other two types. Maybe this object was created by a method that has completed execution, for example, so the reference that pointed to it from the stack is now gone. Whatever the situation, this object is just taking up space that could be used for something else. In other words, it's garbage.

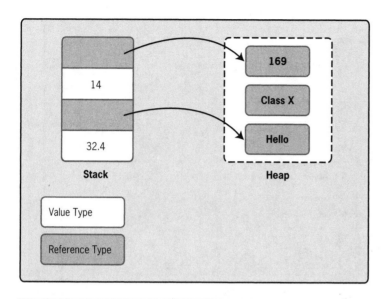

Figure 2-10   The space occupied on the heap by the object of class X is garbage.

When the garbage collector runs, it scans the heap looking for this kind of garbage. Once it knows which parts of the heap are garbage, it rearranges the heap's contents, packing more closely together those values that are still being used. For example, after garbage collection, the very simple case shown earlier would now look as illustrated in Figure 2-11. The garbage from the object of class X is gone, and the space it formerly occupied has been reused to store other information that's still in use.

Garbage collection can reposition the contents of the heap

As this example suggests, longer-lived objects will migrate toward one end of the heap over time. In real software, it's typical for the most recently allocated objects also to be the ones that most quickly become garbage. When looking for garbage, it makes sense to look first at the part of the heap where the most recently allocated objects will be. The CLR's garbage collector does exactly this, examining first this most recent generation of objects and reclaiming any unused space occupied by garbage. If this doesn't free up sufficient memory, the garbage collector

The garbage collector views objects in generations

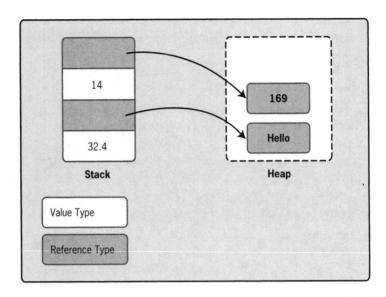

Figure 2-11   The garbage collector rearranges data on the heap to free more memory.

will examine the next generation of objects, those that were allocated somewhat less recently. If this still doesn't free up enough space to meet current needs, the collector will examine all remaining objects in the managed heap, freeing anything that's no longer being used.

Finalizers

An object's finalizer runs just before the object is destroyed

Every object on the heap has a special method called a *finalizer*. By default, however, this method does nothing. If a type needs to perform some final clean-up operations before it is destroyed, the developer creating it can override the default finalizer, adding code to do whatever is required. Before an object with a finalizer is freed, it is placed on the finalize list. Eventually, each object on this list will have its finalizer run.

Finalizers are non-deterministic

Note that a finalizer is not the same thing as the notion of a destructor provided in languages such as C++. You can't be sure when the finalizer will run, or even if it will run (the program could crash before this happens). If an object needs deterministic finalization behavior, guaranteeing that a particular method will run at a specific time before the object is destroyed, it should implement its own method to do this and then require its users to call this method when they're finished using the object.

Application Domains

The CLR is implemented as a DLL, which allows it to be used in a quite general way. It also means, however, that there must typically be an EXE provided to host the CLR and the DLLs in any assemblies it loads. A *runtime host* can provide this function. The runtime host loads and initializes the CLR and then typically transfers control to managed code. ASP.NET provides a runtime host, as does SQL Server 2005, Internet Explorer, and other applications. The Windows shell also acts as a runtime host for loading standalone executables that use managed code.

A runtime host is an EXE that hosts the CLR

A runtime host creates one or more *application domains* within its process. Each process contains a default application domain, and each assembly is loaded into some application domain within a particular process. Application domains are commonly called *app domains,* and they're quite a bit like a traditional operating system process. Like a process, an app domain isolates the application it contains from those in all other app domains. But because multiple app domains can exist inside a single process, communication between them can be much more efficient than communication between different processes.

An app domain isolates the assemblies it contains

Yet how can app domains guarantee isolation? Without the built-in support for processes provided by an operating system, what guarantee is there that applications running in two separate app domains in the same process won't interfere with each other? The answer is, once again, verification. Because managed code is checked for type safety when it's JIT compiled, the system can be certain that no assembly will directly access anything outside its own boundaries.

App domain isolation depends on verification

*An app domain
provides the benefits
of a process without
the overhead*

App domains can be used in a variety of ways. For example,
ASP.NET runs each Web application in its own app domain.
This allows the applications to remain isolated from each other,
yet it doesn't incur the overhead of running many different
processes. Internet Explorer, another runtime host, can download Windows Forms controls from the Internet and then run
each one in its own app domain. Once again, the benefit is
isolation, along with the added security this implies, without
the expense of cross-process communication. And because
applications can be started and stopped independently in
different app domains in the same process, this approach
also avoids the overhead of starting a new process for each
application.

Figure 2-12 shows how this looks. App domain 1, the default
app domain, contains assemblies A, B, and C. Assemblies D and
E have been loaded into app domain 2, while assembly F is running in app domain 3. Even though all of these assemblies are
running in a single process, each app domain's assemblies are
completely independent from those in the other app domains.

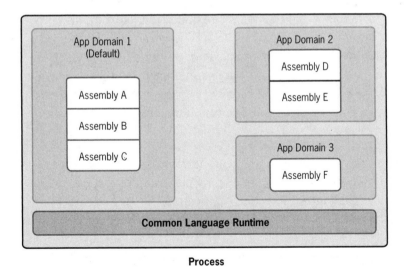

Figure 2-12   A process can contain one or more application domains.

App domains also serve another purpose. Recall that the .NET Framework is intended to run on Windows and at least potentially on other operating systems. Different systems have quite different process models, especially systems used on small devices. By defining its own "process" model with app domains, the .NET Framework can provide a consistent environment across all of these platforms.

App domains provide a consistent environment on multiple platforms

Conclusion

The CLR introduces many new ideas for Windows developers. To help tie together the concepts described in this chapter, Figure 2-13 shows a process running a CLR-based application.

All CLR-based applications have much in common

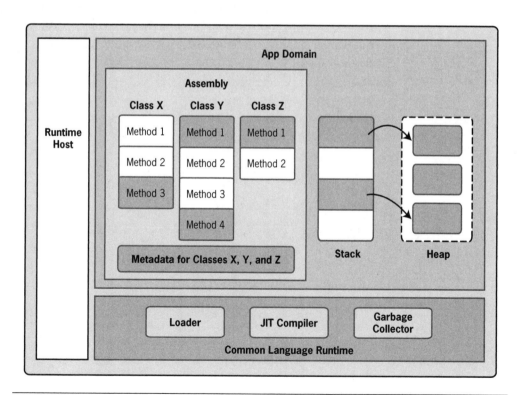

Figure 2-13   Managed code, software built on the .NET Framework, relies on the CLR to provide many different services.

The process includes a runtime host, a single app domain, and the CLR itself. Some of the CLR's more important components are shown, including the loader, the JIT compiler, and the garbage collector. Within the app domain, there's a single loaded assembly containing the three classes X, Y, and Z along with their metadata. Some methods in the classes have already been JIT-compiled, while others have not. And as the figure shows, variables of various value and reference types are in use by this running code. There's even some garbage on the heap waiting to be collected.

Understanding the CLR is important

Creating software on the .NET Framework requires using the CLR, but it doesn't really require understanding how the CLR provides all of its services. Still, having a good conceptual model of what's going on will help in understanding how .NET Framework applications work. This knowledge will help you make better choices and build better applications using the .NET Framework.

3

.NET Languages

The Common Language Runtime (CLR) is explicitly designed to support multiple languages. In general, though, languages built on the CLR tend to have a good deal in common. By defining a large set of core semantics, the CLR also defines a large part of a typical programming language built using it. For example, a substantial chunk of learning any CLR-based language is seeing how the standard types defined by the CLR are mapped into that language. You must also learn the language's syntax, of course, including the control structures the language provides. Yet once you know what the CLR offers, you're a long way down the path to learning any language built on top of it.

This chapter describes C# and Visual Basic (VB), the most important CLR-based languages. It also takes a brief look at C++/CLI, extensions that allow C++ developers to write CLR-based code. The goal is not to provide exhaustive coverage of every language feature—that would require three more books—but rather to give you a sense of how these languages look and how they express the core functionality provided by the CLR. Throughout, the language versions described are those provided with Visual Studio 2005.

Understanding a CLR-based language starts with understanding the CLR

■ Perspective: What About Java for the .NET Framework?

From the beginning, Microsoft has provided J#, a version of the Java programming language for the .NET Framework. This language implements Java's syntax and behavior on top of the CLR. It's nice to have the option, but when does it really make sense to use J#?

There are two main situations when J# is the right choice. The first is when existing Java code needs to be moved to the .NET Framework. This code might have been created using Visual J++, Microsoft's pre-.NET Java tool, or a more mainstream Java tool such as Eclipse. In either case, the existence of J# makes it easier to port this code to the .NET world. It's important to realize, though, that the .NET Framework doesn't implement commonly used Java technologies such as Java Server Pages and Enterprise JavaBeans, so not all Java code can be easily ported. Still, typical Java business logic can be made to run on the .NET Framework without too much work. There's even a binary converter tool that can directly convert Java bytecode into MSIL, a useful thing to have if an application's source is no longer available.

The second situation in which J# might be a good language choice is when an experienced Java developer moves to the .NET Framework. People often feel an enormous attachment to their syntax, and so working in a familiar language might make the transition easier. Still, it's hard to argue that creating new .NET Framework code in Java is really a good thing. Microsoft is clearly focused on C# and VB as the main languages for building new .NET applications, and so there's some risk in choosing anything else. Also, the absence of standard Java packages in .NET means that this transitioning Java developer still won't feel completely at home—there's still a lot to learn. And given the strong similarities between Java and C#, even the biggest Java fan shouldn't be too upset at switching to C# instead.

Microsoft's Java support is clearly focused on migrating code and developers to the .NET Framework, rather than on helping developers create great new software in Java. The battle lines are clear: It's .NET vs. the Java world. This is unquestionably a good thing. Having two powerful technology camps, each with a strong position, is the ideal world. Each provides innovations that the other can learn from, and in the end, the competition benefits everyone.

C#

As its name suggests, C# is a member of the C family of programming languages. Unlike C, C# is explicitly object-oriented. Unlike C++, however, which was once the most widely used object-oriented language in this family, C# isn't fiendishly complicated. Instead, C# was designed to be easily approachable by anyone with a background in C++ or Java.

C# is an object-oriented language with a C-like syntax

Designed by Microsoft, C# first appeared with the release of Visual Studio .NET in 2002. Building on this initial version, Visual Studio 2005 implements C# 2.0. As with everything else in this book, the version of the language described here is the one provided in this 2005 release.

Visual Studio 2005 implements version 2.0 of the C# language

The most popular tool today for creating C# code is Microsoft's Visual Studio. It's not the only choice, however. Microsoft also provides a command-line compiler with the .NET Framework called csc.exe, and the open source world has also created a C# compiler. Given the strong support Visual Studio provides for building CLR-based applications in C#, however, it's hard to imagine that other alternatives will attract a large share of developers.

Microsoft provides the dominant C# compilers but not the only ones

A C# Example

Like most programming languages, C# defines data types, control structures, and more. Unlike older languages, however, C# does this by building on the CLR. To illustrate this, here's a simple C# example:

```
// A C# example
interface IMath
{
    int Factorial(int f);
    double SquareRoot(double s);
}

class Compute : IMath
{
```

```
public int Factorial(int f)
{
    int i;
    int result = 1;
    for (i=2; i<=f; i++)
        result = result * i;
    return result;
}

public double SquareRoot(double s)
{
    return System.Math.Sqrt(s);
}
}

class DisplayValues
{
    static void Main()
    {
        Compute c = new Compute();
        int v;
        v = 5;
        System.Console.WriteLine(
            "{0} factorial: {1}",
            v, c.Factorial(v));
        System.Console.WriteLine(
            "Square root of {0}: {1:f4}",
            v, c.SquareRoot(v));
    }
}
```

Every C# program is made up of one or more types

The program begins with a comment, indicated by two slashes, giving a brief description of the program's purpose. The body of the program consists of three types: an interface named IMath and the two classes Compute and DisplayValues. All C# programs consist of some number of types, the outermost of which must be classes, interfaces, structures, enums, or delegates. (Namespaces, discussed later, can also appear here.) All methods, fields, and other type members must belong to one of these types, which means that C# doesn't allow either global variables or global methods.

A C# interface is an expression of a CTS interface

The IMath interface, which is a C# incarnation of the Common Type System (CTS) interface type described in Chapter 2, defines the methods Factorial and SquareRoot. Each of these methods takes one parameter and returns a numeric result. These parameters are passed by value, the default in C#. This means that changes made to the parameter's value within the method won't be seen by the caller once the method returns. Placing the keyword *ref* in front of a parameter causes that parameter to be passed by reference, so any changes made within the method will be reflected back to the caller.

Each class in this example is also a C# incarnation of the underlying CTS type. C# classes can implement one or more interfaces, inherit from at most one other class, and do all of the other things defined for a CTS class. The first class shown here, Compute, implements the IMath interface, as indicated by the colon between Compute and IMath. Accordingly, this class must contain implementations for both of the interface's methods. The body of the Factorial method declares a pair of integer variables (known as *fields* in the jargon of the CTS), initializes the second of them to 1, then uses a simple for loop to calculate the factorial of its parameter (and doesn't bother to check for overflow, which is admittedly bad programming practice). Compute's second method, SquareRoot, is even simpler. It relies on the .NET Framework class library, calling the Sqrt function provided by the Math class in the System namespace.

A C# class is an expression of a CTS class

The last type in this simple example, the class DisplayValues, contains only a single method named Main. Much like C and C++, a C# program begins executing with this method in whatever type it appears. Main must be declared as static, and although it's not shown here, it can take arguments passed in when the program is started. In this example, Main returns void, which is C#'s way of saying that the method has no return value. The type void cannot be used for parameters as in C and C++, however. Instead, its only purpose is to indicate that a method returns no value.

Execution of a C# program begins with the method named Main

In this example, Main creates an instance of the Compute class using C#'s *new* operator. When this program is executed, new will be translated into the MSIL instruction newobj described in Chapter 2. Main next declares an int variable and sets its value to 5. This value is then passed as a parameter into calls to the Factorial and SquareRoot methods provided by the Compute instance. Factorial expects an int, which is exactly what's passed in this call, but SquareRoot expects a double. The int will automatically be converted into a double, since this conversion can be done with no loss of information. C# calls this an *implicit* conversion, distinguishing it from type conversions that are marked explicitly in the code.

The Console class's WriteLine method writes formatted output to the console

The results are written out using the WriteLine method of the Console class, another standard part of the .NET Framework's System namespace. This method uses numbers that are wrapped in curly braces and that correspond to the variables to be output. Note that in the second call to WriteLine, the number in braces is followed by ":f4." This formatting directive means that the value should be written as a fixed-point number with four places to the right of the decimal. Accordingly, the output of this simple program is

```
5 factorial: 120
Square root of 5: 2.2361
```

This example is unrealistically simple, but the goal is to give you a feeling for the general structure and style of C#. There's much more to the language, as described next.

C# Types

C# types are built on CTS types

Each type defined by C# is built on an analogous CTS type provided by the CLR. Table 3-1 shows most of the CTS types and their C# equivalents. As mentioned earlier in this book, all of these data types are defined in the System namespace. The C# equivalents shown here are in fact just shorthand synonyms for

Table 3-1   Some CTS Types and Their C# Equivalents

CTS	C#
Byte	byte
Char	char
Int16	short
Int32	int
Int64	long
UInt16	ushort
UInt32	uint
UInt64	ulong
Single	float
Double	double
Decimal	decimal
Boolean	bool
Class	class
Interface	interface
Delegate	delegate

these alternative definitions. In the example just shown, for instance, the line

```
int i;
```

could have been replaced with

```
System.Int32 i;
```

Both work, and both produce exactly the same results.

Note that C# is case sensitive. Declaring a variable as "Double" rather than "double" will result in a compiler error. For people accustomed to languages derived from C, this will seem normal. To others, however, it might take a little getting used to.

Classes

Like a CTS class, a C# class can inherit directly from only one other class

C# classes expose the behaviors of a CTS class using a C-derived syntax. For example, CTS classes can implement one or more interfaces but inherit directly from at most one other class. A C# class Calculator that implements the interfaces IAlgebra and ITrig and inherits from the class MathBasics would be declared as

```
class Calculator : MathBasics, IAlgebra, ITrig { ... }
```

Note that the base class, if there is one, must come first in this list, followed by any interface names. C# classes can also be labeled as sealed or abstract, as defined in Chapter 2, and can be assigned a visibility of public or internal (which is the default). These translate into the CTS-defined visibilities public and assembly, respectively. All of this information is stored in the metadata for the class once it has been compiled.

A C# class can include fields, methods, and properties

A C# class can contain fields, methods, and properties, all of which are defined for any CTS class. Each of these has an accessibility, which is indicated in C# by an appropriate access modifier such as public or private. Fields and methods were both illustrated in the simple example program shown earlier, but properties are important enough to deserve their own example.

A property forces all access to a value to use get and set methods

Any field marked as public can be accessed directly by code in another class. But suppose the class in which this field is defined needs to control how that access happens. Maybe every assignment to this field should be checked against pre-defined limits, for example, and maybe every attempt to read this field should be verified in some way. One way to address this would be to mark the field as private, then create methods through which the field could be modified and read. Because this pattern is so common, however, C# provides properties as an easier way to accomplish the same thing. Here's a simple example:

```
class PriorityValue
{
    private int pValue;
```

```
    public int Priority
    {
        get
        {
            return pValue;
        }
        set
        {
            if (value > 0 && value < 11)
                pValue = value;
        }
    }
}
class PropertyExample
{
    static void Main()
    {
        PriorityValue p = new PriorityValue();
        p.Priority = 8;
        System.Console.WriteLine("Priority: {0}",
            p.Priority);
    }
}
```

The class PriorityValue declares the private field pValue followed by a property named Priority. You can tell that Priority is a property because it contains the two accessors *get* and *set*. All access to a property goes through the code contained in these accessors. Here, for example, an attempt to read the Priority property executes the *get* code, which just returns whatever is in pValue. An attempt to modify Priority executes the *set* code, which updates this property only if the new value is between 1 and 10. The keyword *value* contains whatever the calling code is trying to assign to this property.

Why are properties an improvement over writing your own methods to get and set a field's value? Because rather than requiring explicit calls to get and set methods, code using a property views that property just as it would a field—the syntax is the same. This lets the calling code be simple while still letting the property control how it is read and modified. In fact, there's a strong argument that public fields should never be used. Properties are always a better choice.

Properties can be accessed just like fields

Classes can provide constructors, override methods in their parent, and redefine operators

A class can implement one or more constructors, which are methods called when an instance of this class is created. Each class can also provide at most one destructor, which is actually the name C# uses for a finalizer, a concept described in Chapter 2. If the class inherits from another class, it can potentially override one or more of the type members, such as a method, in its parent. To do this, the member in the parent must be declared with the keyword *virtual*, and the child class must label the new member with the keyword *override*. A class can also define overloaded operators. An overloaded operator is one that has been redefined to have a special meaning when used with instances of this class. For example, a class representing workgroups in an organization might redefine the + operator to mean combining two workgroups into one.

Interfaces

A C# interface can inherit directly from one or more other interfaces

Interfaces are relatively simple things, and the basic C# syntax for describing an interface was shown in the earlier example. Not shown there was how C# expresses multiple interface inheritance, that is, one interface inheriting from more than one parent. If, for example, the interface ITrig inherits from the three interfaces, ISine, ICosine, and ITangent, it could be declared as

```
Interface ITrig: ISine, ICosine, ITangent { ... }
```

ITrig will contain all the methods, properties, and other type members defined in its three parent interfaces as well as anything it defines on its own.

Structures

C# structures are like slightly simplified C# classes

The CTS doesn't explicitly define a structure type. Instead, C# structures are based on classes, and so like a class, a structure can implement interfaces, contain methods, fields, and properties, and more. Unlike classes, however, structures are value types (they inherit from System.ValueType) rather than reference types, which means they're allocated on the stack. Recall that value types are also prohibited from participating in inheritance, so unlike a class, a structure can't inherit from another type. It's also not possible to define a type that inherits from a structure.

Here's a simple example of a C# structure:

```
struct employee
{
    string name;
    int age;
}
```

In this example, the structure contains only fields, much like a traditional C-style structure. Yet a structure can be much more complex. The Compute class shown earlier, for instance, could be converted to a structure, methods and all, by just changing the keyword *class* in its definition to *struct*. If this were done, things would be slightly different during execution, but the program's output would be unchanged.

Arrays

As in other languages, C# arrays are ordered groups of elements of the same type. Unlike many other languages, however, C# arrays are objects. In fact, as described in Chapter 2, they are reference types, which means they get allocated on the heap. Here's an example that declares a single-dimensional array of integers:

Like CTS arrays, C# arrays are reference types

```
int[] ages;
```

Since ages is an object, no instance exists until one is explicitly created. This can be done with

```
ages = new int[10];
```

which allocates space for ten integers on the heap. As this example shows, a C# array has no fixed size until an instance of that array type is created. It's also possible to both declare and create an array instance in a single statement, such as

```
int[] ages = new int[10];
```

Arrays of any type can be declared, but exactly how an array gets allocated depends on whether it's an array of value types or reference types. The example just shown allocates space for ten integers on the heap, while

```
string[] names = new string[10];
```

allocates space for ten references to strings on the heap. An array of value types, such as ints, actually contains the values, but an array of reference types, such as the strings in this example, contains only references to values.

C# arrays can be multidimensional

Arrays can also have multiple dimensions. For example, the statement

```
int[,] points = new int[10,20];
```

creates a two-dimensional array of integers. The first dimension has 10 elements, while the second has 20. Regardless of the number of dimensions in an array, however, the lower bound of each one is always zero.

Standard methods and properties can be accessed on all C# arrays

C#'s array type is built on the core array support provided by the CLR. As mentioned in the previous chapter, all CLR-based arrays, including all C# arrays, inherit from System.Array. This base type provides various methods and properties that can be accessed on any instance of an array type. For example, the GetLength method can be used to determine the number of elements in a particular dimension of an array, while the CopyTo method can be used to copy all of the elements in a one-dimensional array to another one-dimensional array.

Delegates and Events

Passing a reference to a method as a parameter is often useful

Passing a reference to a method is a reasonably common thing to do. For example, suppose you need to tell some chunk of code what method in your code should be called when a specific event occurs. You need some way to pass in the identity of this callback function at runtime. In C++, you can do this by passing the address of the method, that is, a pointer to the code you want to be called. In the type-safe world of the .NET Framework, however, passing raw addresses isn't allowed. Yet the problem doesn't go away. A type-safe way to pass a reference to a method is still useful.

As described briefly in Chapter 2, the CTS defines the reference type *delegate* for this purpose. A delegate is an object that contains a reference to a method with a specific signature. Once it has been created and initialized, it can be passed as a parameter into some other method and then invoked. Here's a simple example of creating and using a delegate in C#:

A C# delegate provides a type-safe way to pass a reference to a method

```
delegate void SDelegate(string s);
class DelegateExample
{
    public static void Main()
    {
        SDelegate del = new SDelegate(WriteString);
        CallDelegate(del);
    }
    public static void CallDelegate(SDelegate Write)
    {
        System.Console.WriteLine("In CallDelegate");
        Write("A delegated hello");
    }
    public static void WriteString(string s)
    {
        System.Console.WriteLine("In WriteString:
            {0}", s);
    }
}
```

The example begins by defining SDelegate as a delegate type. This definition specifies that SDelegate objects can contain references only to methods that take a single string parameter. In the example's Main method, a variable del of type SDelegate is declared and then initialized to contain a reference to the WriteString method. This method is defined later in the class, and as required, has a single parameter of type string. Main then invokes the CallDelegate method, passing in del as a parameter.

CallDelegate is defined to take an SDelegate as its parameter. In other words, what gets passed to this method is a delegate object that contains the address of some method. Because it's an SDelegate, that method must have a single parameter of type string. Inside CallDelegate, the method identified by the passed-in parameter is referred to as Write, and after printing a simple message, CallDelegate invokes this Write method. Because Write is actually a delegate, however, what really gets called is the method this delegate references, WriteString. The output of this simple example is

```
In CallDelegate
In WriteString: A delegated hello
```

Note that the CallDelegate method executes first, followed by WriteString.

A delegate can be combined with other delegates

Delegates can be significantly more complicated than this. They can be combined, for example, so that calling a single delegate results in calls to the two or more other delegates it contains. Yet even simple delegates can be useful. By providing a type-safe way to pass a reference to a method, they offer this important feature in a way that's significantly less risky than previous languages.

The .NET Framework and C# provide delegate-based support for events

One very popular use of delegates is for handling events. In a GUI, for instance, the user's mouse clicks, key presses, and other inputs can be received as events, and events are also useful in other contexts. Because events are so common, C# and the .NET Framework provide special support for using delegates to handle events in a consistent way. The delegate an event uses is referred to as an *event handler*, but it's really just an ordinary delegate. The Framework defines two conventions for these event handlers, however:

- An event handler doesn't return a value, i.e., its return type is void.

- An event handler always takes two arguments. The first argument, identifying the source of the event, is by convention named *sender* and is of type System.Object (or in C#, just the type object, which is an alias for System.Object). This makes it easy for the receiver of an event to communicate back to whatever object raised the event by, say, invoking a method in that object. The second argument, containing any data that the source passes when it calls this event handler, is traditionally named *e* and is of type System.EventArgs or a type that inherits from System.EventArgs.

Here's an example declaration for an event handler:

```
public delegate void MyEventHandler(object sender,
  MyEventArgs e);
```

Delegates used for events follow specific conventions

In this example, the type MyEventArgs must be derived from System.EventArgs, extending that base type as needed to carry the event's data. For events that generate no event-specific information, the type used for the data passed into the event handler can be just System.EventArgs. (Even when no data is being passed, the convention for events requires that this parameter still appear in the call.) Because it's so common for an event not to have any event-specific data, the System namespace also includes a built-in type called EventHandler. This type is just a delegate with two arguments: an object followed by a System.EventArgs.

Once an appropriate event handler (i.e., a delegate that follows the conventions just described) has been declared, it's possible to define an event using this delegate. Here's an example:

C# provides the event keyword for declaring events

```
public event MyEventHandler MyEvent;
```

As this example shows, the declaration must include the *event* keyword and the type must be a delegate type.

Given these basics, the clearest way to understand how events work is to look at an example. The simple illustration below contains three classes: EventSource, which defines the event; EventSink, which receives and responds to the event; and EventMain, which creates instances of these two classes, then actually raises the event. Here's the code:

```
public class EventSource
{
    public event System.EventHandler EventX;
    public void RaiseEventX()
    {
        if (EventX != null)
            EventX(this, System.EventArgs.Empty);
    }
}
public class EventSink
{
    public EventSink(EventSource es)
    {
        es.EventX += new
            System.EventHandler(ReceiveEvent);
    }
    public void ReceiveEvent(object sender,
        System.EventArgs e)
    {
        System.Console.WriteLine("EventX raised");
    }
}
public class EventMain
{
    public static void Main()
    {
        EventSource source = new EventSource();
        EventSink sink = new EventSink(source);
        source.RaiseEventX();
    }
}
```

Events are initial-
ized to null

The event used in this example, EventX, is declared at the begin-ning of the EventSource class. Because the event has no associ-ated data, this declaration uses the Framework's standard System.EventHandler class rather than declaring a custom event hander. Following this declaration is the RaiseEventX method. An event that has no event handlers registered for it will have the value of null, and so after making sure that EventX isn't null—there's actually something to call—this method invokes the event. (System.EventArgs.Empty indicates that no data is being passed with the event.) Since an event is in fact a delegate, what's actually called is whatever method this delegate points to. And while this example doesn't show this, a delegate can point to multiple methods, so raising an event will cause all of the methods that have registered for it to be executed.

The second class, EventSink, illustrates one approach to registering for and processing an event. The class's constructor, which like all constructors has the same name as the class itself and runs whenever an instance of the class is created, expects to be passed an instance of an EventSource object. It then registers an event handler for EventX using the += operator. In this simple example, EventSink's constructor registers the class's ReceiveEvent method. ReceiveEvent has the standard arguments used for events, and once it's called, this method will write a simple message to the console. (Although this example doesn't show it, event handlers can also be unregistered using the –= operator.)

EventSinks can register for events using C#'s += operator

The final class, EventMain, contains the example's Main method. This method first creates an instance of EventSource, then creates an instance of EventSink, passing in the just-instantiated EventSource object. This causes EventSink's constructor to execute, registering the ReceiveEvent method with EventX in EventSource. In its final line, the Main method invokes the RaiseEventX method defined in EventSource. The result is the invocation of ReceiveEvent, and the program writes out

```
EventX raised
```

In the interest of simplicity, this example doesn't quite follow all of the conventions of events. Still, this example illustrates the fundamentals of how delegates are slightly enhanced by C# and some .NET Framework conventions to provide more direct support for events.

Direct support for events makes using this common paradigm easier

Generics

Suppose you wish to write a class that can work with data of various types. Maybe a particular application must work with information in pairs, for example, manipulating two values of the same type. One approach to doing this would be to define a different class for each kind of pair: one class for a pair of integers, another for a pair of strings, and so on. A more general solution would be to create a Pair class that stores two values of the type System.Object. Since every .NET type inherits from System.Object, an instance of this class could store integers, strings, and anything else. Yet System.Object can be anything, and so nothing would prevent an instance of this Pair class from storing one integer and one string rather than a pair of identically-typed values. For this and other reasons, working directly with System.Object types isn't an especially attractive solution.

What's really needed is a way to create an instance of a Pair type that allows specifying at creation time exactly what kind of information this Pair will contain, then enforces that specification. To address this, version 2.0 of C# in Visual Studio 2005 has added support for *generic* types, commonly known as just *generics*. When a generic type is defined, one or more of the types it uses is left unspecified. The actual type(s) that should be used are spelled out only when an instance of the generic type is created. Those types can be different for different instances of the same generic type.

For example, here's a simple illustration of defining and using a generic Pair class:

```
class Pair<T>
{
    T element1, element2;

    public void SetPair(T first, T second)
    {
        element1 = first;
        element2 = second;
    }
```

```
    public T GetFirst()
    {
        return element1;
    }

    public T GetSecond()
    {
        return element2;
    }
}

class GenericsExample
{
    static void Main()
    {
        Pair<int> i = new Pair<int>();
        i.SetPair(42,48);
        System.Console.WriteLine("int Pair: {0} {1}",
            i.GetFirst(), i.GetSecond());

        Pair<string> s = new Pair<string>();
        s.SetPair("Carpe", "Diem");
        System.Console.WriteLine(
            "string Pair: {0} {1}",
            s.GetFirst(), s.GetSecond());
    }
}
```

The definition of the Pair class uses T, wrapped in angle brackets in its first appearance, to represent the type of information that an instance of this type will contain. The class's fields and methods work with T just as if it were any other type, using it for parameters and return values. Yet what T actually is—an integer, a string, or something else—isn't determined until an actual Pair instance is declared.

As this example's Main method shows, creating an instance of a generic type requires specifying exactly what type should be used for T. Here, the first Pair will contain two integers, and so the type int is supplied when it is created. That Pair instance is then set to contain two integers, and its contents are written out. The second instance of Pair, however, will contain two strings, and so the type string is supplied when it is created. This time,

What's New in C# 2.0

Generics are perhaps the most important addition in version 2.0 of C#, but several other new aspects are also worth mentioning. Those additions include the following:

- **Partial types:** Using the new term *partial*, the definition of a class, an interface, or a struct can be spread across two or more source files. One common example of where this is useful is when a tool, such as Visual Studio, generates code that gets added to by a developer. With partial types, there's no need for a developer to directly modify the code produced by the tool. Instead, the tool and the developer each create a partial type, and the two types are combined to create the final definition. One important example of where partial classes are used is ASP.NET, described in Chapter 5.

- **Nullable types:** It's sometimes useful for a value to be set to an undefined state, often referred to as *null*. The most common example of this is in working with relational databases, where null is often a legitimate value. To support this idea, C# 2.0 allows an instance of any value type to be declared with its name followed by a question mark, such as

```
int? x;
```

A variable declared this way can take on any of its usual values. Unlike an ordinary int, however, it can also be explicitly set to a null value.

- **Anonymous methods:** One way to pass code as a parameter is to explicitly declare that code inside a delegate. In C# 2.0, it's also possible to pass code directly as a parameter—there's no requirement that the code be wrapped inside a separately declared delegate. In effect, the code passed acts like a method, but since it has no name, it's referred to as an anonymous method.

the Pair instance is set to contain two strings, which are also written out. The result of executing this example is:

```
int Pair: 42 48
string Pair: Carpe Diem
```

Generics can be used with classes, structs, interfaces, delegates (and thus events), and methods, although they'll probably be most common with classes. They aren't appropriate for every application, but for some kinds of problems, generic types can help in creating the right solution.

C# Control Structures

C# provides the traditional set of control structures for a modern language. Among the most commonly used of these is the if statement, which looks like this:

The control structures in C# are typical of a modern high-level language

```
if (x > y)
    p = true;
else
    p = false;
```

Note that the condition for the if must be a value of type bool. Unlike C and C++, the condition can't be an integer.

C# also has a switch statement. Here's an example:

```
switch (x)
{
    case 1:
        y = 100;
        break;
    case 2:
        y = 200;
        break;
    default:
        y = 300;
        break;
}
```

Depending on the value of x, y will be set to 100, 200, or 300. The break statements cause control to jump to whatever statement follows this switch. Unlike C and C++, these (or similar) statements are mandatory in C#, even for the default case. Omitting them will produce a compiler error.

C# includes while, do/while, for, and foreach loops

C# also includes various kinds of loops. In a while loop, the condition must evaluate to a bool rather than an integer value, which again is different from C and C++. There's also a do/while combination that puts the test at the bottom rather than at the top and a for loop, which was illustrated in the earlier example. Finally, C# includes a foreach statement, which allows iterating through all the elements in a value of a *collection* type. There are various ways a type can qualify as a collection type, the most straightforward of which is to implement the standard interface System.IEnumerable. A common example of a collection type is an array, and so one use of a foreach loop is to examine or manipulate each element in an array.

C# also includes a goto statement, which jumps to a particular labeled point in the program, and a continue statement, which immediately returns to the top of whatever loop it's contained in and starts the next iteration. In general, the control structures in this relatively new language are not very new, so most of them will be familiar to anybody who knows another high-level language.

Other C# Features

The fundamentals of a programming language are in its types and control structures. There are many more interesting things in C#, however—too many to cover in detail in this short survey. This section provides brief looks at some of the more interesting additional aspects of the language.

Working with Namespaces

C#'s using statement makes it easier to reference the contents of a namespace

Because the underlying class libraries are so fundamental, namespaces are a critical part of programming with the .NET Framework. One way to invoke a method in the class libraries is by giving its fully qualified name. In the example shown earlier, for instance, the WriteLine method was invoked with

```
System.Console.WriteLine(...);
```

To lessen the amount of typing required, C# provides the *using* directive. This allows the contents of a namespace to be referenced with shorter names. It's common, for example, to start each C# program with the line

```
using System;
```

If the example shown earlier had included this, the WriteLine method could have been invoked with just

```
Console.WriteLine(...);
```

A program can also contain several using directives if necessary, as some of the examples later in this book will illustrate.

Using the *namespace* keyword, it's also possible to define your own namespaces directly in C#. Each namespace can contain one or more types or perhaps even other namespaces. The types in these namespaces can then be referenced either with fully qualified names or through appropriate using directives, just as with externally defined namespaces.

Handling Exceptions

Errors are an inescapable fact of life for developers. In the .NET Framework, errors that occur at runtime are handled in a consistent way through exceptions. As in so much else, C# provides a syntax for working with exceptions, but the fundamental mechanisms are embedded in the CLR itself. This not only provides a consistent approach to error handling for all C# developers, but also means that all CLR-based languages will deal with this potentially tricky area in the same way. Errors can

Exceptions provide a consistent way to handle errors across all CLR-based languages

even be propagated across language boundaries as long as those languages are built on the .NET Framework.

An exception can be raised when an error occurs

An exception is an object that represents some unusual event, such as an error. The .NET Framework defines a large set of exceptions, and it's also possible to create custom exceptions. An exception is automatically raised by the runtime when errors occur. For example, in the code fragment

```
x = y/z;
```

what happens if z is zero? The answer is that the CLR raises the System.DivideByZeroException. If no exception handling is being used, the program will terminate.

Exceptions can be handled using try/catch blocks

C# makes it possible to catch exceptions, however, using try/catch blocks. The code above can be changed to look like this:

```
try
{
    x = y/z;
}
catch
{
    System.Console.WriteLine("Exception caught");
}
```

The code within the braces of the try statement will now be monitored for exceptions. If none occurs, execution will skip the catch statement and continue. If an exception is raised, the code in the catch statement will be executed, in this case printing out a warning, and execution will continue with whatever statement follows the catch.

Different exceptions can be handled differently

It's also possible to have different catch statements for different exceptions and to learn exactly which exception occurred. Here's another example:

```
try
{
    x = y/z;
}
catch (System.DivideByZeroException)
{
    System.Console.WriteLine("z is zero");
}
catch (System.Exception e)
{
    System.Console.WriteLine("Exception: {0}",
        e.Message);
}
```

In this case, if no exceptions occur, x will be assigned the value of y divided by z, and the code in both catch statements will be skipped. If z is zero, however, the first catch statement will be executed, printing a message to this effect. Execution will then skip the next catch statement and continue with whatever follows this try/catch block. If any other exception occurs, the second catch statement will be executed. This statement declares an object e of type System.Exception and then accesses this object's Message property to retrieve a printable string indicating what exception has occurred.

Since CLR-based languages such as C# use exceptions consistently for error handling, why not define your own exceptions for handling your own errors? This can be done by defining a class that inherits from System.Exception and then using the throw statement to raise this custom exception. These exceptions can be caught with a try/catch block, just like those defined by the system.

Custom exceptions can also be defined

Although it's not shown here, it's also possible to end a try/catch block with a finally statement. The code in this statement gets executed whether or not an exception occurs. This option is useful when some final cleanup must take place no matter what happens.

Using Attributes

Once it's compiled, every C# type has associated metadata stored with it in the same file. Most of this metadata describes

A C# program can contain attributes

the type itself. As described in the previous chapter, however, metadata can also include attributes specified with this type. Given that the CLR provides a way to store attributes, it follows that C# must have some way to define attributes and their values. As described later in this book, attributes are used extensively by the .NET Framework class library. They can be applied to classes, interfaces, structures, methods, fields, parameters, and more. It's even possible to specify attributes that are applied to an entire assembly.

For example, suppose the Factorial method shown earlier had been declared with the WebMethod attribute applied to it. Assuming the appropriate using directives were in place to identify the correct namespace for this attribute, the declaration would look like this in C#:

```
[WebMethod] public int Factorial(int f) {...}
```

This attribute is used by ASP.NET, part of the .NET Framework class library, to indicate that a method should be exposed as a SOAP-callable Web service. (For more on how this attribute is used, see Chapter 5.) Similarly, including the attribute

```
[assembly:AssemblyCompanyAttribute
  ("QwickBank")]
```

in a C# file will set the value of an assembly-wide attribute, one that gets stored in the assembly's manifest, containing the name of the company creating this assembly. This example also shows how attributes can have parameters, allowing their user to specify particular values for the attribute.

Custom attributes can also be defined

Developers can also create their own attributes. For example, you might wish to define an attribute that can be used to identify the date a particular C# type was modified. To do this, you can define a class that inherits from System.Attribute, then define the information you'd like that class to contain, such as a date. You can then apply this new attribute to types in your program and have the information it includes be automatically placed into the metadata for those types. Once they've been created, custom attributes can be read using the GetCustomAttributes method defined by the Attribute class, part of the System.Reflection namespace in the .NET Framework class library. Whether standard or custom, however, attributes are a commonly used feature in CLR-based software.

Writing Unsafe Code

C# normally relies on the CLR for memory management. When an instance of a reference type is no longer in use, for example, the CLR's garbage collector will eventually free the memory occupied by that type. As described in Chapter 2, the garbage collection process also rearranges the elements that are on the managed heap and currently in use, compacting them to free more space.

C# developers typically rely on the CLR's garbage collection for memory management

What would happen if traditional C/C++ pointers were used in this environment? A pointer contains a direct memory address, so a pointer into the managed heap would reference a specific location in the heap's memory. When the garbage collector rearranged the contents of the heap to create more free space, whatever the pointer pointed to could change. Blindly mixing pointers and garbage collection is a recipe for disaster.

Pointers and garbage collection don't mix well

Yet this kind of mixing is sometimes necessary. For example, suppose you need to call existing non-CLR-based code, such as the underlying operating system, and the call includes a structure with embedded pointers. Or perhaps a particular section of an application is so performance critical that you can't rely on the garbage collector to manage memory for you. For situations like these, C# provides the ability to use pointers in what's known as *unsafe code*.

C# allows creating unsafe code that uses pointers

Unsafe code can use pointers, with all of the attendant benefits and pitfalls pointers entail. To make this "unsafe" activity as safe as possible, however, C# requires that all code that does this be explicitly marked with the keyword *unsafe*. Within an unsafe method, the *fixed* statement can be used to lock one or more values of a reference type in place on the managed heap. (This is sometimes called *pinning* a value.) Here's a simple example:

```
class Risky
{
    unsafe public void PrintChars()
    {
        char[] charList = new char[2];
        charList[0] = 'A';
        charList[1] = 'B';

        System.Console.WriteLine("{0} {1}",
            charList[0], charList[1]);
        fixed (char* f = charList)
        {
            charList[0] = *(f+1);
        }
        System.Console.WriteLine("{0} {1}",
            charList[0], charList[1]);
    }
}

class DisplayValues
{
    static void Main()
    {
        Risky r = new Risky();
        r.PrintChars();
    }
}
```

The PrintChars method in the class Risky is marked with the keyword unsafe. This method declares the small character array charList and then sets the two elements in this array to "A" and "B," respectively. The first call to WriteLine produces

```
A   B
```

just as you'd expect. The fixed statement then declares a character pointer f and initializes it to contain the address of the charList array. Within the fixed statement's body, the first element of this array is assigned the value at address f+1. (The asterisk in front of the expression means "return what's at this address.") When WriteLine is called again, the output is

```
B    B
```

The value that is one beyond the start of the array, the character "B," has been assigned to the array's first position.

This example does nothing useful, of course. Its intent is to make clear that C# does allow declaring pointers, performing pointer arithmetic, and more, as long as those statements are within areas clearly marked as unsafe. The language's creators really want you to be sure about doing this, so compiling any unsafe code requires explicitly setting an "unsafe" option for the C# compiler. Also, unsafe code can't be verified for type safety, which means that the CLR's built-in code access security features described in Chapter 2 can't be used. Unsafe code can be run in only a fully trusted environment, which makes it generally unsuitable for software that will be downloaded from the Internet. Still, there are cases when unsafe code is the right solution to a difficult problem.

Unsafe code has limitations

Preprocessor Directives

Unlike C and C++, C# has no preprocessor. Instead, the compiler has built-in support for the most useful features of a preprocessor. For example, C#'s preprocessor directives include #define, a familiar term to C++ developers. This directive can't be used to define an arbitrary replacement string for a word, however—you can't define macros. Instead, #define is used to define only a symbol. That symbol can then be used together with the directive #if to provide conditional compilation. For example, in the code fragment

```
#define DEBUG
#if DEBUG
        // code compiled if DEBUG is defined
#else
        //code compiled if DEBUG is not defined
#endif
```

■ Perspective: Is C# Just a Copy of Java?

C# certainly does look a lot like Java. Given the additional similarities between the CLR and the Java virtual machine, it's hard to believe that Microsoft wasn't at least somewhat inspired by Java's success. By uniting C-style syntax with objects in a more approachable fashion than C++, Java's creators found the sweet spot for a large population of developers. Before the arrival of .NET, I saw more than one project that chose the Java environment primarily because neither Visual Basic 6 (VB 6) nor C++ was seen as a good language for large-scale enterprise development.

The arrival of C# and a .NET-based version of VB has certainly shored up Microsoft's language technology against the Java camp. The quality of the programming language is no longer an issue. Yet this once again begs the question: Isn't C# like Java?

In many ways, the answer is yes. The core semantics of the CLR are very Java-esque. Being deeply object-oriented, providing direct support for interfaces, allowing multiple interface inheritance but only single implementation inheritance—these are all similar to Java. Yet C# also added features that weren't available in Java. C#'s native support for properties, for instance, built on the support in the CLR, reflects the VB influence on C#'s creators. Attributes, also a CLR-based feature, provide a measure of flexibility beyond what Java originally offered, as does the ability to write unsafe code. Fundamentally, C# is an expression of the CLR's semantics in a C-derived syntax. Since those semantics are much like Java, C# is necessarily much like Java, too. But it's not the same language.

Is C# a better language than Java? There's no way to answer this question objectively, and it wouldn't matter if there were. Choosing a development platform based solely on the programming language is like buying a car because you like the radio. You can do it, but you'll be much happier if your decision takes into account the complete package.

If Sun had allowed Microsoft to modify Java a bit, C# might not exist today. For understandable reasons, however, Sun resisted Microsoft's attempts to customize Java for the Windows world. The result is two quite similar languages, each targeting a different development environment. Competition is good, and both languages have a long future ahead of them.

DEBUG is defined, so the C# compiler would process the code between the #if and #else directives. If DEBUG were undefined, something that's accomplished using the preprocessor directive #undef, the compiler would process the code between the #else and #endif directives.

C# is an attractive language. It combines a clean, concise design with a modern feature set. Introducing a new development technology is hard—the world is littered with the carcasses of unsuccessful programming languages—yet Microsoft has clearly succeeded with C#. As one of the two most widely used .NET languages, it's now squarely in the mainstream of software development.

Visual Basic

Before the release of .NET, VB 6 was by a large margin the most popular programming language in the Windows world. The first .NET-based release of VB, dubbed Visual Basic .NET (VB .NET), brought enormous changes to this widely used tool. The version supported by Visual Studio 2005, officially called Visual Basic 2005, builds on this foundation. It's nowhere near as big a change as the move from VB 6 to VB .NET, but this new version does offer a number of interesting new features.

Like C#, VB is built on the Common Language Runtime, and so large parts of the language are effectively defined by the CLR. In fact, except for their syntax, C# and VB are largely the same language. Because both owe so much to the CLR and the .NET Framework class library, the functionality of the two is very similar.

Except for syntax, C# and VB are very similar

VB can be compiled using Visual Studio or vbc.exe, a command-line compiler supplied with the .NET Framework. Unlike C#, however, Microsoft has not submitted VB to a standards body. Accordingly, while the open source world or some other third party could still create a clone, the Microsoft tools

Only Microsoft provides VB compilers today

are likely to be the only viable choices for working in this language for the foreseeable future.

A VB Example

The quickest way to get a feeling for VB is to see a simple example. The one that follows implements the same functionality as did the C# example shown earlier in this chapter. As you'll see, the differences from that example are largely cosmetic.

```
' A VB example
Module DisplayValues

Interface IMath
  Function Factorial(ByVal F As Integer) _
    As Integer
  Function SquareRoot(ByVal S As Double) _
    As Double
End Interface

Class Compute
  Implements IMath

  Function Factorial(ByVal F As Integer) _
    As Integer Implements IMath.Factorial
    Dim I As Integer
    Dim Result As Integer = 1

    For I = 2 To F
      Result = Result * I
    Next
    Return Result
  End Function

  Function SquareRoot(ByVal S As Double) _
    As Double Implements IMath.SquareRoot
    Return System.Math.Sqrt(S)
  End Function
End Class

Sub Main()
  Dim C As Compute = New Compute()
  Dim V As Integer
  V = 5
  System.Console.WriteLine( _
    "{0} factorial: {1}", _
```

```
    V, C.Factorial(V))
  System.Console.WriteLine( _
    "Square root of {0}: {1:f4}", _
    V, C.SquareRoot(V))
End Sub

End Module
```

·The example begins with a comment, indicated by the single quote that begins the line. Following the comment is an instance of the Module type that contains all of the code in this example. Module is a reference type, but it's not legal to create an instance of this type. Instead, its primary purpose is to provide a container for a group of VB classes, interfaces, and other types. In this case, the module contains an interface, a class, and a Sub Main procedure. It's also legal for a module to contain method definitions, variable declarations, and more that can be used throughout the module.

A Module provides a container for other VB types

The module's interface is named IMath, and as in the earlier C# example, it defines the methods (or in the argot of VB, the functions) Factorial and SquareRoot. Each takes a single parameter, and each is defined to be passed by value, which means a copy of the parameter is made within the function. (The trailing underscore is the line continuation character, indicating that the following line should be treated as though no line break were present.) Passing by value is the default, so the example would work just the same without the ByVal indications[1].

Like C#, VB's default is to pass parameters by value

The class Compute, which is the VB expression of a CTS class, implements the IMath interface. Unlike C#, each of the functions in this class must explicitly identity the interface method it implements. Apart from this, the functions are just as in the earlier C# example except that a VB–style syntax is used. Note

A VB class is an expression of a CTS class

---

1. Passing by reference was the default in VB 6, one example of how VB was changed to match the underlying semantics of the CLR.

■ Perspective: C# or VB?

Before .NET, the language choice facing Microsoft-oriented developers was simple. If you were a hard-core developer, deeply proud of your technical knowledge, you embraced C++ in all its thorny glory. Alternatively, if you were more interested in getting the job done than in fancy technology, and if that job wasn't too terribly complex or low level, you chose VB 6. Sure, the C++ guys abused you for your lack of linguistic savoir faire, but your code had a lot fewer obscure bugs.

This divide ended with the arrival of .NET. C# and VB are very nearly the same language. Except for relatively uncommon things such as writing unsafe code, they're equally powerful. Microsoft may change this in the future, making the feature sets of the two languages diverge significantly. Until this happens, however (if it ever does), the main issue in making the choice is personal preference, which is really another way of saying "syntax."

Developers get very attached to how their language looks. C-oriented people love curly braces, while VB developers feel at home with Dim statements. In the years since .NET's original 2002 release, both languages have become popular, and both have ardent fans. Microsoft generally treats them equally, too, and even the .NET Framework documentation is quite even-handed, providing examples in both languages. Neither will go away anytime soon, and so either one is a safe choice for developers and the organizations that pay them.

In spite of this, however, I believe that any developer who knows C# can (and should) acquire at least a reading knowledge of VB, and vice versa. The core semantics are nearly identical, and after all, this is the really hard part of learning a language. In fact, to illustrate the equality of these two languages, the examples in the following chapters of this book alternate more or less randomly between the two. In the world of .NET, you shouldn't think of yourself as a VB developer or a C# developer. Whichever language you choose, you will in fact be a .NET Framework developer.

particularly that the call to System.Math.Sqrt is identical to its form in the C# example. C#, VB, and any other language built on the CLR can access services in the .NET Framework class library in much the same way.

This simple example ends with a Sub Main procedure, which is analogous to C#'s Main method. The application begins executing here. In this example, Sub Main creates an instance of the Compute class using the VB *New* operator (which will eventually be translated into the MSIL instruction newobj). It then declares an Integer variable and sets its value to 5.

Execution begins in the Sub Main Procedure

As in the C# example, this simple program's results are written out using the WriteLine method of the Console class. Because this method is part of the .NET Framework class library rather than any particular language, it looks exactly the same here as it did in the C# example. Not too surprisingly, then, the output of this simple program is

```
5 factorial: 120
Square root of 5: 2.2361
```

just as before.

To someone who knows VB 6, the .NET version of VB will look familiar. To someone who knows C#, this version of VB will act in a broadly familiar way since it's built on the same foundation. But the VB implemented in Visual Studio 2005 is not the same as either VB 6 or C#. The similarities can be very helpful in learning this new language, but they can also be misleading.

VB's similarities to VB 6 both help and hurt in learning this new language

VB Types
Like C#, the types defined by VB are built on the CTS types provided by the CLR. Table 3-2 shows most of these types and their VB equivalents.

Table 3-2   Some CTS Types and Their VB Equivalents

CTS	VB
Byte	Byte
Char	Char
Int16	Short
Int32	Integer
Int64	Long
UInt16	UShort
UInt32	UInteger
UInt64	ULong
Single	Single
Double	Double
Decimal	Decimal
Boolean	Boolean
Class	Class
Interface	Interface
Delegate	Delegate

VB is not case sensitive

Unlike C#, VB is not case sensitive. There are some fairly strong conventions, however, which are illustrated in the example shown earlier. For people coming to .NET from VB 6, this case insensitivity will seem entirely normal. It's one example of why both VB and C# exist, since the more a new environment has in common with the old one, the more likely people are to adopt it.

Classes

VB classes expose the behaviors of a CTS class using a VB-style syntax. Accordingly, VB classes can implement one or more interfaces, but they can inherit from at most one other class. In VB, a class Calculator that implements the interfaces IAlgebra and ITrig and inherits from the class MathBasics looks like this:

Like a CTS class, a VB class can inherit directly from only one other class

```
Class Calculator
    Inherits MathBasics
    Implements IAlgebra
    Implements ITrig
. . .
End Class
```

Note that, as in C#, the base class must precede the interfaces. Note also that any class this one inherits from might be written in VB or in C# or perhaps in some other CLR-based language. As long as the language follows the rules laid down in the CLR's Common Language Specification, cross-language inheritance is straightforward. Also, if the class inherits from another class, it can potentially override one or more of the type members, such as a method, in its parent. This is allowed only if the member being overridden is declared with the keyword Overridable, analogous to C#'s keyword virtual.

VB classes can be labeled as NotInheritable or MustInherit, which means the same thing as sealed and abstract, respectively, the terms used by the CTS and C#. VB classes can also be assigned various accessibilities, such as Public and Friend, which largely map to visibilities defined by the CTS. A VB class can contain variables, methods, properties, events, and more, just as defined by the CTS. Each of these can have an access modifier specified, such as Public, Private, or Friend. A class can also contain one or more constructors that get called whenever an instance of this class is created. And new with the 2005 version, VB supports operator overloading, like C#.

VB supports operator overloading

VB classes can also have properties. Here's the C# property shown earlier, this time expressed in VB:

```
Module PropertyExample
  Class PriorityValue
    Private m_Value As Integer
    Public Property Priority() As Integer
      Get
        Return m_Value
      End Get
      Set(ByVal Value As Integer)
        If (Value > 0 And Value < 11) Then
          m_Value = Value
        End If
      End Set
    End Property
  End Class

  Sub Main()
    Dim P As PriorityValue = New PriorityValue()
    P.Priority = 8
    System.Console.WriteLine("Priority: {0}", _
      P.Priority)
  End Sub
End Module
```

As in the C# example, a property relies on a private value within the class to contain its information. The property's Get and Set methods look much like that earlier example, too, with the syntax changes required for VB. And access to the property once again looks just like accessing a public field in a class, with the advantage that both reading and writing its value rely on developer-defined code.

Like a CTS interface, a VB interface can inherit directly from one or more other interfaces

Interfaces

Interfaces as defined by the CTS are a fairly simple concept. VB essentially just provides a VB-derived syntax for expressing what the CTS specifies. Along with the interface behavior shown earlier, CTS interfaces can inherit from one or more other interfaces. In VB, for example, defining an interface ITrig that inherits

▪ Perspective: Is Inheritance Really Worthwhile?

Inheritance is an essential part of object technology. Until .NET, VB didn't really support inheritance, and so (quite correctly) it was not viewed as an object-oriented language. VB now has inheritance, since it's built on the CLR, and so it is unquestionably truly object-oriented.

But is this a good thing? Microsoft certainly could have added inheritance to VB long ago, yet the language's keepers chose not to. Whenever I asked Microsoft why this was so, the answers revolved around two main points. First, inheritance can be tricky to understand and to get right. In a class hierarchy many levels deep, with some methods overridden and others overloaded, figuring out exactly what's going on isn't always easy. Given that the primary target audience for VB was not developers with formal backgrounds in computer science, it made sense to keep it simple.

The second point often made about why VB didn't have inheritance was that in many contexts, inheritance was not a good thing. This argument was made most strongly with COM, a technology that had no direct support for implementation inheritance. Inheritance binds a child class to its parent very closely, which means that a change in the parent can be catastrophic for the child. This "fragile base class" issue is especially problematic when the parent and child classes are written and maintained by completely separate organizations or when the parent's source isn't available to the creator of the child. In the component-oriented world of COM, this is a more than plausible argument.

So why did Microsoft change its mind about inheritance? Inheritance still can be problematic if changes in a parent class aren't communicated effectively to all developers who depend on that class, and it can also be complicated. The arguments Microsoft made are not incorrect. Yet the triumph of object technology is complete: Objects are everywhere. To create new languages in a completely new environment—that is, to create the .NET Framework and the current Visual Studio—without full support for inheritance would brand any organization as irretrievably retro. And the benefits of inheritance, especially those gained by providing a large set of reusable classes such as the .NET Framework class library, are huge. The pendulum has swung, and inheritance is now essential.

from the three interfaces, ISine, ICosine, and ITangent, would look like this:

```
Interface ITrig
    Inherits ISine
    Inherits ICosine
    Inherits ITangent
...
End Interface
```

Structures

VB structures can contain fields, implement methods, and more

Structures in VB are much like structures in C#. Like a class, a structure can contain fields, members, and properties, implement interfaces, and more. Like a C# structure, a VB structure is a value type, which means that it can neither inherit from nor be inherited by another type. A simple employee structure might be defined in VB as follows:

```
Structure Employee
    Public Name As String
    Public Age As Integer
End Structure
```

To keep the example simple, this structure contains only data members. As described earlier, however, VB structures are in fact nearly as powerful as classes.

Arrays

Unlike VB 6, array indexes in VB start at zero

Like arrays in C# and other CLR-based languages, arrays in VB are reference types that inherit from the standard System.Array class. Accordingly, all of the methods and properties that class makes available are also usable with any VB array. Arrays in VB look much like arrays in earlier versions of VB. Perhaps the biggest difference is that the first member of a VB array is referenced as element zero, while in pre-.NET versions of this language, the first member was element one. The number of elements in an array is thus one greater than the number that appears in its declaration. For example, the following statement declares an array of eleven integers:

```
Dim Ages(10) As Integer
```

Unlike C#, there's no need to create explicitly an instance of the array using New. It's also possible to declare an array with no explicit size and later use the ReDim statement to specify how big it will be. For example, this code

```
Dim Ages() As Integer
ReDim Ages(10)
```

results in an array of eleven integers just as in the previous example. Note that the index for both of these arrays goes from 0 to 10, not 1 to 10.

VB also allows multidimensional arrays. For example, the statement

```
Dim Points(10,20) As Integer
```

creates a two-dimensional array of integers with 11 and 21 elements, respectively. Once again, both dimensions are zero-based, which means that the indexes go from 0 to 10 in the array's first dimension and 0 to 20 in the second dimension.

Delegates and Events

The idea of passing an explicit reference to a procedure or function and then calling that procedure or function was not something that the typical VB 6 programmer was accustomed to. Yet the CLR provides support for delegates, which allows exactly this. Why not make this support visible in today's VB? Even more important, why not make events easy to use?

VB's creators chose to do both of these things, allowing VB programmers to create callbacks and other event-oriented code easily. Here's an example, the same one shown earlier in C#, of creating and using a delegate in VB:

VB allows creating and using delegates

```
Module DelegatesExample

  Delegate Sub SDelegate(ByVal S As String)
```

```
Sub CallDelegate(ByVal Write As SDelegate)
  System.Console.WriteLine("In CallDelegate")
  Write("A delegated hello")
End Sub

Sub WriteString(ByVal S As String)
  System.Console.WriteLine( _
    "In WriteString: {0}", S)
End Sub

Sub Main()
  Dim Del As New SDelegate( _
    AddressOf WriteString)
    CallDelegate(Del)
End Sub

End Module
```

Although it's written in VB, this code functions exactly like the
C# example shown earlier in this chapter. Like that example,
this one begins by defining SDelegate as a delegate type. As
before, SDelegate objects can contain references only to methods that take a single String parameter. In the example's Sub
Main method, a variable Del of type SDelegate is declared and
then initialized to contain a reference to the WriteString subroutine. (A VB subroutine is a method that, unlike a function, returns no result.) Doing this requires using VB's AddressOf
keyword before the subroutine's name. Sub Main then invokes
CallDelegate, passing in Del as a parameter.

CallDelegate has an SDelegate parameter named Write. When
Write is called, the method in the delegate that was passed into
CallDelegate is actually invoked. In this example, that method is
WriteString, so the code inside the WriteString procedure exe-
cutes next. The output of this simple example is exactly the
same as for the C# version shown earlier in this chapter:

```
In CallDelegate
In WriteString: A delegated hello
```

Delegates are another example of the additional features VB has
acquired from being rebuilt on the CLR. While this rethinking of

the language certainly requires lots of learning from developers
using it, the reward is a substantial set of features.

One idea that's not new to VB is direct language support for
events. Unlike the pre-.NET versions of VB, events are now built
on delegates. Still, using events in VB can be relatively straightforward, simpler even than using them in C#. Here's the events
example shown earlier recast into VB:

*VB events rely
on delegates*

```
Module EventsExample
  Public Class EventSource
    Public Event EventX()
    Sub RaiseEventX()
      RaiseEvent EventX()
    End Sub
  End Class

  Public Class EventSink
    Private WithEvents Source As EventSource
    Public Sub New(ByVal Es As EventSource)
      Me.Source = Es
    End Sub
    Public Sub ReceiveEvent() _
      Handles Source.EventX
      System.Console.WriteLine("EventX raised")
    End Sub
  End Class

  Sub Main()
    Dim Source As EventSource = New EventSource()
    Dim Sink As EventSink = New EventSink(Source)
    Source.RaiseEventX()
  End Sub
End Module
```

Like the earlier example, this one includes an EventSource
class, an EventSink class, and a Main that creates and uses an
instance of each class. As this illustration shows, however, it's
possible to use events in VB without explicitly working with
any delegate types. Instead, an event can be declared using
just the Event keyword, as is done in the first line of the
EventSource class. There's no requirement to reference either
a system-defined delegate such as System.EventHandler or

*Events can be
declared with the
keyword Event*

a custom delegate (although it's certainly possible to do this). Also, raising an event doesn't necessarily require explicitly conforming to the argument convention used in C#. Instead, as shown in EventSource's RaiseEventX method, the RaiseEvent keyword can be used. The VB compiler fills in everything else that's required.

Events in VB can be simpler than in C#

The way that event handlers are attached to events can also be somewhat simpler than in C#. In this example's EventSink class, for instance, the WithEvents keyword indicates that the Source field can raise events. The definition for a method that handles an event can use the Handles keyword to indicate which event this method should receive. This is exactly what's done by EventSink's ReceiveEvent method. And while like the earlier C# example, this code attaches the event's source to its receiver in EventSink's constructor (the New method), the details are different. Here, the Source field in EventSink is assigned whatever instance of the EventSource class is passed in when the EventSink is created. Finally, the Main method does just the same things as before: it creates instances of the two classes, then invokes the method that will ultimately raise the event. As before, the program's output is

```
EventX raised
```

There are also other ways to work with events in VB. It's possible to explicitly declare events using delegates as in C#, for example, and to attach event handlers using the AddHandler keyword. However it's done, events (and the delegates they rely on) are an important part of application development, used by Windows Forms, ASP.NET, and other fundamental parts of the .NET Framework.

■ Perspective: Has VB Become Too Hard?

Maybe. There have been lots of complaints about the changes, and certainly some VB 6 developers have been left behind. Microsoft historically targeted quite separate developer markets with VB and C++, yet the .NET Framework greatly blurred this distinction. VB and C# are functionally almost identical.

The .NET Framework is certainly simpler in many ways than the Windows DNA environment it replaced. But the Framework is also harder for a certain class of developers, especially those with no formal training in computer science. One reason for Microsoft's success in the developer market was the approachability of VB. The people who create software tools often forget that they're almost always much better software developers than the people who will use those tools. As a result, they tend to create tools that they themselves would like to use, powerful tools that are too complex for many of their potential customers.

The original creators of VB didn't make this mistake. Despite the opprobrium heaped on the language and its users by C++ developers, Microsoft kept a clear focus on the developer population and skill level they wished to target. This was a good decision, as VB was once the world's most widely used programming language.

And yet many VB developers wanted more. The .NET-based versions of VB certainly gave them more, but it also required *all* VB developers to step up a level in their technical knowledge. Still, the skills required to build the GUI-based client of a two-tier application, the original target for VB, are almost entirely unrelated to what's needed to build today's scalable, multitier, Web-accessible solutions. Given this, perhaps the original audience Microsoft targeted for VB, some of whom were just a step above power users, no longer has a role. With its complete object orientation and large set of more advanced features, VB is certainly too complex for many of them.

Yet building modern applications effectively was becoming more and more difficult with the old VB. Between a rock and a hard place, Microsoft chose to make this popular language both more powerful and more complex. Some developers have been very happy about this, but some haven't. Even when you have Microsoft's vast resources, you can't please everybody.

Generics

Just as with C#, the 2005 release of VB adds support for generic types. Here's the Pair example shown earlier expressed in VB:

```
Module GenericsExample
  Class pair(Of t)
    Dim element1, element2 As t
    Sub SetPair(ByVal first As t, ByVal second As t)
      element1 = first
      element2 = second
    End Sub

    Function GetFirst() As t
      Return element1
    End Function

    Function GetSecond() As t
      Return element2
    End Function
  End Class

  Sub Main()
    Dim i As New pair(Of Integer)
    i.SetPair(42, 48)
    System.Console.WriteLine( _
      "int Pair: {0} {1}", _
      i.GetFirst(), i.GetSecond())

    Dim s As New pair(Of String)
    s.SetPair("Carpe", "Diem")
    System.Console.WriteLine( _
      "string Pair: {0} {1}", _
      s.GetFirst(), s.GetSecond())
  End Sub
End Module
```

The syntax is different from the C# version shown earlier, most obviously in how the generic class is defined:

```
Class pair(Of t)
```

rather than C#'s

```
class Pair<T>
```

These superficial differences aside, however, generics in VB function as they do in C#.

Like C#, the 2005 version of VB also supports partial types, including partial classes and more. Unlike C#, however, it does not provide nullable types or anonymous methods. As was true in their original incarnations, the 2005 versions of C# and VB are functionally almost identical while still retaining a few small differences.

■ Perspective: Are Generics Worth It?

There's probably no better indication of the distance the VB language has traveled from its humble origins than the addition of generics. Generics are similar to templates in C++, a feature that's sometimes cited as an example of that language's excessive complexity. Do generics belong in VB?

One answer is to realize that generics are optional. Developers writing new applications can avoid using generics if they find the concept confusing. The trouble with this perspective is that Microsoft itself has begun using generics in the new programming interfaces it makes available. Given this, VB developers might be forced to confront this concept whether they like it or not.

Another view is to argue that generics just aren't that hard. Once you get your mind around the idea, they can actually make code simpler and less error-prone. This is certainly true for some percentage of .NET developers, but it's just as certainly not true for many others. Especially for developers focused more on solving business problems than on technicalities—the traditional heart of the VB community—the subtleties of generics might be a bridge too far.

Whatever the truth turns out to be, the addition of generics to VB makes very clear that, despite its name, the traditional simplicity of the Basic language is gone for good.

VB Control Structures

While the CLR says a lot about what a .NET Framework–based language's types should look like, it says essentially nothing about how that language's control structures should look. Accordingly, adapting VB to the CLR required making changes to VB's types, but the language's control structures are fairly standard. An If statement, for example, looks like this:

```
If (X > Y) Then
    P = True
Else
    P = False
End If
```

while a Select Case statement analogous to the C# switch shown earlier looks like this:

```
Select Case X
    Case 1
        Y = 100
    Case 2
        Y = 200
    Case Else
        Y = 300
End Select
```

As in the C# example, different values of x will cause y to be set to 100, 200, or 300. Although it's not shown here, the Case clauses can also specify a range rather than a single value.

The loop statements available in VB include a While loop, which ends when a specified Boolean condition is no longer true; a Do loop, which allows looping until a condition is no longer true or until some condition becomes true; and a For...Next loop, which was shown in the example earlier in this section. And like C#, VB includes a For Each statement, which allows iterating through all the elements in a value of a collection type.

VB also includes a GoTo statement, which jumps to a labeled point in the program, a Continue statement which returns to the top of the loop it's contained in and starts the next iteration (new in the 2005 version of the language), and a few more choices. The innovation in the .NET Framework doesn't focus on language control structures (in fact, it's not easy to think of the last innovation in language control structures), and so VB doesn't offer much that's new in this area.

Other VB Features

The CLR provides many other features, as seen in the description of C# earlier in this chapter. With very few exceptions, the creators of VB chose to provide these features to developers working in this newest incarnation of VB. This section looks at how VB provides some more advanced features.

VB exposes most of the CLR's features

Working with Namespaces

Just as in C#, namespaces are an important part of writing applications in VB. As shown earlier in the VB example, access to classes in .NET Framework class library namespaces looks just the same in VB as in C#. Because the CTS is used throughout, methods, parameters, return values, and more are all defined in a common way. Yet how a VB program indicates which namespaces it will use is somewhat different from how it's done in C#. Commonly used namespaces can be identified for a module with the Imports statement. For example, preceding a module with

VB's Imports statement makes it easier to reference the contents of a namespace

```
Imports System
```

would allow invoking the System.Console.WriteLine method with just

```
Console.WriteLine( . . .)
```

VB's Imports statement is analogous to C#'s using directive. Both allow developers to do less typing. And as in C#, VB also allows defining and using custom namespaces.

Handling Exceptions

One of the greatest benefits of the CLR is that it provides a common way to handle exceptions across all .NET Framework languages. This common approach allows errors to be found in, say, a C# routine and then handled in code written in VB. The exact syntax for how these two languages work with exceptions is different, but the underlying behavior, specified by the CLR, is the same.

As in C#, try/catch blocks are used to handle exceptions in VB

Like C#, VB uses Try and Catch to provide exception handling. Here's a VB example of handling the exception raised when a division by zero is attempted:

```
Try
    X = Y/Z
Catch
    System.Console.WriteLine("Exception caught")
End Try
```

Any code between the Try and Catch is monitored for exceptions. If no exception occurs, execution skips the Catch clause and continues with whatever follows End Try. If an exception occurs, the code in the Catch clause is executed, and execution continues with what follows End Try.

VB offers essentially the same exception handling options as C#

As in C#, different Catch clauses can be created to handle different exceptions. A Catch clause can also contain a When clause with a Boolean condition. In this case, the exception will be caught only if that condition is true. Also like C#, VB allows defining your own exceptions and then raising them with the Throw statement. VB also has a Finally statement. As in C#, the code in a Finally block is executed whether or not an exception occurs.

Using Attributes

A VB program can contain attributes

Code written in VB is compiled into MSIL, so it must have metadata. Because it has metadata, it also has attributes. The designers of the language provided a VB-style syntax for specifying attributes, but the result is the same as for any CLR-based language: Extra information is placed in the metadata of some assembly. To repeat once again an example from earlier in this chapter, suppose the Factorial method shown in the complete VB example had been declared with the WebMethod attribute applied to it. This attribute instructs the .NET Framework to expose this method as a SOAP-callable Web service, as described in Chapter 7. Assuming the appropriate Imports statements were in place to identify the correct namespace for this attribute, the declaration would look like this in VB:

```
<WebMethod()> Public Function Factorial(ByVal F _
As Integer) As Integer Implements IMath.Factorial
```

This attribute is used by ASP.NET to indicate that a method should be exposed as a SOAP-callable Web service. Similarly, including the attribute

```
<assembly:AssemblyCompanyAttribute("QwickBank")>
```

in a VB file will set the value of an attribute stored in this assembly's manifest that identifies QwickBank as the company that created this assembly. VB developers can also create their own attributes by defining classes that inherit from System.Attribute and then have whatever information is defined for those attributes automatically copied into metadata. As in C# or another CLR-based language, custom attributes can be read using the GetCustomAttributes method defined by the System.Reflection namespace's Attribute class.

Attributes are just one more example of the tremendous semantic similarity of VB and C#. Which one a developer prefers will be largely an aesthetic decision.

The My Namespace

The 2005 version of VB provides an interesting addition that's not part of C#: the My namespace. The goal is to move VB just a little closer to its roots by making it easier for developers to do common but potentially complex things. Toward this end, the

◾ Perspective: Why Provide All of These Languages?

Microsoft says that more than 20 languages have been ported to the CLR. Along with the languages shipped by Microsoft itself, .NET developers have plenty of options to choose from. Yet given the CLR's central role in defining these languages, they often have much in common. What's the real benefit of having multiple languages based on the CLR?

For Microsoft, there are two key advantages. First, the pre-.NET population of Windows developers was split into two primary language camps: C++ and VB. Microsoft needed to move both groups of developers forward, and both certainly have some attachment to their language. Although the semantics of the CLR (and of languages built on it such as C# and VB) are different from either C++ or VB 6, the fundamental look of these new languages will be familiar. If Microsoft chose to provide only, say, C#, it's a safe bet that developers who were wedded to VB 6 would be resistant to moving to .NET. Similarly, providing only a CLR-based language derived from VB 6 wouldn't make C++ developers very happy. People who write code get attached to the oddest things (curly braces, for example), and so providing both C# and a CLR-based version of VB is a good way to help the current Windows developer population move forward.

The second benefit in providing multiple languages is that it gives the .NET Framework something the competition doesn't have. One complaint about the Java world has been that it requires all developers always to use the same language. The .NET Framework's multilingual nature offered more choice, so it gave Microsoft something to tout over its competitors.

In fact, however, there are some real benefits to having just one language. Why add extra complexity, such as a different syntax for expressing the same behavior, when there's no clear benefit? Java's traditional one-language-all-the-time approach has the virtue of simplicity. Even in the .NET world, organizations would do well to avoid multilanguage projects if possible. It's true that code written in different CLR-based languages can interoperate with no problems, and that developers who know C# should have no trouble understanding VB (and vice versa). Still, having two or more separate development groups using distinct languages will complicate both the initial project and the maintenance effort that follows. It's worth avoiding if possible.

So far, the diverse set of languages that are officially available for the .NET Framework hasn't mattered much. Because of Microsoft's strong support, expressed most powerfully in Visual Studio, C# and VB are by far the most widely used choices for creating new CLR-based applications. The other languages might be interesting for universities, but for professional developers, Visual Studio and the languages it supports rule.

My namespace includes a number of objects that simplify life for VB developers. Some of those objects are:

- **My.Application:** This object lets developers more easily access information about the current application. For example, the My.Application.CommandLineArgs property allows a VB developer to access any arguments supplied on the command line when the application was invoked, while the My.Application.ChangeCulture method allows modifying the culture (e.g., from United States English to French) used for formatting dates and other things.

- **My.User:** This object provides access to the current user of an application. Accessing the My.User.Name property returns the name of the current user, for example, while the IsInRole method can be used to determine whether this user belongs to a particular role, such as Administrator.

- **My.Computer:** This object provides access to various aspects of whatever machine the current application is running on. My.Computer contains a set of properties that return other objects for different kinds of access. Some examples include My.Computer.Audio for playing .wav files, My.Computer.Clock for accessing the current time, My.Computer.FileSystem for working with files and directories, My.Computer.Network for uploading and downloading files, and My.Computer.Registry for accessing the local machine's registry.

- ■ **My.Settings:** This object allows working with an application's settings, such as information for connecting to a database or user preferences.

There's no inherent reason why the My namespace classes couldn't be made accessible to developers working in C# or other CLR-based languages. Given VB's historic orientation toward less technical developers, however, it isn't surprising that this simplifying set of classes shows up here first.

C++

C++ was too popular for the .NET Framework's creators to ignore

C# was a brand new language created just for the .NET Framework. The .NET-based version of VB was essentially the same thing, although its name and syntactic style were borrowed from VB 6. But C++ existed well before .NET, and it's been in wide use for many years. Given this, Microsoft decided that while providing some way to create CLR-based software in C++ was essential, so was maintaining compatibility with the existing language. Unlike VB, Microsoft believed that making everyone move to a purely CLR-based version of C++ wasn't a good idea. Accordingly, Visual Studio 2005, like its predecessors, still supports standard C++.

The semantics of C++ differ from those of the CLR

Yet mapping C++ to the CLR presented some challenges. Most important, the original semantics of C++ don't exactly match those of the CLR. They have much in common—both are object-oriented, for example—but there are also many differences. C++, for instance, supports multiple inheritance, the ability of a class to inherit simultaneously from two or more parent classes, while the CLR does not.

Unlike VB, Microsoft isn't free to change C++ unilaterally to fit the CLR

VB 6 also differed substantially from the CLR, but Microsoft owned VB. The company was free to change it as they wished, so VB's .NET-based incarnation was designed to match the CLR. Microsoft does not own C++, however. Unilaterally changing the language itself to match the CLR would have met with howls of protest. Yet providing no way to create .NET Framework–based applications in C++ would also have left many developers unhappy. What's the solution?

The original answer Microsoft chose was to create a set of extensions to the base C++ language. Officially known as *Managed Extensions for C++*, the resulting dialect is commonly referred to as just *Managed C++*. C++ is not simple to begin with, and Managed C++ added new complexities. Despite this, Managed C++ was used by a number of organizations for creating .NET applications.

Microsoft originally defined a set of Managed Extensions for C++

With the 2005 release of the Visual Studio, Microsoft has provided another way to create managed code in C++. While the

▨ Perspective: C++ or C#?

C++ has legions of die-hard fans. And why shouldn't it? It's a powerful, flexible tool for building all kinds of applications. It's complicated, too, which means that learning to exploit all that power and flexibility takes a substantial amount of effort. Anyone who's put in the time to master C++ is bound to be less than thrilled about leaving it behind.

Yet for brand-new applications built from scratch on the .NET Framework, C++ probably should be left behind. For a C++ developer, learning C# isn't difficult. In fact, learning C# will probably be easier than using either C++/CLI or Managed C++ to write .NET Framework–based applications. As the short summary in this chapter suggests, these language extensions add even more complexity to an already complex language. For new applications, C# is probably a better choice.

For extending existing C++ applications with managed code, however, C++/CLI is a good choice. And if you plan to port an existing C++ application to run on the Framework, C++/CLI is also a good choice, since it saves you from rewriting large parts of your code. Although it's not as widely used in the .NET Framework world as either VB or C#, C++ is nevertheless an important part of .NET's language arsenal.

The 2005 release of C++ adds direct language extensions for creating managed code

original managed extensions are still supported, they're now deprecated. Instead, the C++ language itself has been modified, adding new keywords and more for creating applications that run on the CLR. Expressly designed for creating managed code, this language dialect is known as *C++/CLI*. These extensions are following the standardization path originally defined for the CLI, with the goal of potentially making the C++/CLI dialect available in non-Microsoft environments. This section provides a brief introduction to both C++/CLI and the Managed C++ dialect it replaces.

C++/CLI

Before looking at a C++/CLI example, it's useful to briefly describe some of the extensions made to the language. To make writing CLR-based code as natural as possible, Microsoft chose to add several keywords to the language. To avoid breaking existing C++ code, these keywords use two interesting approaches:

- *Contextual* keywords have meaning only in a specific context. For example, the keyword *sealed* on a declaration specifies that no other type can inherit from this one, just as in C#. This keyword only has meaning when it appears in the context of a declaration, however. This allows existing programs that use the identifier *sealed* in another way, such as for a variable name, to work unchanged.

- *Spaced keywords* are pairs of terms that are treated as a single unit. For instance, a C++/CLI interface is defined using the spaced keywords *interface class*. As with a contextual keyword, the identifier *interface* has a special meaning only in this context, so existing code that uses it in other ways won't break.

With these ideas in mind, we can now make some sense out of an example.

A C++/CLI Example

Here's the same simple program shown earlier in C# and VB, this time expressed in C++/CLI. As before, the semantics are essentially the same. What's changed is the syntax in which those semantics are expressed.

```cpp
// A C++/CLI example
#include "stdafx.h"

interface class IMath
{
    int Factorial(int f);
    double SquareRoot(double s);
};

ref class Compute : public IMath
{
    public: virtual int Factorial(int f)
    {
        int i;
        int result = 1;
        for (i=2; i<=f; i++)
            result = result * i;
        return result;
    };

    public: virtual double SquareRoot(double s)
    {
        return System::Math::Sqrt(s);
    }
};

void main(void)
{
    Compute ^c = gcnew Compute;
    int v;
    v = 5;
    System::Console::WriteLine(
      "{0} factorial: {1}",
      v, c->Factorial(v));
    System::Console::WriteLine(
      "Square root of {0}: {1:f4}",
      v, c->SquareRoot(v));
}
```

The first thing to notice is how much this example resembles the C# version. Most of the basic syntax and many of the operators are the same. Yet it's different, too, beginning with the #include statement necessary for creating managed code in C++. Following these, the interface IMath is defined, just as before. This time, however, it uses the spaced keyword interface class,

C++/CLI resembles C#

described above. The result is a C++ incarnation of a CTS-defined interface.

A CTS class is defined with ref class

Next comes the class Compute, which implements the IMath interface. This class is prefaced with C++/CLI's *ref class* keyword, which indicates that this is a CTS reference class, one whose lifetime is managed by the CLR using garbage collection. The class itself varies a bit in syntax from the C# example, since C++ doesn't express things in exactly the same way, but it's nonetheless very similar.

Instances of CTS reference types are created using gcnew

The example ends with a standard C++ main function. Just as in the earlier examples, it creates an instance of the Compute class and then calls its two methods, all using standard C++ syntax. The most visible difference from those earlier examples (and from standard C++) is the use of the *gcnew* keyword. This keyword indicates that an instance of a CTS class (i.e., a garbage-collected class, hence the "gc" in "gcnew") is being created. In other words, the Compute class is being created on the heap managed by the CLR rather than on the native heap maintained by C++. (Objects instantiated using the standard C++ new operator are created on this native heap, just as always.)

A CTS class is referenced via a handle

Another difference is the appearance of the ^ symbol, commonly called a *caret* or, more informally, a *hat*, in the declaration of the Compute class. Standard C++ uses the traditional asterisk to indicate a reference. To make immediately clear that a CTS reference type is involved, however, C++/CLI introduces the idea of a *handle*. Identified by this new symbol, a handle like the one declared here can sometimes be used in ways similar to an ordinary C++ pointer, as shown by the calls to Factorial and SquareRoot later in the program. Because it's actually a reference to a garbage-collected object on the CLR-managed heap, however, it is in fact quite different from an ordinary C++ pointer. This new syntax makes that difference very visible to developers. And just as you'd expect, the output of this example is the same as before: the factorial and square root of five.

C++/CLI Types

C++/CLI allows full access to the .NET Framework, including the types defined by the CLR and more. It's important to note that managed and unmanaged code, classes defined with and without ref, can be defined in the same file, and they can exist in the same running process. Only the managed classes are subject to garbage collection, however; unmanaged classes must be explicitly freed as usual in C++. Table 3-3 shows some of the major CTS types and their equivalents in C++/CLI.

Managed and unmanaged C++ code can coexist in a process

Other C++/CLI Features

Because it fully supports the CLR, there's much more in C++/CLI. Properties can be created using the *property* keyword, for example, while delegates can be created using the *delegate*

C++/CLI allows full access to what the CLR provides

Table 3-3   Some CTS Types and Their C++/CLI Equivalents

CTS	C++/CLI
Byte	unsigned char
Char	wchar_t
Int16	short, signed short
Int32	int, signed int, long, signed long
Int64	__int64, signed __int64
UInt16	unsigned short
UInt32	unsigned int, unsigned long
UInt64	unsigned __int64
Single	float
Double	double, long double
Decimal	Decimal
Boolean	bool
Class	ref class, ref struct
Interface	interface class
Delegate	delegate

keyword. C++/CLI supports both CLR-defined generics and their cousins, standard C++ templates. Namespaces can be referenced with a *using namespace* statement, such as

```
using namespace System;
```

Exceptions can be handled using try/catch blocks, and custom CLR exceptions that inherit from System::Exception can be created. Attributes can also be embedded in code using a syntax much like that used in C#.

C++ is the only language in Visual Studio 2005 that can compile directly to native code

Except for C++, all languages in Visual Studio compile only to MSIL, and they require the .NET Framework to run. Since all C++/CLI classes are compiled to MSIL, the language can obviously be used to generate Framework-based code. Yet C++ is unique among Microsoft's .NET-based languages in that it also allows compiling directly to a machine-specific binary. For building Windows applications that don't require the CLR, this makes C++ the only way to go.

Managed C++

Using Managed C++ is deprecated today

Visual Studio .NET, Microsoft's original tool for creating .NET applications, introduced Managed C++ for creating CLR-based software in C++. With the release of Visual Studio 2005, the use of Managed C++ is now discouraged. Still, plenty of people wrote (or more often extended) C++ applications using this original attempt at combining C++ and the CLR. Given this, it's worth taking a quick look at this now-deprecated dialect. It's also interesting to compare it with its successor, C++/CLI.

Like C++/CLI, Managed C++ defined several new keywords

Before looking at a Managed C++ example, though, it's useful to describe some of the extensions made to the language. Like C++/CLI, several keywords were added to allow access to CLR services. These keywords all begin with two underscores, following the convention defined in the ANSI standard for C++ extensions. Among the most important of these are the following:

- __gc: Indicates a CTS type that is subject to garbage collection, i.e., a CTS reference type.

- __value: Indicates a CTS type that is not subject to garbage collection, i.e., a CTS value type.

- __interface: Used to define a CTS interface type.

- __box: An operation that converts a CTS value type to a reference type. Unlike C#, VB, and C++/CLI, Managed C++ does not implicitly perform boxing and unboxing operations. Instead, developers are required to indicate explicitly where these conversions should occur.

- __unbox: An operation that converts a boxed CTS value type back to its original form.

As before, an example is now in order.

A Managed C++ Example
Here's this chapter's standard example, this time in Managed C++:

```
// A Managed C++ example
#include "stdafx.h"
#using <mscorlib.dll>

__gc __interface IMath
{
    int Factorial(int f);
    double SquareRoot(double s);
};

__gc class Compute : public IMath
{
    public: int Factorial(int f)
    {
        int i;
        int result = 1;
        for (i=2; i&lt;=f; i++)
            result = result * i;
        return result;
    };
```

```
        public: double SquareRoot(double s)
        {
            return System::Math::Sqrt(s);
        }
};

void main(void)
{
    Compute *c = new Compute;
    int v;
    v = 5;
    System::Console::WriteLine(
      "{0} factorial: {1}",
      __box(v), __box(c->Factorial(v)));
    System::Console::WriteLine(
      "Square root of {0}: {1:f4}",
      __box(v), __box(c->SquareRoot(v)));
}
```

Managed C++ resembles C++/CLI and C#

Not too surprisingly, this example looks similar to the versions shown earlier in C# and C++/CLI. The differences are interesting, however, and they start with the #include and #using statements necessary for creating Managed C++ code. The interface IMath is once again defined, but this time, it uses the __interface keyword and precedes it with the __gc keyword. The combination has the same meaning as *interface class* in C++/CLI. The Compute class is also declared with the __gc keyword, expressing in a different way what C++/CLI says with *ref*.

Managed C++ requires explicit boxing

The example ends with a standard C++ main function. Just as before, it creates an instance of the Compute class and then calls its two methods, all using standard C++ syntax. The only substantive difference is in the calls to WriteLine. Because this method expects reference parameters, the __box operator must be used to pass the numeric parameters correctly. Boxing also occurred for this parameter in C# and VB, but it was done automatically. Because C++ was not originally built for the CLR, however, a Managed C++ developer must explicitly request this operation.

Managed C++ Types

Managed C++ is functionally similar to C++/CLI

Like C++/CLI, Managed C++ allows full access to the .NET Framework, lets managed and unmanaged code be defined in

Table 3-4 Some CLR Types and Their Managed C++ Equivalents

CLR	Managed C++
Byte	unsigned char
Char	wchar_t
Int16	short
Int32	int, long
Int64	__int64
UInt16	unsigned short
UInt32	unsigned int, unsigned long
UInt64	unsigned __int64
Single	float
Double	double
Decimal	Decimal
Boolean	bool
Class	__gc class
Interface	__gc __interface
Delegate	__delegate

the same file, and more. To a very large degree, the two C++ dialects just provide different ways of expressing identical semantics. Table 3-4 shows some of the major CLR types and their equivalents in Managed C++.

Other Managed C++ Features

Like C++/CLI, Managed C++ provides full access to the CLR. Delegates can be created using the __*delegate* keyword, namespaces can be referenced with *using namespace*, just as in C++/CLI, exceptions and attributes can be used, and more. Managed C++ isn't a weak tool, and its use wasn't deprecated because it lacked power. Rather, the people at Microsoft who control this technology felt that their first attempt at mapping

Managed C++ also allows full access to the CLR's features

■ Perspective: Is C++ a Dying Language?

C++ was the workhorse of professional software developers for most of the 1990s. It's been used to write Lotus Notes, a surfeit of business applications, and even parts of Windows. Yet in a world that offers C#, a modern version of VB, and Java, where does C++ fit? Has its usefulness come to an end?

Certainly not. C#, VB, and Java are much better than C++ for many types of applications, even many for which C++ has commonly been used. But all three of these languages operate in a virtual machine environment. This has many benefits, but there's also a price: performance and size. Some categories of software, such as certain real-time applications or system-level code, can't afford this.

Still, the day when C++ was the default choice for building a broad range of new applications has ended. In the Microsoft world, C# and VB are the new defaults, while Java dominates elsewhere. Yet in cases where none of these is appropriate—and they do exist—C++ will still dominate. Its role has surely shrunk, but C++ is not about to disappear.

C++ to the CLR wasn't good enough, and so going forward, new C++ managed code should be created using C++/CLI instead.

Conclusion

The .NET Framework brings a new approach to programming language design

Programming languages are a fascinating topic. There now appears to be wide agreement on what fundamental features a modern general-purpose programming language should have and how it should behave. These features and behaviors are essentially what the CLR provides. There is little agreement on how a modern programming language should look, however, with everyone voting for his or her preferred syntax. By providing a common implementation of the core and then allowing diverse expressions of that core, the .NET Framework brought a new approach to language design. Even without Microsoft's backing, this would be an attractive model for creating a development environment. Combined with the support of the world's largest software company, it has improved the lives of many, many developers.

4

Surveying the .NET Framework Class Library

All software built on the .NET Framework uses the Common Language Runtime (CLR). Yet even the simplest CLR-based program also requires using some part of the .NET Framework class library, and more capable software will use a much larger set of the services this library provides. Understanding .NET requires having a clear idea of what the .NET Framework class library offers to software developers. This chapter provides a survey of this very large library, then takes a closer look at some of its more fundamental parts.

The .NET Framework class library is essential for building .NET Framework applications

An Overview of the Library

The .NET Framework class library is organized into a hierarchy of namespaces. Each namespace can contain types, such as classes and interfaces, as well as other subordinate namespaces. The root namespace is System, and every .NET Framework application will use some of the types it contains. Yet the types

The library is a hierarchy of namespaces

■ Perspective: How Big Is Big?

If there's any one fact about the .NET Framework class library that you should internalize, it is that the library is big—very, very big. Many, many people have been working on the .NET Framework for several years, and a large chunk of them were designing and building this class library. The steepest learning curve for developers moving to .NET will be learning the .NET Framework class library.

Fortunately, you don't need to learn the whole thing. Unless you have a great deal of free time and remarkably catholic interests, you're unlikely ever to understand every type in the library. Instead, any developer working in the .NET world should first decide which parts of this mountain of software she absolutely needs to understand and then determine which parts she's really interested in. Every developer will need to understand some of its namespaces, but most will be able to ignore many others quite safely.

Providing a large set of generally useful code is clearly a good idea. While the initial .NET Framework class library wasn't exactly on the mark in every way—the 2005 release of version 2.0 includes changes big and small—its straight forward design makes it as approachable as something this big can ever be.

in several other namespaces are also likely to be commonly used by a broad swathe of developers. System is the foundation, but it's by no means the whole story.

The System Namespace

System is the root namespace of the .NET Framework class library

The System namespace is the ultimate parent—the root—of the .NET Framework class library. Along with its large set of subordinate namespaces, System itself contains many different types. Among the most interesting of these are the following:

- The core types defined by the CLR's Common Type System, including Int16, Int32, Char, Boolean, and all other standard value types, along with reference types such as Array and Delegate. The fundamental base type Object is also defined here.

- **Console,** the class whose WriteLine method was used in the previous chapter to output simple information. This class also provides a corresponding ReadLine method and several others.

- **Math,** the class whose Sqrt method was used in the previous chapter to compute the square root of a number. This class has more than two dozen methods that provide standard ways to compute sines, cosines, tangents, logarithms, and other common mathematical functions.

- **Environment,** a class used to access information about the environment of the currently running application. An application can learn what its current directory is, find out what operating system it's running on, determine how much memory it's using, and more.

- **GC,** a class used to affect how and when garbage collection happens. By invoking this class's Collect method, an application can force garbage collection to happen immediately. (This isn't likely to be a good idea, however, since the CLR knows better than you when garbage collection should occur.)

- **Random,** a class whose members can be used to compute pseudorandom numbers.

Except for the base CLR types, the types in System sometimes seem to have been placed here because there was no obviously better namespace for them. Still, these types can be useful in a broad range of applications.

The types in System are a diverse lot

A Survey of System's Subordinate Namespaces

Directly below System are more than two dozen other namespaces, many of which have subnamespaces of their own. Providing even a short survey of these is a daunting task. Nonetheless, before moving on to examine the most important namespaces in this and later chapters, it's important at least to attempt a broad view. With this lofty goal in mind, this section takes an alphabetical look at most of the namespaces directly below System, providing a brief description of what each one

System directly contains more than two dozen namespaces

offers. Note that this chapter (and, in fact, this book) doesn't describe every namespace in this library, and so what follows isn't a complete list.

System.CodeDom provides a way to generate code for CLR-based programs

System.CodeDom includes types that can be used to create a program directly in memory. This large set of types includes classes for generating declarations, assignments, if statements, and everything else required to construct a complete program. Even comments are supported. Once a program is created, it can be output in C#, Visual Basic (VB), or some other language. The types in this namespace can be used by any .NET developer, and they're also used by some parts of the .NET Framework itself, such as ASP.NET.

System.Collections defines generic types such as stacks and queues

System.Collections includes types for creating and working with hash tables, arrays, queues, stacks, lists, and other generally useful data structures. These types are defined quite generally. For example, the Stack and Queue classes contain Objects, which lets them contain values of any CTS type. A subordinate namespace, *System.Collections.Generic*, contains essentially the same group of types, this time defined using generics rather than simple Objects. System.Collections also contains the subordinate namespace *System.Collections.Specialized*, which provides types for more narrowly applicable uses, such as a collection of Strings (although the types in System.Collections.Generic effectively make many of these specialized collection types redundant).

System.Component-Model provides a foundation for building software components

System.ComponentModel contains types for creating various kinds of .NET Framework–based components. Among the types it includes is the Component class, which serves as the basis for components used by Windows Forms, described in this chapter, and for many other classes in the .NET Framework class library. Components, which implement the IComponent interface defined in this namespace, exist inside instances of the Container class, also defined in this namespace. Each Container object implements two more interfaces defined in this namespace: one occurrence of the IContainer interface, along with one ISite interface for each component the container hosts. This namespace also contains types for licensing components. If you're familiar with the older COM-based mechanisms for building ActiveX controls, the types defined in this namespace should suggest those once-popular models for building components.

System.Configuration provides types such as the ConfigurationsSettings class that allow accessing configuration information for a .NET Framework–based application. It also contains subordinate namespaces such as *System.Configuration.Assemblies* for working with assembly-specific configuration information and *System.Configuration.Install* for building custom installers for CLR-based software.

System. Configuration supports configuring assemblies and creating installers

System.Data is among the most important namespaces in the .NET Framework class library. The types in this namespace implement ADO.NET, the standard approach to accessing data for .NET Framework applications. Its subordinate namespaces include *System.Data.SqlClient,* which allows access to data stored in Microsoft's SQL Server, *System.Data.OracleClient,* which allows access to data stored in an Oracle database, *System.Data.OleDb,* which allows access to data sources using OLE DB providers, and *System.Data.Odbc,* which allows access to data sources through ODBC. ADO.NET is described in more detail in Chapter 6.

System.Data contains the types that make up ADO.NET

System.Diagnostics contains a large set of classes, interfaces, structures, and other types that help with debugging .NET Framework applications. For example, the Trace class allows adding assertions to code that verify key conditions, writing messages that trace the flow of execution, and performing other useful functions in released software. The Debug class, also defined in this namespace, provides similar services but is designed to be used during development rather than in a released product.

System.Diagnostics supports tracing, assertions, and more

System.Directory-Services provides an API to Active Directory

System.DirectoryServices contains types for accessing Active Directory and other directory services. Prior to .NET, the standard way to expose Windows services was through COM-based interfaces. Active Directory, for instance, can be accessed via the Active Directory Services Interface (ADSI), which is defined as a collection of COM objects. The .NET Framework has superseded COM for new interface definitions, however, and so new ways to expose services must be created using managed code. The types in the System.DirectoryServices namespace are the .NET Framework's analog to ADSI. A subordinate namespace, *System.DirectoryServices.Protocols*, provides an interface for accessing directories using the standard Lightweight Directory Access Protocol (LDAP).

System.Drawing supports creating text and several kinds of graphics

System.Drawing provides a large set of types for using the services of the current version of Microsoft's Graphics Device Interface (GDI), known as GDI+. System.Drawing itself includes classes for working with pens, brushes, and other drawing tools, while several subordinate namespaces contain types for related uses. *System.Drawing.Drawing2D*, for example, contains types for vector graphics and other two-dimensional drawing functions; *System.Drawing.Imaging* contains types for working with metafiles and other more advanced GDI imaging; *System.Drawing.Printing* contains types for controlling printers; and *System.Drawing.Text* contains types for manipulating fonts. A *System.Drawing.Design* namespace is also included that provides types for customizing the user interface developers see at design time.

System.Enterprise-Services allows access to COM+ services

System.EnterpriseServices contains types for accessing the services provided by COM+, including support for distributed transactions, role-based authorization, and object pooling. Unlike most of the functions provided by the .NET Framework class library, the types contained here largely provide a wrapper around the existing COM+ software rather than reimplementing it as managed code. This important namespace is described in more detail in Chapter 7.

System.Globalization contains types for creating national calendars, converting to national code pages, formatting dates and times, and other aspects of building software that supports multiple cultures. Globalized software is important, and so many of the .NET Framework's basic functions are automatically culture-aware. For example, conversion to a currency value can automatically examine the caller's culture setting to format the currency appropriately.

System. Globalization helps developers write software that works in diverse cultures

System.IO provides a large set of types for reading and writing files, directories, and in-memory streams. While access to a database management system (DBMS) is often the main route applications take to data, the ability to work with files is still important. System.IO also contains a few subordinate name-spaces that provide related services. *System.IO.Compression*, for example, allows reading and writing compressed data using the GZIP standard. The basics of System.IO are described later in this chapter.

System.IO supports access to files and directories

System.Management provides types for accessing Windows Management Instrumentation (WMI) data from managed code. WMI is Microsoft's implementation of the Web-Based Enterprise Management (WBEM) initiative supported by many different vendors. A number of the types in this namespace provide support for the WMI Query Language (WQL), a dialect of SQL focused on accessing WMI-related information.

System. Management supports working with WMI data

System.Media includes classes for working with sounds. For example, this simple namespace provides a SoundPlayer class with methods such as Play and Stop, allowing a CLR-based application to start and stop playing of a sound file.

System.Media provides a simple way to play sounds

System.Messaging contains types for accessing Microsoft Message Queuing (MSMQ), Microsoft's solution for Windows-to-Windows message queuing. MSMQ has several other application programming interfaces (APIs), including a COM-

System.Messaging provides an API for MSMQ

based API and an API defined as a set of C function calls. System.Messaging's types define the MSMQ API that managed code should use.

System.Net supports access to HTTP, TCP, and other protocols

System.Net provides types for accessing several common protocols, including HTTP, FTP, and the Domain Name System (DNS). It also contains the abstract classes WebRequest and WebResponse, which allow building applications that are unaware of what protocol is being used to communicate. These applications can simply make requests to and get responses from specified URLs and let the underlying software worry about the details. Version 2.0 of the .NET Framework adds the HttpWebListener class, which allows a developer on newer versions of Windows to create simple Web servers. System.Net also contains a number of subordinate namespaces. *System.Net.Sockets*, for example, provides a managed implementation of the traditional sockets interface to TCP and UDP—it's WinSock for the .NET generation—while *System.Net.Mail* allows sending mail to an SMTP server.

System.Reflection allows access to an assembly's metadata

System.Reflection contains a large set of types for examining an assembly's metadata. A subordinate namespace, *System.Reflection.Emit*, contains types that can be used to create other types dynamically. Reflection is described in more detail later in this chapter.

System.Resources allows manipulating resources

System.Resources provides types that allow managed code to work effectively with resources. Resources are parts of an application that can be separated from the source code, such as message strings, icons, and bitmaps. A primary use of this namespace's types is to allow an application to display different resources easily when used in different cultures. This makes the contents of this namespace especially relevant for internationalized software that must work in many different countries and languages.

System.Runtime is a parent namespace that contains several important subordinate namespaces. One of these, *System.Runtime.InteropServices*, is one of the .NET Framework class library's most important namespaces. It contains types that help in interoperating with non-CLR-based software, such as COM classes, and is described in more detail later in this chapter. *System.Runtime.Remoting* is another important namespace, as the types it contains allow accessing managed objects in other processes and other machines. This technology, known as .NET Remoting, is described in more detail in Chapter 7. *System.Runtime.Serialization* contains types for serializing a managed object's state. Serializing a managed object means copying its state (although not its code) into either memory or some more permanent medium such as a file. The ability to work with an object's state in this way is a fundamental feature of the .NET Framework—it's used by .NET Remoting, for example—and this namespace is also described in more detail later in this chapter.

System.Runtime provides interoperability, remoting, serialization, and other fundamental services

System.Security contains classes, interfaces, enumerations, and subordinate namespaces that provide various security-related functions. The namespace directly contains several fundamental classes, such as the SecurityManager class, which is the primary access point for working with the security system. The subordinate namespace *System.Security.Cryptography* contains types for using secret and public key cryptography services. Those types provide access to the Windows Cryptographic Service Providers (CSP) that actually implement algorithms such as DES, RC2, and RSA. System.Security.Cryptography itself also contains a few subordinate namespaces. One of them, *System.Security.Cryptography.X509Certificates*, contains classes for creating and using X.509 version 3 public key certificates for use with Microsoft's Authenticode technology, while another, *System.Security.Cryptography.Xml*, implements the World Wide Web Consortium (W3C) standard for digitally signing data described using XML.

System.Security provides cryptography support and other security services

System.Security also contains a few other subordinate namespaces. They include *System.Security.Permissions*, which defines types such as a class representing each of the possible permissions for code access security, and *System.Security.Policy*, which defines classes such as Site, URL, Publisher, Zone, and others used in defining security policy. How these concepts are used by the CLR was described briefly in Chapter 2's section on code access security. Another child namespace of System.Security, *System.Security.Principal*, contains types for working with security principals. These classes are used by the CLR in implementing the role-based security described in Chapter 2.

System.Service Process allows creating Windows services

System.ServiceProcess contains types for building .NET Framework applications that run as long-lived processes called *Windows services*. This kind of application was previously known as an *NT service* and is also sometimes referred to as a *daemon*.

System.Text supports text conversion and working with regular expressions

System.Text contains a group of classes for working with text. For example, this namespace's UTF8Encoding class can convert Unicode characters from their default encoding into UTF-8 and vice versa. UTF stands for *Unicode Transformation Format,* and UTF-8 is compatible with the familiar ASCII character representation (although it allows representing multibyte non-ASCII characters, too). System.Text also contains the namespace *System.Text.RegularExpressions*. The types in this namespace allow access to a generic regular expression engine that can be used from any CLR-based language.

System.Threading provides standard threading services used by all CLR-based languages

System.Threading is another of the .NET Framework's more important namespaces. The types it contains provide a standard way for developers working in any .NET language to build multithreaded applications. In the pre-.NET era, VB, C++, and other languages all had their own unique approach to threading, with COM's apartments serving as a (complicated) cross-language solution. With the .NET Framework, all CLR-based languages can use the contents of System.Threading to work with threads in a consistent way. Perhaps the most important type in this namespace is the Thread class, which provides methods to start a thread, stop one, cause it to wait for another thread, and more. The namespace also contains classes for using fundamental synchronization constructs, such as mutexes and monitors, and for working with a thread pool.

System.Timers contains types for specifying and handling recurring events. The most important class in this namespace is Timer, which allows a developer to specify an interval at which an Elapsed event, defined as part of the Timer class, will be raised in his application. The application can then catch this event and perform some function. For example, an application may wish to check for new mail once every ten minutes. Using this mechanism, the developer could cause the Elapsed event to take place every ten minutes, then put mail-checking code in the handler for this event.

System.Timers supports working with regularly occurring events

System.Transactions, a new namespace in version 2.0 of the .NET Framework, contains types that let applications use transactions. Prior to this 2005 release, applications could use ADO.NET for handling database transactions or Enterprise Services for working with more complex, multisystem transactions. With System.Transactions, Microsoft rethought how applications should use transactions on Windows. This important new technology is described in more detail later in this chapter.

System. Transactions provides support for applications using transactions

System.Web is, after System itself, perhaps the most important namespace in the .NET Framework class library. Comprising many types and many subordinate namespaces, the software it contains implements ASP.NET. The two most important children of System.Web are *System.Web.UI*, which contains types for building browser-accessible applications, and *System. Web.Services*, which contains types for creating applications that expose Web services. ASP.NET's support for creating

System.Web implements ASP.NET and ASP.NET Web services

■ Perspective: The Risks and Rewards of a Standard Class Library

The goal of creating a class library is to make life easier for developers. Rather than reinvent wheels from scratch, a developer can reuse existing wheels. Class libraries aren't a new idea, and several useful collections of code exist today. Before the arrival of .NET, the most popular was surely the large set of packages defined for the Java environment, which collectively define a set of services that look much like the .NET Framework class library. (In fact, a Java package is very similar to a namespace in the .NET Framework.) The existence of this large set of prepackaged functionality was a major reason for Java's success.

There have been attempts to create broad class libraries that were doomed by their own ambition, however. One of the most visible (and probably most expensive) of these was a project undertaken by the joint Apple/IBM venture Taligent. I once gave a seminar for the technical staff at Taligent, and I don't think I've ever spoken to a more intelligent audience—those people were amazing. Yet in part because the class libraries they produced were so complex and had such a long learning curve, they ultimately weren't successful.

Does the .NET Framework class library suffer from this problem? I don't think so. It's certainly big, but a developer doesn't need to understand the whole thing to use just one part of it. Some degree of compartmentalization is critical to a successful class library, since the number of people willing to devote the necessary time to achieve complete mastery is much smaller than those who can benefit from exploiting some parts of it.

The success of the .NET Framework suggests that the creators of its library made mostly the right choices. Overall, the .NET Framework class library appears to strike a good balance between power and complexity. While the library certainly requires effort to understand, the popularity of .NET today suggests that developers believe the payoff is worth it.

browser-based applications is described in Chapter 5, while Chapter 7 looks at the support it provides for Web services.

System.Windows.Forms contains types used to construct local Windows Graphical User Interfaces (GUI). Local GUIs are somewhat less important for application developers than they once were—a browser interface is now more common—but they're nonetheless an important topic. Accordingly, this namespace is described in more detail later in this chapter.

System.Windows. Forms supports building local Windows GUIs

System.XML contains types useful for working with XML documents. The .NET Framework is shot through with support for XML, and the contents of this namespace provide a significant amount of technology for developers working with XML-defined data. This namespace is also described in more detail later in this chapter.

System.XML includes a wide range of support for working with XML-defined data

Code provided by a standard library isn't useful unless you know it's there. Accordingly, while memorizing the entire .NET Framework class library isn't necessary, any developer writing CLR-based code should have a broad grasp of what the library makes available. One way to think about what's available is to group the library's services into a few broad categories:

Every .NET Framework developer needs a basic knowledge of the class library

- Fundamental services such as performing basic input and output, serializing an object's state, accessing metadata via reflection, working with XML, using transactions, interoperating with other Windows software, and building native Windows GUIs.

- Services for creating Web applications that interact with people. This critically important area is addressed by the browser-oriented aspects of ASP.NET.

- Services for working with data. This mostly means support for working with data in DBMSs, such as that provided by ADO.NET, but XML data is also important.

■ Services for creating distributed applications. This includes the Web services aspects of ASP.NET, along with .NET Remoting and Enterprise Services.

The rest of this book is structured in this way. The remainder of this chapter describes some of the library's most important general services, while the chapters that follow examine the other three categories.

Fundamental Namespaces

The .NET Framework class library provides so many services that it's challenging to decide which ones are most fundamental. One developer might use something in every application that another developer never needs. Still, a basic knowledge of the .NET technologies described next—input and output, serialization, reflection, transactions, and inter operability—should be part of every .NET developer's arsenal.

Input and Output: System.IO

File access is a basic service

Like most software, .NET Framework applications need some way to input and output data. These operations are most commonly done against some kind of disk storage, but there are other possibilities too. The .NET Framework class library's System.IO namespace contains a group of types that developers can use to read and write files, work with directories in a file system, and do other kinds of straightforward data access.

A Stream object contains a sequence of bytes and provides methods to access those bytes

Among the most important of these types is the Stream class. This class defines the useful abstraction of a *stream*, which is a sequence of bytes together with methods to read the stream's contents, write those contents, perhaps seek a specific location in the stream, and perform other operations. Stream is an abstract class, and so a number of specialized classes inherit from it. The goal is to let developers work with various kinds of information in a consistent way.

Information stored in files can be accessed using the File class. While an instance of File provides familiar methods for working with files such as Create, Delete, and Open, it doesn't provide methods for reading and writing a file's contents. Instead, a File object's Create and Open methods return an instance of a FileStream that can be used to get at the file's contents. Like all streams, a FileStream object provides Read and Write methods for synchronous access to a file's data, that is, for calls that block waiting for data to be read or written. Also like other streams, FileStream objects allow asynchronous access using the paired BeginRead/EndRead and BeginWrite/EndWrite methods. These methods allow a .NET Framework application to begin a read or write operation and then check later to get the result. Each FileStream also provides a Seek method to move to a designated point in the file, a Flush method to write data to the underlying device (such as a disk), a Close method to close the FileStream, and many more.

A FileStream object allows access to a file's contents as binary data

FileStreams work only with binary data, however, which isn't always what's needed. System.IO provides other standard classes to work with file data in other formats. For example, a class called FileInfo can be used to create FileStreams, but it can also be used to create instances of the classes StreamReader and StreamWriter. Unlike File, whose methods are mostly static, an instance of a FileInfo class must be explicitly created before its methods can be used. Once a FileInfo object exists, its OpenText method can be used to create a new StreamReader object. This StreamReader can then be used to read characters from whatever file is associated with the FileInfo object.

A FileInfo object allows access to a file's contents as text

Here's a C# example that illustrates how these classes can be used:

```csharp
using System;
using System.IO;

class FileIOExample
{
    static void Main()
    {
```

```
FileStream fs;
FileInfo f;
StreamReader sr;
byte[] buf = new byte[10];
string s;
int i;

for (i=0; i<10; i++)
    buf[i] = (byte) (65 + i);
fs = File.Create("test.dat");
fs.Write(buf, 0, 10);
fs.Close();

f = new FileInfo("test.dat");
sr = f.OpenText();
s = sr.ReadToEnd();

Console.WriteLine("{0}", s);
    }
}
```

This admittedly unrealistic example begins with appropriate using directives and then defines the single class FileIOExample. This class contains only a Main method, which begins with several declarations. After this, the 10-byte buffer buf is populated with the characters "A" through "J." Because buf can accept only bytes, this is done by explicitly calculating each character's value and then forcing the result to be of type byte. (This forced type conversion is called *casting*.) File's Create method is then used to create a file, followed by a call to File's Write method. This method writes buf's ten characters into that file and is followed by a Close call that closes the file. Because the File class declares all of these methods to be static, they can be invoked without explicitly creating a File instance.

The example next opens the same file using an instance of the FileInfo class. Calling the FileInfo object's OpenText method returns a StreamReader object whose ReadToEnd method can be used to read the characters just written into a string. Stream Readers also provide methods to read single characters, blocks of characters, and lines of characters. Finally, the characters read from the file are written to the console, yielding the result

```
ABCDEFGHIJ
```

System.IO also defines several other useful types. The Directory class, for instance, provides methods such as CreateDirectory to create a new directory, Delete to destroy an existing directory and its contents, and several more. The MemoryStream class allows the typical operations defined for a stream, such as Read, Write, and Seek, to be carried out on an arbitrary set of bytes in memory. StringWriter and StringReader provide analogous functions to StreamWriter and StreamReader, except that instead of working with files, they work with in-memory strings. BinaryReader and BinaryWriter allow reading and writing values of types such as integers, decimals, and characters from a stream. While information stored in relational databases is more important for many applications, data stored in files still matters. The classes in System.IO provide a flexible set of options for working with that data.

Many other classes are also defined for working with files, directories, and streams

Serialization: System.Runtime.Serialization

Objects commonly have state. An instance of a class, for example, can have one or more fields, each of which contains some value. It's often useful to extract this state from an object, either to store the state somewhere or to send it across a network. Performing this extraction is called *serializing* an object, while the reverse process, recreating an object from serialized state, is known as *deserializing*. Somewhat confusingly, the term *serialization* is commonly used to refer to the ability to do both.

Serialization extracts an object's state

The .NET Framework class library provides support for serialization. The work of serialization is done by a particular *formatter,* each of which provides a Serialize and Deserialize method. The NET Framework class library provides two varieties of formatter. The binary formatter, implemented by the BinaryFormatter class in the System.Runtime.Serialization.Formatters.Binary namespace, serializes an object into a straightforward binary form designed to be compact and quick to parse. The SOAP formatter, implemented by the SoapFormatter class in the System.Runtime.Serialization.Formatters.Soap namespace, serializes an object into a SOAP message.

A formatter can be used to serialize an object

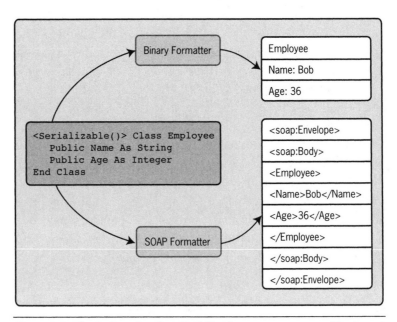

Figure 4-1 The System.Runtime.Serialization namespace provides two different formatters to serialize an object's state.

Both a binary formatter and a SOAP formatter are provided

Figure 4-1 illustrates the serialization process. As the figure shows, an instance of a class can be run through a formatter that extracts the state of this object in a particular form. The binary formatter emits that state information in a simple and compact form, while the SOAP formatter generates the same information wrapped in XML and formatted as a SOAP message[1]. While the outputs shown in the figure are simplified—the binary formatter actually stores integers in binary form, for instance—they illustrate the key difference between the two serialization options built into the .NET Framework class library.

An object's state is serialized into a stream

When a formatter serializes an object, the resulting state is placed into a stream. As described in the previous section, a stream is an abstraction of a sequence of bytes and so can hold

---

1. For a description of SOAP messages, see the W3C's SOAP specification at www.w3.org.

any serialization format. Once it's in a stream, an object's state can be stored on disk (or in the jargon of objects, be made *persistent*), sent across a network to another machine, or used in some other way.

For a type to be serializable, its creator must mark it with the Serializable attribute, as Figure 4-1 illustrates. The Serializable attribute can be assigned to classes, structures, and other types or just to specific fields within a type to indicate that only they should be serialized. Also, a type marked with the Serializable attribute can indicate that certain fields should not be saved when an instance of this type is serialized by marking them with the NonSerialized attribute.

Not every type is serializable

Here's a simple VB example that shows how serialization works:

```
Imports System
Imports System.IO
Imports System.Runtime.Serialization
Imports _
    System.Runtime.Serialization.Formatters.Binary

Module SerializationExample

    <Serializable()> Class Employee
        Public Name As String
        Public Age As Integer
    End Class

    Sub Main()
        Dim E1 As Employee = New Employee()
        Dim E2 As Employee = New Employee()
        Dim FS As FileStream
        Dim BinForm As BinaryFormatter = _
            New BinaryFormatter()

        E1.Name = "Bob"
        E1.Age = 36

        FS = File.Create("test.dat")
        BinForm.Serialize(FS, E1)
        FS.Close()

        FS = File.Open("test.dat", FileMode.Open)
        E2 = BinForm.Deserialize(FS)
```

```
                      Console.WriteLine("E2 Name: {0}", E2.Name)
                      Console.WriteLine("E2 Age: {0}", E2.Age)
                End Sub
          End Module
```

This example begins with several Imports statements, the VB analog to C#'s using directive. As always, these statements aren't required, but they make the code that follows more readable by removing the need to type fully qualified names. Following these, the module begins with the definition of a very simple Employee class. This class contains just two fields representing an employee's name and age and has no methods at all. (This is unrealistic, of course, but information about methods isn't stored anyway when a class is serialized.)

The example's Sub Main routine creates two instances of the Employee class, E1 and E2, and then declares a FileStream called FS. It next creates an instance of the BinaryFormatter class that will be used to serialize and deserialize the objects' state. Once that state has been created by initializing E1's fields to contain a name and an age, the file test.dat is created to hold the serialized state. The binary formatter's Serialize method is then called, which serializes the state in E1 into the stream FS. When the stream is closed, its contents are written to the file test.dat.

The example then reopens test.dat, associating it once again with the stream FS. This stream is passed into the binary formatter's Deserialize method, with the result assigned to E2. Although E2 has had just its default state so far, the deserialization process gives it the state that was extracted earlier from E1. Accordingly, the output of this simple program is

```
E2 Name: Bob
E2 Age: 36
```

Serialization has options

Serialization can also be customized. For example, if a class implements the ISerializable interface, it can participate in its own serialization. This interface has only a single method that allows controlling the details of what gets serialized. Also, although it's not shown in this simple example, serializing an object will also serialize objects it refers to, causing them all to be serialized (or deserialized) at once. And for the brave, it's possible to build your own formatter that does serialization in a completely customized way by inheriting from the abstract class System.Runtime.Serialization.Formatter. However it's done, serialization is useful, and in its basic form, at least, it's simple to use. As described later, serialization plays a role in several parts of the .NET Framework class library.

Reflection: System.Reflection

Every assembly includes metadata. Always having metadata available is handy, since it allows creating useful features such as Visual Studio's IntelliSense, which automatically displays the methods available for a class and other useful information. But metadata is just information sitting in a file. It's useless without software that knows how to read and interpret that metadata. To support this software, it's useful to have a standard interface to an assembly's metadata, one that can be used by all kinds of applications.

An assembly's metadata is useless without some way to access it

For managed code, that interface is provided by the types contained in the System.Reflection namespace. Before taking a look at these types, recall what metadata consists of: information about the types in an assembly, such as what methods they implement, along with information about the assembly itself, stored in the assembly's manifest. As mentioned in Chapter 2, the Ildasm tool can be used to examine an assembly's metadata. Figure 4-2 shows how Ildasm displays the metadata stored with the simple example application from Chapter 3. The manifest appears first, followed by entries for each of the three outermost types in the program: the classes Compute and DisplayValues and the interface IMath. Each of these has associated information, the most interesting of which is the methods each type implements. Note that along with the methods shown in Chapter 3's code, each class also has a constructor, labeled ".ctor" in the Ildasm display.

The types in System.Reflection allow managed code to access metadata

Figure 4-2   The metadata stored with Chapter 3's simple example application can be displayed using Ildasm.

Each kind of meta-data is represented by a specific class

To allow programmatic access to this information, the System.Reflection namespace includes a class for each type of information in an assembly's metadata. An application can create instances of these classes as needed and then populate them with the appropriate information from a particular assembly. As Figure 4-3 shows, instances of these classes are organized into a hierarchy. Once the appropriate instances have been created—Figure 4-3 shows a fairly complete picture for Chapter 3's sample application—the assembly's metadata can be accessed[2]. Although it's not shown in the diagram, it's also possible to access any attributes this metadata contains.

For example, to list all methods contained in this assembly's Compute class, an application could create an instance of the Assembly class and then call this class's LoadFrom method with

---

2. It's worth reiterating that full access to metadata requires appropriate code access security permissions.

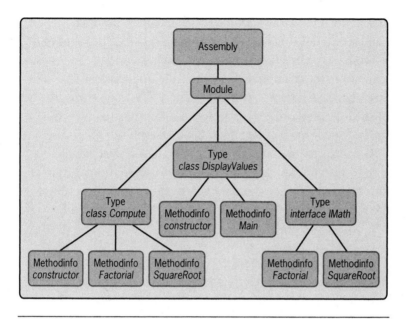

Figure 4-3   The classes in System.Reflection can be used to create a hierarchical in-memory structure that contains an assembly's metadata.

the name of the file containing the assembly. The Assembly class also provides a GetModule method that can be used to return an instance of the Module class that describes the module containing the Compute class. Once this Module instance exists, the application can call GetType with the name of the desired type in this module, which in this case is Compute. The result is an object of the class Type that contains information about the Compute class. The Type class provides a large set of methods and properties for learning about its contents. For example, a call to Type.GetMethods can return a description of all methods that type implements, each contained in an instance of the class MethodInfo. In this case, three MethodInfo objects would be returned, each containing information about one of Compute's three methods. By examining the properties of each MethodInfo, the application can learn whatever it needs to know about these methods. Among the information available is the method's name, the types of its parameters, its return type, whether the method is final (sealed), and much more.

The types in Reflection.Emit allow creating assemblies dynamically

The Reflection namespace also contains the subordinate namespace Reflection.Emit. To understand what the types in this namespace do, it's first important to understand the two types of assemblies that can be used by the .NET Framework. As described in Chapter 2, the most common variety, *static* assemblies, are stored on and loaded from disk. All assemblies described so far have in fact been static assemblies. It's also possible to create *dynamic* assemblies, assemblies that are created directly in memory. With this approach, a running application creates MSIL code and metadata, building an assembly on the fly, and then executes it. The types in the Reflection.Emit namespace are used to do this.

Types in Reflection.Emit allow applications to generate and then execute MSIL code

Creating dynamic assemblies is not for the faint of heart. Reflection.Emit contains types that do very low-level things, including generating MSIL code one instruction at a time. (The CodeDom, described briefly earlier in this chapter, provides a somewhat simpler way to generate dynamic CLR-based applications.) Yet while most developers probably won't work directly with Reflection.Emit, it's useful to know that these types exist. Class libraries are meant to make developers' lives easier, and you can't use code in a library if you don't know the code is there.

XML: System.Xml

XML is a fundamental technology for many kinds of applications

XML is certainly among the most important new technologies to emerge in the last few years. Recognizing this, Microsoft has chosen to use XML in many different ways throughout the .NET Framework. The company also recognizes that its customers wish to use XML in a variety of ways. Accordingly, the .NET Framework class library includes a substantial amount of support for working with XML technologies, most of it contained in the System.Xml namespace.

The XML Technology Family

XML is more than angle brackets

To get a sense of what the System.Xml namespace provides requires understanding a bit about the family of XML technologies. From its beginning as a way to define documents, elements in those documents, and namespaces for those elements,

XML has evolved into a significantly more powerful—and significantly more complex—group of technologies.

The familiar angle bracket form of XML implies a logical hierarchy of related information. This abstract set of information and relationships is known as the XML document's *Information Set*, a term that's usually shortened to just *Infoset*. An Infoset consists of some number of *information items*, each of which represents some aspect of the XML document from which this Infoset was derived. For example, every Infoset has a *document* information item that acts as the root of the tree, with a single root *element* information item just beneath it. Most Infosets have some number of child element information items below this root element.

An Infoset provides an abstract view of the information in an XML document

For example, consider this simple XML document:

```
<employees>
    <employee>
        <name>Bob</name>
        <age>36</age>
    </employee>
    <employee>
        <name>Casey</name>
    </employee>
</employees>
```

The Infoset for this document can be represented as shown in Figure 4-4. The root of the Infoset's tree is a document information item, while below it is a hierarchy of element information items, one for each element in the XML document. The leaves of the tree are the values of the elements in this simple document.

XML documents and the Infosets they imply can provide the foundation for tools that manipulate a document's data. Among the most important of these is XPath, which provides a mechanism for identifying a subset of an Infoset. A simple and quite accurate way to think of XPath is as a query language for information in XML documents (that is, for XML Infosets). Just as SQL provides a standard language for querying information contained in a relational database, XPath provides a language for querying information represented as a hierarchy.

XPath allows querying an XML document

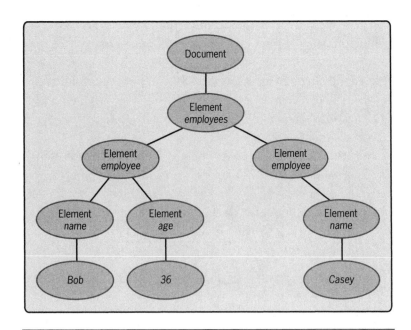

Figure 4-4   An XML document's Infoset is an abstract representation of the document's contents.

Using an XPath expression, a user can identify specific nodes in a tree. For example, imagine that this query is issued against the simple XML document just described:

```
/employees/employee/name
```

This simple XPath request first identifies each employee element below the root employees element and then identifies the values of each name element in each of those employee elements. Far more complex queries are also possible, including queries that use comparison operators, compute sums, include wildcards, and much more. With XPath, a developer need not write her own code to search through information. Instead, this standard language can be used to find information represented as an in-memory XML document.

XSLT allows transforming XML documents

Another technology built on the abstract foundation provided by XML Infosets is the Extensible Stylesheet Language Transformations, universally referred to as XSLT. XSLT is a mechanism for specifying transformations of XML documents using an XSLT stylesheet. For instance, a set of XSLT rules that transforms an XML document from one schema to another can be defined. XSLT also relies on the abstract form of an XML document represented by its Infoset, and it relies on XPath for some of its functionality.

Figure 4-5 summarizes the relationships among the fundamental XML technologies. An XML Schema definition describes the structure and contents of an XML document—it defines a group of types—while an XML document itself can be thought of as an instance of the document type defined by some schema[3]. This

XML today is a unified family of technologies

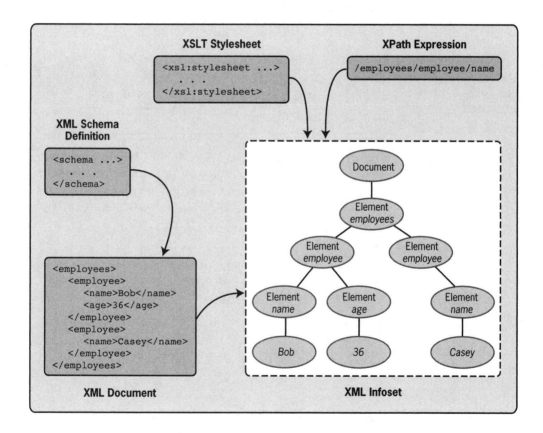

Figure 4-5   XML is a family of technologies, with the Infoset at the center.

---

3. In effect, an XML document's metadata is provided by its associated XML Schema definition.

XML document, in turn, is the foundation for an Infoset, which provides an abstract view of the document's data. Technologies for working with that data, such as XPath and XSLT, are effectively defined to work against the Infoset, allowing them to remain independent of the specific representation used for the XML document itself. Note that because these technologies rely on the Infoset rather than the familiar angle bracket–based syntax of an XML document, they can actually be used with any data that can be represented in a strict hierarchy. That data need not necessarily come from a traditional XML document as long as it can be represented as an Infoset. For example, hierarchical data such as a file system or the Windows registry might be accessed in this way.

SAX is a streaming API for accessing XML-defined information

The XML standards don't mandate any particular approach to processing the information in an XML document. As it happens, two styles of APIs have come into common use. In one approach, the information in an XML document is read sequentially, traversing a document's tree in a depth-first search. An API that supports this kind of access is referred to as a *streaming* API, and one common choice for this is the Simple API for XML (SAX). SAX was created by a group of volunteers independent of the W3C or other formal standards groups, but it is supported by many vendors today.

The DOM is a navigational API for accessing XML-defined information

In the second approach, the entire document is represented as an in-memory data structure (conceptually, at least), which allows an application to navigate through it, moving back and forth as needed. The most commonly used API for this option is an implementation of the Document Object Model (DOM) defined by the W3C. Because of the style of access it allows, the DOM is an example of a *navigational* API.

What System.Xml Provides

System.Xml includes support for XPath, XSLT, the DOM, and more

The System.Xml namespace has a variety of support for working with XML. Among the features available are support for both streaming and navigational APIs, the ability to use XPath queries, the ability to perform XSLT transformations, and more.

While describing all of these features in any detail is well beyond the scope of this book, this section provides an overview of their most important aspects.

The most fundamental types for handling XML-defined data are contained directly in System.Xml itself. Among these fundamental types is the class XmlReader, which provides a streaming interface for reading the information in an XML document sequentially. (Note while this is similar to the SAX API, the .NET Framework does not directly support SAX; instead it bases all streaming access on XmlReader.) This is the fastest option for reading XML-defined data, but it's also somewhat limited in that no navigation is possible through the document.

The XmlReader class allows streaming access to XML-defined information

The XmlReader class provides a Create method that can be passed an instance of the XmlReaderSettings class. Based on the properties specified in XmlReaderSettings, the newly created XmlReader instance can behave in different ways. The properties that can be specified via XmlReaderSettings include (among many others) the following:

- **ConformanceLevel:** indicates whether this XML document should be checked for conformance. This means making sure that the document is well-formed by ensuring that elements are properly nested and performing other checks. Conformance checking of the entire document is the default.

- **ValidationType:** indicates whether this XML document should be validated, i.e., verified for correctness, when it is read. The document can be validated against either an XML schema or a document type definition (DTD), which is an older way of defining the structure of XML documents. By default, no validation is done.

- **CheckCharacters:** indicates whether this XML document should be checked for characters that aren't legal in XML and for invalid XML names. This property's default value is true.

- **IgnoreComments:** indicates whether comments should be ignored when this XML document is read. The default is false.

It's worth pointing out that this style of working with an XmlReader is new in version 2.0 of the .NET Framework. Previous releases provided a standard set of more specialized classes that inherited from XmlReader, such as XmlTextReader and XmlValidatingReader, allowing a developer to choose whichever class best met her needs. Given version 2.0's more flexible approach, these classes are now deprecated.

The XmlWriter class allows writing XML documents

System.Xml also includes an XmlWriter class. The methods in this class allow writing XML information, angle brackets and all, to a stream. As described earlier in this chapter, a stream can be maintained in memory, written to a file, or used in some other way. Much like XmlReader, version 2.0 of the .NET Framework provides a Create method on the XmlWriter class, along with an XmlWriterSettings class that can be passed in when a new XmlWriter instance is created. Some example properties that can be specified using XmlWriterSettings are:

- **Encoding:** determines how characters in the XML document will be encoded. The default is UTF8, but the choices include ASCII, Unicode, and others.

- **Indent:** determines whether elements in the XML document are indented. The default is false.

- **IndentChars:** If Indent is true, determines the characters used to indent, such as a tab or three spaces. The default is two spaces.

An XmlDocument object allows navigational access to XML-defined information

System.Xml also includes the XmlDocument class. This class provides an implementation of the DOM API. While using an XmlReader is the fastest way to access information in an XML document, the XmlDocument class is more general because it allows navigation, moving backward and forward through the document at will. A developer is free to choose whichever approach best meets the needs of his application.

The methods and properties provided by XmlDocument give some idea of the kinds of operations the DOM allows. Those methods include the following:

- **Load:** Loads an XML document and parses it into its abstract tree form

- **Save:** Saves an in-memory document to a stream, file, or some other location

- **InsertBefore:** Inserts a new node, represented as an instance of a class called XmlNode, in front of the currently referenced node in the tree

- **InsertAfter:** Inserts a new node, once again an XmlNode instance, in back of the currently referenced node in the tree

- **SelectNodes:** Allows selecting nodes using an XPath expression

XmlDocument also exposes a number of properties that allow navigation through the tree. They include the following:

- **HasChildNodes:** Indicates whether the current node has any nodes beneath it

- **FirstChild:** Returns the first child of the current node

- **LastChild:** Returns the last child of the current node

- **ParentNode:** Returns the parent, that is, the node immediately above the current node

In version 2.0 of the .NET Framework, it's also possible to use an XmlDocument object to create an object of the class XPathNavigator. An XPathNavigator provides a way to use XPath expressions to navigate through and modify the information in this XmlDocument.

Types for XPath, XSLT, and XML Schema support are provided in separate namespaces

Several other namespaces are defined beneath System.Xml:

- **System.Xml.Schema:** Contains classes for creating and working with XML Schema definitions. Because this language is quite complex, this namespace contains a large set of classes, including a class for each of the elements in the XML Schema language. Microsoft refers to these classes collectively as the Schema Object Model (SOM).

- **System.Xml.XPath:** Contains types that support using XPath expressions to query hierarchical data. Among them are the XPathDocument class, which allows read-only access to an XML document via an instance of the XPathNavigator class mentioned earlier, and the XPath Expression class, which can contain a compiled XPath query.

- **System.Xml.Xsl:** Contains types that support using XSLT. The most important of these is the XslCompiledTransform class, which allows transforming data using an XSLT style sheet.

- **System.Xml.Serialization:** Contains types that allow serializing data into an XML format. This is another large namespace, but a key type within it is the XmlSerializer class. This class provides Serialize and Deserialize methods that write and read an object's state in XML. The System.Xml.Serialization namespace also contains many other classes that allow customizing the serialization process and other aspects of converting between state information stored in a language object and the XML form of that information.

The .NET Framework class library has a great deal of support for XML

XML has become an essential part of modern computing. By providing a standard way to describe information, it fills an important hole in the complex, multivendor world we live in. The .NET Framework's large set of namespaces and types devoted to XML are intended to make this important technology significantly easier to use.

Transactions: System.Transactions

The idea of a transaction—a group of two or more operations that succeed or fail as a single unit—is fundamental to many applications. The idea itself is simple: Either everything happens or nothing happens. Yet because of the thousand natural shocks that software is heir to, ensuring that a group of operations can result in only these two outcomes isn't simple at all. Accordingly, the .NET Framework provides services that make it easier to create transactional applications.

Transactions ensure that a group of operations succeed or fail as a whole

Transactions are most commonly used with DBMSs. As described in Chapter 6, a .NET developer can use ADO.NET to explicitly start a DBMS transaction, perform operations inside that transaction such as updating records in the DBMS, then explicitly commit or abort the transaction. (In the jargon of transactions, a DBMS and anything else capable of correctly carrying out transactional requests is known as a *resource manager* or *RM*, a more general term that will be used from now on.) This simple approach works well when all of a transaction's operations are requested from one application and are performed by a single RM, such as a DBMS.

ADO.NET lets developers control DBMS transactions

A developer's life gets more complicated when the operations in a single transaction can be issued from multiple entities, such as two or more objects in the same application, or carried out by multiple RMs. While these situations are less common, they're nonetheless important. The .NET Framework's support for this more complex style of transactional application is provided by Enterprise Services. This technology allows grouping operations issued by one or more objects into a single transaction, and it also allows the operations in a single transaction to be carried out by multiple RMs. Enterprise Services does more than just support transactions, however. It also provides services for managing object lifetimes and more, sometimes inextricably mingling these services together with transactions. (For more on this, see the description of Enterprise Services in Chapter 7.)

Enterprise Services lets developers control more complex transactional scenarios

*System.
Transactions
focuses purely on
transactions*

New with version 2.0 of the .NET Framework, System.
Transactions provides another way for developers to work with
transactions. Rather than bundling transaction control together
with object lifetime management and other things, as is done in
Enterprise Services, System.Transactions is focused entirely on
controlling transactions. It's important to emphasize that the
advent of System.Transactions doesn't break anything; Enterprise
Services still works just as before, as does the transaction support in ADO.NET. System.Transactions does make using transactions somewhat simpler, however, since they're no long bound
up with other unrelated ideas.

Controlling Transactions with Transaction Scopes

*Transactions can be
created using
TransactionScope
objects*

The easiest way to control transactional behavior with
System.Transactions is to use an object of the type
TransactionScope. Here's the basic skeleton of how an application can use this class to create a new transaction, do work
within it, then commit that transaction:

```
using System.Transactions;

using (TransactionScope ts = new TransactionScope())
{
  // Do work, e.g., update different DBMSs
  ts.Complete;
}
```

As this example shows, System.Transactions allows *using*
transactions in concert with a using statement. Unlike using a
namespace at the start of a C# program (a usage that's actually
an example of a using *directive*), a using statement allows
creating an instance of an object, then having this object
automatically disposed of when the statement's scope is
exited. In this example, the using statement creates a
TransactionScope object, then automatically disposes of it when
the using statement ends. The TransactionScope object defines a
new transaction, sometimes referred to as the *ambient* transaction. All of the operations within the using block belong to the
same transaction scope, and so all will become part of this
transaction.

The last line in this example, calling the TransactionScope object's Complete method, is effectively a vote to commit the transaction when the block is exited. If all goes well—if all RMs involved can successfully commit the transaction—and if this block isn't nested within a larger transaction scope (a notion described later in this section), the transaction will commit, making all work done within it permanent. If Complete is not called within the scope, however, or if an unhandled exception is raised within the scope, the transaction will abort. In this case, all of the work done within the transaction will revert to the state it was in before the transaction began. Interestingly, TransactionScope provides no method that's the opposite of Complete. Since either raising an exception or just failing to call Complete before leaving the scope will cause the transaction to abort, there's no need to add this extra option.

Calling a TransactionScope's Complete method votes to commit the transaction

Starting and ending a transaction using a TransactionScope object is simple to understand and simple to do. Other aspects of a transaction's behavior are a bit more complex, however. What happens when the transaction scopes defined using TransactionScope objects are combined, for example? Controlling this and other aspects of a transaction's behavior are described next.

Controlling the Behavior of a Transaction
From 50,000 feet, a transaction is just a group of operations that either all succeed or all fail. Closer to the ground, however, more complexity emerges. For example, it's legal to explicitly nest transaction scopes, like this:

Transaction scopes can be nested

```
using System.Transactions;

using(TransactionScope ts1 = new TransactionScope())
{
    // Do work, e.g., update two different DBMSs
    using(TransactionScope ts2 = new
      TransactionScope())
    {
        // Do more work, e.g., issue two more DBMS
          updates
```

```
            ts2.Complete;
        }
        ts1.Complete;
    }
}
```

Nested transaction scopes can be grouped into transactions in various ways

It's also possible for one TransactionScope to invoke a method that in turn contains a TransactionScope of its own. In both this case and the example above, one TransactionScope winds up nested inside another one. Are the two scopes separate, so that two independent transactions are created? Or is the work done inside both scopes combined into a single transaction? The answer depends on the value specified when each TransactionScope is created. Rather than creating a scope with just new TransactionScope( ), it's possible to pass in a value on creation that controls how this scope will behave when it's combined with other scopes. The possible values and their meanings are as follows:

- **Required:** indicates that a scope must always run inside a transaction. If a scope created with Required is at the root of a hierarchy of nested transactions, or if it's a standalone scope that's not part of any hierarchy, a new transaction will be created. If a scope marked with Required is nested inside some other transactional scope, however, it will join that scope's ambient transaction—no new transaction will be created. Required is the default value, so it's what will be applied to all of the scopes in the examples shown so far.

- **RequiresNew:** indicates that a scope always requires its own transaction. Whether a scope created with this value stands on its own or is nested inside a transaction hierarchy, a new transaction will always be created for it.

- **Suppress:** indicates that the work within a scope will run without a transaction. If there is an ambient transaction from some outer transaction scope, it will be ignored—this scope's work won't be done inside that transaction.

These options can be set whenever a new TransactionScope object is created. For example, a scope set to RequiresNew can be created with

Different options can be specified when a TransactionScope object is created

```
using (TransactionScope ts =
  new TransactionScope(RequiresNew)) {...}
```
and one with a scope set to Suppress can be created with

```
using (TransactionScope ts =
  new TransactionScope(Suppress)) {...}
```

Scopes can be combined in arbitrarily complex ways. However they're grouped together, each scope always votes on how it wishes to end the transaction it's part of. If the code in every scope contained within a particular transaction calls that TransactionScope's Complete method, that transaction will commit (assuming no errors occur in the RMs the transaction accesses or elsewhere). If the code in any scope contained within a particular transaction fails to call its TransactionScope's Complete method or raises an unhandled exception, the transaction will abort. In this case, all changes made to any RMs in all of the scopes in this transaction will be rolled back.

A transaction commits only if all of the scopes within it vote to commit

Other aspects of a transaction's behavior, such as its timeout value, can also be set via options passed in when a new TransactionScope is created. Whatever the details, though, transactions have been important since the early days of mainframe computing, and they're still important today. System.Transactions provides a straightforward and focused way for .NET developers to create transactional applications.

Transactions are important in many .NET applications

Interoperability: System.Runtime.InteropServices

Before the release of the .NET Framework, the world of Windows development was dominated by the Windows DNA technologies. Lots of applications were built using COM, Active Server Pages, COM+, and the rest of the DNA family, and those applications still exist. Many of them play an important role in

Software using pre-.NET technologies will not just disappear

running businesses, so they're certain to remain in use for at least the next few years. No matter how successful the .NET Framework is, the Windows DNA technologies that preceded it are not going away anytime soon.

The types in System.Runtime. InteropServices allow interoperability with existing Windows software

Given the huge investment Microsoft's customers have made in these applications, the .NET Framework must provide some way for new applications to connect with them. Just as important, the Framework must provide an effective way for managed code to access existing DLLs that weren't built using COM and to invoke the raw services provided by the underlying operating system. Solutions to all of these problems are provided by the classes in the System.Runtime.InteropServices namespace.

Accessing COM Objects

A key aspect of interoperability is mapping from COM types to CLR types

Interoperating with COM objects requires mapping between the CLR's type system and that defined by COM. Changing COM to better match the CLR wasn't an option for Microsoft. Even though they own the technology, COM is frozen in stone. The millions of lines of existing COM-based code in the world won't change to accommodate the new type system of the CLR, so the .NET Framework's solution for COM interoperability must adapt itself to the reality of the installed base.

Mapping between COM and managed objects can be simple, but it can also be complex

Doing this can be simple. In some cases, mapping from a COM interface to a CLR type is straightforward. It can also be quite difficult, however, especially when the COM interface involved uses complex types. While it's virtually always possible to map the two together in some way, it isn't always easy. To make even difficult mappings possible, the classes in System.Runtime.InteropServices provide very fine-grained control over how the mapping is done as well as many, many options. While most people won't use most of these options most of the time, it's still good to know that they're available.

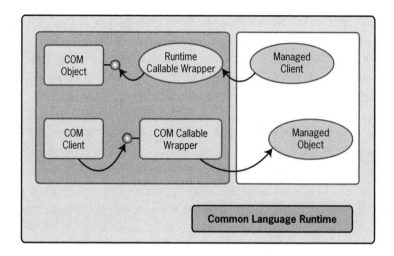

Figure 4-6 The .NET Framework's COM interoperability services can make a COM object look like managed code and managed code look like a COM object.

The fundamental model for interoperation between managed code and COM-based code is that each side sees the other in the form it expects: Managed code sees COM-based code as managed types, while COM-based code sees managed code as COM objects. How this looks is shown in Figure 4-6. To provide this illusion, the .NET Framework relies on two kinds of wrappers. One, known as a *runtime callable wrapper (RCW)*, allows managed code to call a COM object. The other, a *COM callable wrapper (CCW)*, allows COM code to access managed code.

Interoperability lets COM code and managed code each see the other as being like themselves

But where does the information needed to create these wrappers come from? Managed code sees the world in terms of assemblies, so to access a COM object as managed code, an assembly that mimics the COM class must exist. Furthermore, this assembly must contain metadata that accurately reflects the COM class's interfaces. To create this interoperability assembly, the .NET Framework provides a tool called Tlbimp, also known as the Type Library Importer. The input to this tool is a COM type library, and the output is an assembly that contains metadata for the CLR analogs of the COM types in the type library.

Tools create wrappers for COM objects

The wrapper maps between COM's behavior and what managed code expects

Once this assembly has been created, managed code can treat the library's COM classes just like any other managed code. When the managed code creates an instance of the class, the RCW actually creates the COM object. When the managed code invokes a method, the RCW makes a corresponding method invocation on the COM object. If an error occurs and the COM method returns an error HRESULT, as COM requires, the RCW automatically turns this into an exception that can be caught by the managed code. And when the managed code is finished using the object, it can behave just as it does when using any other managed object. The RCW will decrement the COM object's reference count before it is itself destroyed by the CLR's garbage collector.

Tools also create wrappers for managed objects

When a COM client uses a managed class, the same kinds of things happen in the opposite direction. Rather than producing an assembly from a type library, the developer can now produce a type library from an assembly. The Type Library Exporter tool, known as Tlbexp, provides a way to do this. Also, because COM uses the registry to determine which code should be loaded for a particular class, assemblies that will be accessed by COM clients must have appropriate registry entries. The Assembly Registration tool, Regasm, can be used to do this and optionally to register the assembly's generated type library as well. When a COM client creates and uses an instance of a managed class, translations between the two worlds are performed as before, but this time they're done by the CCW rather than the RCW.

A developer can customize the mapping between these two environments

All of this sounds simple and straightforward, and it often is. Yet what's not been addressed so far is the process of converting between the CLR type system and the COM type system. To do this, the wrappers must translate data between the two environments. Default mappings are defined, and if those defaults work, using code from the other world is simple. Marshaling an integer, for example, is straightforward, since a value of this type is the same in both environments. If the default mappings aren't appropriate, however, a developer's life gets more complex. What should a CLR string map to in the COM world, for example? COM has more than one string format, and it's not always obvious which one should be used. To control this and other marshaling choices, a developer can use the MarshalAs attribute to indicate the choice she prefers. Figuring out the right thing to do isn't always easy, but the fine-grained control the types in this namespace provide at least makes it possible.

One last point worth noting is that making calls across the boundary between managed and unmanaged code is noticeably more expensive than making calls solely within either environment. Marshaling data between the two takes time, and so writing managed code that interoperates with unmanaged code has performance implications. It's a good idea to do as much work as possible on each call across this boundary. If each one does only a small amount of work, an application that makes a large number of calls between the two worlds might not perform especially well.

Calls between managed and unmanaged code are expensive

Accessing Non-COM DLLs

While much of the existing code a .NET Framework application needs to use is accessible as COM classes, much of it isn't. Plenty of useful DLLs that don't use COM have been created. One important example of this is the Win32 API, exposed as a set of DLLs that allow direct access to Windows services. To allow managed code to call functions in these DLLs, the .NET Framework provides what are called *platform invoke* services, a phrase that's commonly shortened to just *PInvoke*.

PInvoke allows managed code to call existing DLLs

To use these services, a developer must specify the name of some DLL he wishes to use, the entry point to be called, the parameter list, and possibly other information. How this is done varies with the language in use. In VB, for example, the Declare statement is used, while C# relies on an attribute called DllImport. Whichever choice is made, once a DLL function has been appropriately specified, it can be invoked as if it were a function in a managed object. The platform invoke services provide the necessary translations, including marshaling of parameter types, to carry out the call.

Interoperability is an essential feature of the .NET Framework

System.Runtime.InteropServices is a critically important part of the .NET Framework class library. Although the notion of legacy software is sometimes viewed pejoratively, it has one enormous thing going for it: It works. If new code written on the .NET Framework had no way to communicate with the installed base, this new platform would have been much less attractive. The Framework's strong support for interoperability with existing code recognizes this reality, doing its part to smooth the transition to the brave new .NET world.

Windows GUIs: System.Windows.Forms

The .NET Framework provides three options for creating user interfaces

Most Windows applications interact with people in some way. To allow this, the .NET Framework provides three primary approaches to creating user interfaces:

- Console applications that interact with users one line at a time. All of the examples shown so far used this approach, which relies on the Console class in the System namespace. This class provides methods such as WriteLine and ReadLine to interact with users through a simple line-at-a-time approach. Even though it's convenient for simple examples, console applications aren't common today— real Windows software seldom uses this approach.

- Windows Forms applications that interact with users via a Windows graphical user interface (GUI). Mostly defined by the types in the System.Windows.Forms namespace, this technology lets developers create applications that interact directly with a local user's display, mouse, and keyboard. Especially for standalone applications, Windows Forms is a common choice for creating user interfaces today.

- ASP.NET applications that interact with users via a Web browser. Relying primarily on the types in the

System.Web.UI namespace, ASP.NET lets developers build applications that interact with users via a Web browser such as Internet Explorer or Firefox. The Web is a staple of modern life, and so it's fair to say that a majority of new .NET Framework applications interact with users through ASP.NET.

ASP.NET applications, a large topic, are described in Chapter 5. This section takes a brief look at creating Windows GUIs with Windows Forms.

Building Application with Windows Forms

It can sometimes seem as if browser-based applications have taken over the world. Many developers who once focused on getting the Windows GUI right now instead sweat technical bullets over details of HTML and JavaScript. Browsers have become the new default interface for a whole generation of software. But Windows GUIs still matter. The ascendancy of browsers notwithstanding, applications that access pixels on a local screen are not going away. Recognizing this fact, the designers of the .NET Framework provided Windows Forms, a full set of classes that allow CLR-based applications to build Windows GUIs.

Native Windows interfaces are important

Stripped to its essentials, an application that presents a GUI displays a form on the screen and then waits for input from the user. This input is typically processed by a message loop, which passes the input on to the appropriate place, generally as one or more events. (Events, which are based on delegates, were described in Chapter 3.) For example, when the user clicks a button or hits a key or moves the mouse, events are sent to the form the user is accessing. Code associated with this form handles these events, perhaps writing output to the screen or performing other tasks.

The typical model for a GUI is a form with code that responds to events

In Windows Forms, every form is an instance of the Form class, while the message loop that accepts and distributes events is provided by a class called Application. Using these and other classes in System.Windows.Forms, a developer can create a single-document interface (SDI) application, able to display only

A Windows Forms application can display many documents at a time or just one

one document at a time, or a multiple-document interface (MDI) application, able to display more than one document simultaneously.

Forms have properties

Each instance of the Form class has a large set of properties that control how that form looks on the screen. Among them are Text, which indicates what caption should be displayed in the title bar; Size, which controls the form's initial on-screen size; DesktopLocation, which determines where on the screen the form appears; and many more. Developers set these properties to customize a form's appearance and behavior.

Forms can contain Windows Forms controls

Forms commonly contain other classes called *Windows Forms controls*. Each of these controls typically displays some kind of output, accepts some input from the user, or both. The System.Windows.Forms namespace provides a large set of controls, many of which will be familiar to anyone who's built or even used a GUI. The control classes available in this namespace include Button, TextBox, CheckBox, RadioButton, ListBox, ComboBox, and many more. Also provided are more complex controls such as OpenFileDialog, which encapsulates the operations that let a user open a file; SaveFileDialog, which encapsulates the operations that let a user save a file; PrintDialog, which encapsulates the operations that let a user print a document; and several others. Version 2.0 of the .NET Framework added even more controls, including a WebBrowser that allows hosting Web pages in a Windows Forms application.

Controls have properties

Like a form, each control has properties that can be set to customize its appearance and behavior. Many of these properties are inherited from System.Windows.Forms.Control, the base class for every control. (In fact, even the Form class inherits from System.Windows.Forms.Control.) The Button control, for example, has a Location property that determines where the button will appear relative to its container and a Size property that determines how big the on-screen button will be, both of which are directly inherited from the parent Control class.

Button also has properties that aren't directly inherited from this parent, such as a Text property that controls what text will appear in the button.

Forms and controls also support events. Some examples of common events include Click, indicating that a mouse click has occurred; GotFocus, indicating that the form or control has been selected by the user; and KeyPress, indicating that a key has been pressed. All of these events and several more are defined in the base Control class from which all forms and controls inherit. As with properties, a control can also support unique events that have meaning only to it.

Both forms and controls can respond to events

As shown in Chapter 3, a developer can create code to handle events received by a form or control. Called an *event handler*, this code determines what happens when the event occurs. Here's a very simple C# example that illustrates the basic mechanics of forms, controls, and event handlers. While this example works, some things are simpler than they really should be, so you shouldn't necessarily view this as paradigmatic for your own code.

Event handlers are used to process events

```csharp
public class ExampleForm : System.Windows.Forms.Form
{
    private System.Windows.Forms.Button myButton;

    public ExampleForm()
    {
        Text = "An Example Form";
        myButton = new System.Windows.Forms.Button();
        myButton.Location = new
            System.Drawing.Point(50, 50);
        myButton.Size = new
            System.Drawing.Size(175, 50);
        myButton.Text = "Click Here";
        myButton.Click += new
            System.EventHandler(myButton_Click);
        Controls.Add(myButton);
    }

    private void myButton_Click(object sender,
        System.EventArgs e)
    {
```

```
            System.Windows.Forms.MessageBox.Show(
                "Button clicked");
        }
    }

    class DisplayForm
    {
        static void Main()
        {
            System.Windows.Forms.Application.Run(
                new ExampleForm());
        }
    }
```

This example begins by declaring the class ExampleForm.
Like all forms, this one inherits from System.Windows.
Forms.Form. (This code contains no using statements, partly
to make it shorter and partly to make clear where the various
types can be found in the .NET Framework class library.) The
ExampleForm class then declares a private instance of the
System.Windows.Forms.Button class, one of the controls men-
tioned earlier, called myButton.

The next thing to appear is the constructor for the ExampleForm
class. The constructor is automatically run whenever an instance
of this class is created, and in this example, the constructor's job
is to initialize appropriately the form and the control it contains.
The first step in that initialization is to set the form's Text property.
The constructor then creates an instance of the Button class and
sets several of its properties. Those properrties include
Location, Size, and Text, all of which were described earlier.
Once this is done, the constructor sets up an event handler for
the Click event on myButton. This is done using EventHandler,
a standard delegate provided in the System namespace. (Like
events in general, the EventHandler type was described in
Chapter 3.) Finally, the myButton control is added to the control
collection for this form, something that must be done to allow
the control's output to be displayed.

Following the ExampleForm class's constructor is the method that
will handle the Click event on myButton. By convention, the

format of this method's name is the name of the control followed by an underscore and the name of the event: myButton_Click. This isn't required, however, and in fact any name can be used. The standard arguments to the event handler method allow learning more about the event, but they're not used in this simple example. Instead, the event handler just calls the Windows Forms MessageBox method to output a simple message.

The example ends with a class containing just one method—Main—which itself has only one statement, a call to the Run method of the System.Windows.Forms.Application class. This method provides a message loop that accepts and processes events. Passing it an instance of a form, as in this case, causes it to make that form visible when the application runs.

The output of this program is shown in Figure 4-7. As you would expect, it consists of a single form containing a button with the text "Click Here." The figure shows how things look after a user has clicked the button, causing the event handler for the Click event to run. The result is the message box that appears to the right of the form.

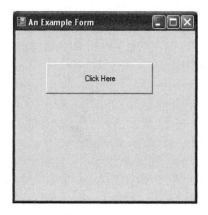

Figure 4-7 The simple application described in this section puts up a form containing a button, then displays a message box when the button is clicked.

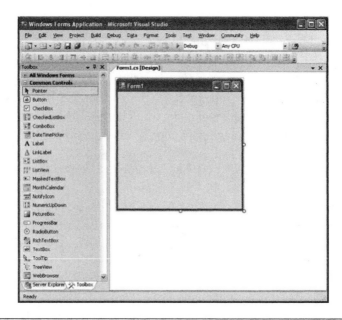

Figure 4-8 **Visual Studio 2005 provides a graphical designer for creating Windows Forms GUIs.**

Visual Studio 2005 allows creating forms interactively

It's certainly possible to hand-code GUIs using the types in System.Windows.Forms, but only a masochist would do it. While it's useful to see a simple example to get a sense of how the mechanism works, the vast majority of Windows GUIs are created using Visual Studio 2005 or some other tool. Like its predecessors, Visual Studio 2005 provides a full-featured designer that allows dragging controls onto a form, directly setting their properties, and adding code to handle events. The full implementation is then generated automatically by this tool. Creating a GUI in this way is faster, more accurate (since you can see what you're doing), and much less error-prone. Figure 4-8 shows a basic picture of how this GUI-builder tool looks to a developer.

Windows Forms Controls

Developers can create custom Windows Forms controls

Windows Forms controls are a useful way to package reusable chunks of functionality. Although the .NET Framework class library provides a large set of controls, the inventiveness of developers knows no bounds. Accordingly, the .NET Framework makes it straightforward to write custom Windows Forms controls. As already mentioned, every Windows Forms control must inherit either directly or indirectly from the class Control. It's also possible to inherit from one of the standard controls provided with the .NET Framework class library, basing a new control on existing functionality, or to combine two controls into one new one. Whatever choice the control's creator makes, a good chunk of the work is done for her.

Windows applications built before the .NET era relied on COM-based components known as ActiveX controls. Despite being fairly complicated to create, huge numbers of these were created by third parties. Many containers capable of running ActiveX controls also exist, such as Internet Explorer. Given this large installed base of both ActiveX controls and containers for those controls, Microsoft needed to provide some way for Windows Forms controls to interoperate with this world.

To use an ActiveX control in a Windows Form environment, the ActiveX Control Importer, Aximp, can be used to create a wrapper for the control. As with other parts of the .NET Framework's support for COM interoperability, this tool reads the ActiveX control's type library and produces an assembly containing analogous metadata. To allow a Windows Forms control to be used in a container that expects only ActiveX controls, the Windows Forms control can inherit from the class UserControl. This class implements everything required to make the Windows Forms control look like an ActiveX control and thus be hostable in the many ActiveX control containers that exist today. Also, because ActiveX controls are COM-based, any Windows Forms control used in this way must have an entry in the Windows registry, just as in the COM interoperability scenarios described earlier in this chapter.

Windows Forms controls can emulate ActiveX controls

Before the creation of the .NET Framework, Visual Basic 6 and C++ had completely different approaches to building GUIs. Because of this, ActiveX controls were based on COM, which allowed them to work with both languages. The predictable

Windows Forms provides a common mechanism for creating GUIs in any CLR-based language

What's Next: Windows Presentation Foundation

In 2006, Microsoft plans to release Windows Presentation Foundation (WPF), the successor to Windows Forms. The basic concepts of WPF are much like those of its predecessor: Interfaces are built from forms (called *panels* in WPF), those panels can contain customizable controls that handle incoming events, and more. Yet WPF is also different in some interesting ways. The structure of a user interface—panels, controls, and the rest—can be specified in an XML-based language called XAML as well as in code. A WPF application can be constructed in pages, much like a Web application, allowing a user to navigate through those pages. Each page might contain its user interface specified in XAML, along with event handlers and other code written in C#, VB, or some other CLR-based language. XAML also allows directly defining documents, providing a Microsoft-define analog to Adobe's Portable Document Format (PDF) files.

WPF is part of Microsoft's larger WinFX technology suite. Like other WinFX technologies, it will be available for Windows Vista, Windows XP, and Windows Server 2003. Once this happens, new applications that target these operating systems can use WPF rather than Windows Forms. These newer systems will still support Windows Forms, and so applications are also free to use this older technology.

result was complexity. Windows Forms swept away the accumulation of GUI technologies that had built up on the Windows platform, replacing them with a single consistent approach for all .NET applications.

Installing Windows Forms Applications Remotely: ClickOnce

Windows Forms interfaces and browser interfaces both have pros and cons

Which is better: a Windows Forms interface or a browser interface? The answer, of course, depends on the situation. Browsers allow access to the entire world of the Web, and since everybody knows how to click links, a browser-based application is instantly familiar to its users. Still, from a pure user interface point of view, Windows Forms applications have a lot going for them. They're much more responsive, since a round trip to a remote Web server isn't required to interact with the application, and they can also be more Windows-specific, since they're not required to adhere largely to Web standards such as HTML. Especially for people who use a custom application frequently, such as workers in a call center, these differences can be very beneficial.

Despite this, a majority of .NET applications written today target browsers. An important reason for this is the challenge of deploying new versions of native Windows applications. If anything changes in the assemblies running on clients, all client systems must be updated. Deploying a new version of a browser-based application, by contrast, typically requires updating only the server(s) on which this application runs. If installation of Windows Forms applications were easier, developers would have one less reason to build browser-based software, allowing the benefits of native Windows applications to be more widely applied.

Browser-based applications have historically been easier to deploy

ClickOnce, a new technology in version 2.0 of the .NET Framework, exists to make deploying and updating Windows Forms applications easier[4]. ClickOnce applications can be installed from a Web page, a shared file system somewhere on the network, or from a local device such as a CD-ROM. Once it's installed, a ClickOnce application can automatically detect when updates have occurred, then copy and install only those parts of itself that were changed. Updates or the entire installation can also be rolled back if necessary.

ClickOnce allows deploying and updating Windows Forms applications more easily

To allow an application to be deployed using ClickOnce, a developer creates an *application manifest* that describes the assemblies in this application, their dependencies, and other information. An administrator must also create a *deployment manifest* that indicates where to find the application manifest,

ClickOnce applications rely on the CLR's code access security

---

4. Although not many people care, ClickOnce can also be used with console applications.

where to check for updates to the application, and more. The deployment manifest is then copied to the location from which this application will be deployed, such as a Web page or file share. The application manifest, along with the application itself, might be placed at this same location or perhaps live somewhere else—both are possible. In either case, a user accesses the deployment manifest, typically by clicking on an icon, and the installation process begins. When the application is executed, it runs in the sandbox created by the .NET Framework's code access security, which was described in Chapter 2.

ClickOnce applications can be automatically updated in various ways

Checks for updates to the application, followed by installation of any changes, are made based on an update strategy specified in the deployment manifest. By default, a ClickOnce application will check for updates in the background while the application is running. If any are found, the user will be prompted to copy and install them the next time he starts this application. It's also possible to configure the application to check for and download any updates each time it's started, or to force users to download and install updates, preventing them from running an earlier version.

Administrative permission isn't required to install a ClickOnce application

ClickOnce installation doesn't require administrative permissions, and it can also do useful things such as making a newly installed application visible in the system's Start menu. Still, ClickOnce isn't appropriate for every Windows Forms application. This approach can't be used to install assemblies in the global assembly cache, for example, nor is it useful for installing device drivers. The standard Windows Installer with its MSI files is a better choice in cases like these. Yet providing the ability to update applications automatically from a remote location is a useful thing. And the simplicity this technology brings—it's not called "ClickOnce" for nothing—also makes it an attractive choice for Windows applications. Browser applications aren't going away any time soon, but the advent of ClickOnce will certainly cause some developers to lean a bit more toward building Windows Forms applications instead.

Conclusion

For a developer moving to the .NET Framework, learning a new language will surely take some time. Yet neither C# nor VB is all that different from other programming languages, so most developers won't have too much trouble learning these new tools. Learning to use the .NET Framework class library will probably take longer. Probably no developer will need to master the entire library, but everybody will need to learn some parts.

Understanding the .NET Framework class library will take time

The good news is that by providing a standard solution to many common problems, Microsoft has given us a large set of code that we'll never need to write again. While it will surely take some effort to master the relevant parts of this new technology, we should receive substantial benefits. And however you feel about it, the .NET Framework is a reality. If you want to write Windows-based software, your choice isn't whether to learn it, but when.

Every Windows developer will need to learn the .NET Framework

5

Building Web Applications: ASP.NET

Accessing software over the Web has become the norm. Most new enterprise applications offer at least the option of a browser interface, while Internet applications offer nothing else. Given this, an application platform that doesn't provide first-class support for building Web-based software is doomed to failure. And yet how we use software via the Web is changing. While communicating with a user through a browser is certainly important, Web services are also on the scene. The Web is expanding from a world driven solely by eyeballs to one that's also driven by applications.

Web-based applications are important

ASP.NET is the .NET Framework's foundation for building Web applications. Implemented primarily as part of the .NET Framework class library, it supports creating both browser applications and Web services applications. Like everything else in the class library, ASP.NET defines a group of types contained in several namespaces. The root namespace for ASP.NET is System.Web, and immediately below it are several more

ASP.NET allows creating browser applications and Web services applications

namespaces. The most important of these are System.Web.UI, which contains the types used to build browser Web applications, and System.Web.Services, which contains the types used to build Web services applications. This chapter describes how ASP.NET 2.0, the version contained in the .NET Framework 2.0 and supported by Visual Studio 2005, allows developers to create browser applications. The ASP.NET Web services technology, a largely independent topic, is described in Chapter 7.

ASP.NET Applications: Basics

Browsers understand HTML

When a user at a Web browser issues a request for an ordinary HTML page, what happens is simple. The request is conveyed to some Web server, which reads the file the user has specified and sends back the HTML this file contains. This kind of simple communication is what browsers were originally designed to do.

Web applications must generate HTML, perhaps with embedded scripts

Creating an environment that lets developers create full-fledged Web applications isn't so simple. The browser still expects the same thing—HTML pages that perhaps contain some embedded code in a language such as JavaScript[1]—and so the job of a Web application must be to create this. Yet like any application, software written for the Web can contain complex logic, access data, and more. Reconciling these requirements with the simple capabilities of a Web browser presents a challenge.

IIS passes requests for pages with the .aspx extension to ASP.NET

The goal of ASP.NET is to meet this challenge. To do this, the technology defines a specific file extension, .aspx, for Web pages. Browser requests made to Internet Information Services (IIS), Microsoft's Web server, for pages with this extension will actually be handed off to ASP.NET. Figure 5-1 shows the broad outlines of how this process works.

---

1. Actually, the language's official name is *ECMAScript*, reflecting its status as an ECMA standard.

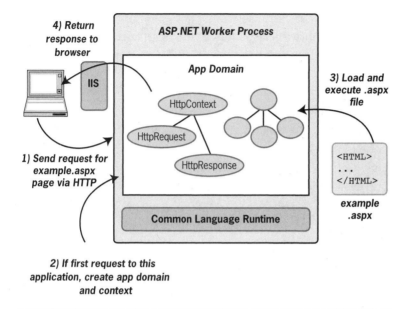

Figure 5-1   When a browser requests a page whose URL ends with .aspx, ASP.NET executes the associated .aspx file.

As the figure suggests, a user issues a request for a page in the usual way (step 1). If the URL for this page ends in .aspx, however, IIS hands this request to an ASP.NET worker process. Each .aspx page is part of a specific ASP.NET application, so this process must determine whether this is the first time this application is being accessed. If so, the worker process creates an app domain for this ASP.NET application, then creates a standard group of *context* objects (step 2). The root object in this group, called HttpContext, allows access to other objects that hold particular kinds of information. Those other objects include HttpRequest, which is populated with information such as the type of browser that made this request and any cookies that accompanied this request, and HttpResponse, which is used to hold the response that's sent back to the user. Once all of this infrastructure is ready, the .aspx file the user specified is loaded and executed (step 3). The execution of this file creates a response, perhaps accessing data or doing other things along the way, then sends the response back to the browser via IIS (step 4).

Each request causes an .aspx file to be executed

Given this big-picture view of what's going on, it's possible to understand how the .aspx files at the heart of any ASP.NET application are constructed. How this is done is described next.

Creating .aspx Files

An .aspx file can mix text, HTML, and code

An .aspx file can contain text, HTML, and executable code. Any code in the file must either be in a *script block*, bracketed by the tags <script> and </script>, or be wrapped in the symbols "<%" and "%>". Here's a very simple example of an .aspx file that contains text, HTML, and a few lines of Visual Basic (VB) code:

```
<html>
The date and time: <% =Now() %>
<hr>
<% ShowNumbersAndBrowser() %>

<script runat="server" language="vb">
    Sub ShowNumbersAndBrowser()
        Dim I As Integer
        For I = 0 To 5
            Response.Write(I)
        Next
        Response.Write("<hr>")
        Response.Write("Browser: " _
            & Request.Browser.Type)
    End Sub
</script>
</html>
```

Code must be contained in a script block or wrapped in <% ... %>

After the opening <html> tag, this file begins with a text string— "The date and time: "—followed by a call to the built-in VB function Now. This call is wrapped in <% and %>, as just described, allowing ASP.NET to distinguish this text from the literal string that precedes it. The horizontal rule tag, <hr>, appears next, followed by a call to the ShowNumbersAndBrowser method. Since it's code, this call also appears inside <% and %>.

Output is written to the Response object

Next comes the ShowNumbersAndBrowser method itself, defined inside a script block. The attributes in the opening <script> tag indicate that this code should be run at the server rather than at the client and that the code is written in VB. (VB is the default language for .aspx pages, so this second attribute isn't strictly required.) The ShowNumbersAndBrowser method begins with a simple loop that writes out the numbers 0 through 5. To accomplish this, that code calls the Write method of ASP.NET's built-in Response object. This object is actually a reference to the HttpResponse object shown in Figure 5-1, and it's used to contain output that will eventually be sent to the browser.

Following this simple loop is another call to Response.Write, this time outputting another <hr> tag. Because we're inside a script block, ASP.NET expects everything to be code, and so the <hr> tag can't appear on its own. Finally, one more call to Response.Write appears that writes out another text string. Concatenated with this string is the result of accessing the Browser.Type property of the built-in Request object. Request is a reference to the HttpRequest object shown in Figure 5-1, and it contains information about the request. Included in this information is the type of browser from which the request for this page was made.

Information about the browser and more is available via the Request object

What this .aspx file is doing is just creating an ordinary HTML page. When this page is accessed from Internet Explorer 6, the result is:

```
The date and time: 12/8/2006 5:25:40 PM
```
_____
```
012345
```
_____
```
Browser: IE6
```

Just for completeness, the actual HTML that is created by this .aspx file looks like this:

```
<html>
The date and time: 12/8/2006 5:25:40 PM
<hr>
012345<hr>Browser: IE6
</html>
```

ASP.NET converts each .aspx file into a class that gets compiled into an assembly

As this simple example shows, creating a basic .aspx file isn't complicated. Yet even though the contents of an .aspx file created using VB look quite different from an ordinary VB program, ASP.NET applications are .NET Framework applications, just like those seen throughout this book. They look different only because the designers of ASP.NET wanted to give developers the familiar, easy-to-use model of Web scripting. The truth is that every .aspx file is automatically turned into a class, then compiled into an assembly the first time it's accessed by a client.

An .aspx file is really just another way to define a class

Figure 5-2 gives an abstracted view of how this simple example file gets converted into a class. (What's shown here isn't literally correct—the complete truth is a bit more complicated.) The generated class's name is derived from the name of the file containing this page, and this new class inherits from the Page class defined in System.Web.UI. As the diagram shows, any code con-

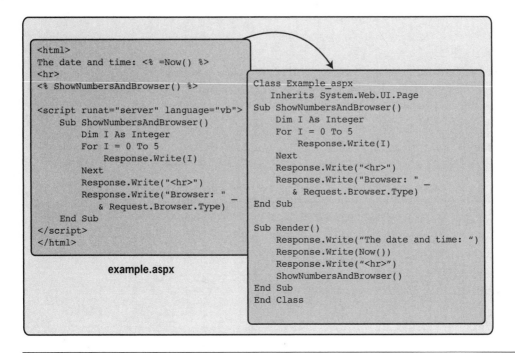

Figure 5-2   Each .aspx file is converted into a class.

tained in a script block is inserted into the class itself. In this case, the page's simple ShowNumbersAndBrowser method becomes a method in the generated class. The rest of this page, including any text, HTML tags, and code wrapped in "<% . . . %>", gets dropped into a single Render method for this class.

The class is then compiled into MSIL and packaged into an assembly. What is produced isn't a static assembly, however, but rather a dynamic assembly built directly in memory using types provided by the System.CodeDom namespace. Once this dynamic assembly has been created, it's written to disk and then used to handle all future requests for this page. If the file is changed, the process happens again, and a new assembly is generated. In the absence of any changes, the original assembly is all that's needed, so only one compilation is required for each .aspx file.

The compiled assembly handles requests until the underlying .aspx file is changed

Each file is turned into a class before it's executed, but how does that execution happen? The answer is that, like Windows Forms, ASP.NET uses an event-driven model. When a file is accessed, the assembly generated from that file is executed, and an instance of that assembly's page class is created. This page object receives a series of events. The object can provide a method to handle each event, and each of those methods can produce output that gets sent to the client's browser. Once all events have been handled, the page object is destroyed.

.aspx files are executed using events

For example, every page object receives a Page_Load event, sent immediately after the page object has been created. Every page object also receives a Page_Unload event just before it is destroyed. In between these two bookend events, the page object can receive and process various other events. Sometime prior to receiving Page_Unload, every page object will receive a Render event. This event causes the object's Render method to execute and thus displays the page's output. Given that a primary goal of ASP.NET is to create effective user interfaces, and that user interfaces are by nature event driven, it makes sense to apply this model here.

Every .aspx page receives several standard events

Using Web Controls

GUIs tend to have many of the same elements

Event-driven user interfaces have always been the norm for graphical Windows applications. But along with events, there's another idea that's long been popular in building Windows graphical user interfaces (GUIs): packaging discrete chunks of reusable functionality into controls. Each control commonly provides some part of a user interface, such as a button or text box, and so controls can be combined as needed to build an effective GUI. Since ASP.NET relies on the notion of event-based programming, why not use reusable interface components to create Web GUIs as well?

Web controls provide packaged functionality for creating a browser GUI

This is exactly what ASP.NET's Web controls do. They're conceptually close to the Windows Forms controls described in Chapter 4 in that each one provides its own user interface and carries out its own function. Unlike Windows Forms controls, however, Web controls run on the server—they're classes that become part of a page class—and they produce their user interfaces by generating appropriate HTML[2]. It's also possible for a Web control to learn what kind of browser it's communicating with, as shown earlier, then send the appropriate output— HTML, Dynamic HTML, or something else—for that browser.

ASP.NET includes many Web controls

ASP.NET provides a large set of standard Web controls. All of them inherit from the base class WebControl in the namespace System.Web.UI.WebControls. The available choices include the common atoms of GUI design, such as Button, TextBox, CheckBox, RadioButton, and ListBox. Several more complex controls are also provided. There's a Calendar control, for instance, that displays months and allows users to select dates and an AdRotator control capable of automatically cycling through a series of Web-based advertisements. There are also controls focused on working with user information, accessing data, and more, as described later. And of course, it's possible to create custom Web controls, just as there are custom Windows Forms

2. By default, all ASP.NET 2.0 pages and Web controls generate XHTML 1.1-compatible output.

controls. Third parties have built a large selection of these in the last few years.

Here's a simple example, once again in VB, that illustrates using Web controls:

```
<html>
<form runat="server">
    <asp:Button runat="server"
        width="175px" height="50px"
        text="Click Here"
        onClick="Button_Click"/>
    <asp:Label id="Output" runat="server"/>
</form>
<script runat="server">
    Sub Button_Click(ByVal Sender As Object, _
        ByVal E As System.EventArgs)
        Output.Text = "Button clicked"
    End Sub
</script>
</html>
```

This .aspx file begins with a standard HTML form element that contains two Web controls: a Button and a Label. The tag identifying both controls begins with asp:, which indicates that these controls are defined by ASP.NET. Both of them, along with many others, are contained in the namespace System.Web.UI.WebControls. The Button element contains a number of attributes that indicate where the control should run, its width and height in pixels, and the text the Button should display. The element ends with the onClick attribute, specifying that a method called Button_Click should be run when this Button receives a Click event. The Label element also contains a few attributes. One of them, id, gives this Label a name so it can be referred to later in the page. This simple Label initially displays no text but is instead used to provide a way to send output to the browser, as described next.

Web controls can handle events

Following the form is a short script containing just the single method Button_Click. When the button is clicked, this method will be executed. The only thing this method does is assign a value to the Label's Text property, causing it to be displayed on

Web controls allow building browser GUIs in a familiar style

**Figure 5-3   The simple .aspx file described in this section shows
a button, then displays a message when the button is clicked.**

the screen. Figure 5-3 shows the result of loading this page and
clicking the button it displays. If you recall the Windows Forms
example from Chapter 4, this should look familiar. Once again,
a Button control is created, its size is determined, and an event
handler is associated with the Button's Click event. By using Web
controls, developers can build browser-based applications in a
familiar style. In fact, by analogy with Windows Forms, ASP.NET
pages are sometimes referred to as *Web forms*.

*Web controls are
similar to, but not
the same as,
Windows Forms
controls*

ASP.NET's event-driven approach certainly is very similar to the
event-driven model used in Windows Forms applications, and
many Web controls even have the same names as their
Windows Forms analogs. Still, there are significant differences
between the controls used in Windows Forms applications and
those used with ASP.NET applications. The most important difference grows out of the fact that while Windows applications
handle events that were generated on the same machine,
ASP.NET events are typically generated on a client machine

and then are handled by a remote server system. This greatly increases the cost of raising an event, since each one results in a round trip across the network from the browser to the ASP.NET application and back. Accordingly, there are some kinds of events that just don't make sense for Web controls.

For example, both Windows Forms and ASP.NET include a Button control. Yet the number of events supported by the Web control Button is much smaller than that supported by its Windows Forms cousin. Both Buttons support an event called Click, for instance, so an application using either one can contain an event handler that runs when the control is clicked, as shown earlier. The Windows Forms control, however, also has an event called MouseMove that occurs when the mouse pointer is moved over the on-screen button, along with many other mouse-related events. None of these is available in the Web control Button. Raising each of these events on a single machine is cheap, but to send an HTTP request to the Web server every time the mouse moves over a new control in the browser would result in an unacceptably large amount of network traffic. Accordingly, Web controls are substantially more limited in the events they can accept and process than their Windows Forms brethren.

Web controls support fewer events than Windows Forms controls

Another difference between Windows Forms controls and those used with ASP.NET is how they maintain their state. Each control has properties, such as the text it displays or its on-screen size. Windows Forms controls maintain this state in the control's memory, which is simple and efficient. Sadly, this isn't possible with Web controls. With an ASP.NET application, every object created to handle a request from a user is destroyed when that request is completed—application scalability would suffer if this weren't done—so an application does not by default maintain any in-memory information about a client between requests. Because it retains no knowledge of the client's state between requests, an ASP.NET application is said to be *stateless*. This makes them more scalable, but it also creates problems. One of those problems is finding a way for Web controls to maintain their state between

Web controls maintain state automatically between requests

client requests. The solution adopted by ASP.NET is to insert each control's state into the Web page sent back to the browser. When the user submits another request, the page is sent back, and this state information is copied back into each Web control. (In ASP.NET 2.0, some control state can also be saved in other ways.)

■ Perspective: Is ASP.NET Too Hard?

Microsoft's original Active Server Pages (ASP) technology, introduced in 1996, was a huge hit. A primary reason for this was that it was incredibly easy to use, and so everybody and his dog Rover wrote ASP applications. This initial ease of use tended to devolve into unmaintainable code for applications of any size, but nonetheless, the barriers to entry for this technology were very low.

ASP.NET was the successor to the very popular ASP. This second generation technology provides much more for developers than the original, and so unsurprisingly, it's also more complex. While using the original ASP required knowing a simple scripting language and a little HTML, using ASP.NET effectively requires understanding the .NET world, since all code must be written in a language based on the Common Language Runtime (CLR), such as VB or C#. With the release of ASP.NET, classes, events, inheritance, and a host of other more advanced concepts descended on unsuspecting ASP developers like fog on a San Francisco evening. While writing ASP applications required some technical knowledge, ASP.NET asks significantly more of its developers.

Suppose Microsoft had shipped ASP.NET in the first place and that the original ASP technology had never existed. Would ASP.NET now be so widely used? I'm inclined to doubt it. Like .NET technologies in general, ASP.NET's barriers to entry are noticeably higher for beginners. Still, this new technology does make some accommodation for newcomers, while still providing plenty of functionality for serious developers. Upping the technical ante has pleased most developers, but as with other parts of the .NET Framework—VB is the most obvious—Microsoft decided that giving its more technical customers what they needed was more important than keeping life simple for the less capable.

The process is arguably inelegant, but given the limitations imposed on Web-based applications, it's an effective solution.

Despite the simple example shown earlier, building browser GUIs by hand makes no more sense than building Windows GUIs by hand. Using a tool that allows creating a browser GUI graphically is a much better approach. Visual Studio 2005, for example, includes a designer referred to as Visual Web Developer that allows a developer to drag and drop Web controls on a form, set their properties, and attach code to the events they generate, just as with Windows Forms. While it's useful to know what's going on under the covers, real applications should be built using real tools whenever possible.

Visual Web Developer can be used to build browser GUIs

Separating User Interface from Code: Code-Behind

One problem with creating browser-based applications is the inescapable need to combine HTML with code written in a language such as VB or C#. Simple pages like those shown earlier in this chapter don't create much of a problem, but real applications can get hard to read and maintain when HTML and code are mingled in the same file. While ASP.NET allows doing this, as the single-file examples so far have shown, it also provides a mechanism known as *code-behind* for separating the GUI-oriented HTML from the code behind that GUI.

Code and HTML can be separated using code-behind

Code-behind is a straightforward idea. Rather than mixing HTML and code in a single file, this approach allows putting all of a page's HTML in its .aspx file and then inserting a reference in that file to another file that contains all of the code for that page. The result is significantly easier to work with, since the two very different worlds of HTML and a CLR-based programming language can remain distinct from one another.

Separating code and HTML can make applications more maintainable

Here's how the simple ASP.NET page just shown might look if the code-beside option were used. The file containing just the code (which might have the filename Example.aspx.vb) is as follows:

```
Partial Class Example
   Inherits System.Web.UI.Page
   Sub Button_Click(ByVal Sender As Object, _
      ByVal E As System.EventArgs)
      Output.Text = "Button clicked"
   End Sub
End Class
```

This is the same Button_Click method that appeared in the script block in the previous example. It's now contained inside the class Example, which is declared using the Partial keyword. As described in Chapter 3, a partial class can be combined with another partial class at compile time to create a complete, fully defined class. With code-behind, a partial class like the one above is combined with another partial class generated by ASP.NET from an .aspx file. For this simple example, that .aspx file might look like this:

```
<%@ Page Language="VB" CodeFile="Example.aspx.vb"
    Inherits="Example" %>
<html>
<form runat="server">
   <asp:Button runat="server"
      width="175px" height="50px"
      Text="Click Here"
      onclick="Button_Click" />
 <asp:Label id="Output" runat="server" />
</form>
</html>
```

This page begins with a Page directive. ASP.NET defines several such directives, each indicated by the "<%@" that precedes them. Different directives are used for different things, but the Page directive is always used to specify page-specific attributes in an .aspx file. As used here, this directive indicates that the associated code is written in VB (optional in this case, since VB is ASP.NET's default language), specifies that the associated code can be found in the file Example.aspx.vb, and that the relevant class is named Example. The rest of the page contains the same form and control definitions shown in the earlier example, defining a button and a label for output. When this page is accessed, it's compiled into a class together with the partial class Example defined in Example.aspx.vb. The result is identical to the earlier example, producing what's shown in Figure 5-3.

This simple example can make code-behind seem like more trouble than it's worth. In any reasonably complex ASP.NET application, however, this approach leads to much more maintainable code, since it cleanly separates HTML from whatever CLR-based language is used to create the application logic. It's also worth mentioning that the example shown here illustrates code-behind as it's implemented in ASP.NET 2.0. The original release of this technology had a similar but slightly more complex mechanism (there were no partial classes) for doing the same thing. While that older approach is still supported, applications created today should use the style provided by this newer version of the technology.

Code-behind is the right choice for all but the simplest ASP.NET applications

Defining Applications

So far, the term "application" has been used in a fairly general way. The truth is that ASP.NET defines quite clearly what it means to be an application. Each ASP.NET application comprises some number of .aspx pages, assemblies, and other files, all of which must be installed beneath a common directory. Each application can also optionally have application-wide logic stored in a file named global.asax. This file can contain code that handles application-wide events that are issued when the application begins executing, when it ends, when an error occurs, and at other times. Each ASP.NET application also has its own Web.config file that controls many aspects of the application's behavior. Web.config files can also be used to configure all ASP.NET applications on a particular machine, specific pages of an application, and in other ways.

An ASP.NET application can contain .aspx pages, assemblies, and more

Figure 5-4 shows one way in which the files that comprise a single ASP.NET application might be organized. In this example, the application consists of only two .aspx files, named page1.aspx and page2.aspx, each of which has an associated

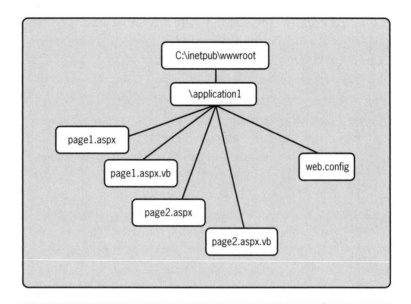

Figure 5-4   An ASP.NET application might include .aspx files, code files, and a Web.config file.

code-behind file containing logic written in VB. The application also has a Web.config file, and all of its files are contained in a directory called application1 that lives beneath the standard root directory for ASP.NET.

Figure 5-5 shows another ASP.NET application. As always, all of its files live below a common root directory, here named application2. Unlike the previous example, however, this application includes a global.asax file containing event handlers for application-level events. It also includes two precompiled assemblies, both stored in a directory named bin, whose classes can be accessed at runtime by the application's .aspx files.

ASP.NET provides several options for how an application is structured

ASP.NET applications can also be structured in other ways; there are possibilities that aren't shown here. Source code written in VB, C#, or another language can be stored in a directory named App_Code, for instance, and other directories with standard

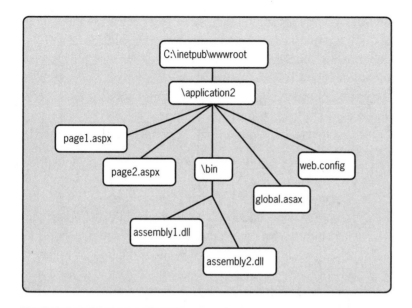

Figure 5-5   An ASP.NET application can also include precompiled assemblies, a global.asax file, and more.

names can be used for other purposes. While there's no formal connection among these various files, the fact that all live below a common root and all follow certain naming conventions groups them together in a single ASP.NET application.

Because ASP.NET applications are .NET Framework applications, installing an ASP.NET application requires just copying the application's files to the target machine. There's no need to restart IIS to begin using the new application. Deleting the application is equally simple—all that's required is deleting the application's files. It's even possible to install new versions of pages or assemblies while an ASP.NET application is running. Requests in progress will complete using the old code, while new requests will automatically use the new version.

ASP.NET applications can be installed by just copying their files

Using Context Information

When a request from a client is processed, the request passes through a series of objects sometimes referred to collectively as

Context information can be accessed via the HttpContext object

the *HTTP pipeline*. These objects all need access to information about the request, so an instance of the HttpContext class, contained in the System.Web namespace, is created for each incoming request. Among other things, this object connects to the HttpRequest and HttpResponse objects shown in Figure 5-1. To access these objects and other information, the HttpContext object contains a large number of properties, including the following:

- **Request:** allows access to the HttpRequest object for this request. As described earlier, this object's properties contain information about the request received from the client, such as what kind of browser it came from, the HTTP query string that accompanied it, any cookies that were sent with the request, and much more.

- **Response:** allows access to the HttpResponse object for this request. This object provides a large group of methods and properties focused on sending information back to the requesting client. Perhaps the most commonly used of these is the Write method illustrated in the example pages shown earlier, which directly sends output back to the client.

- **Application:** allows access to the HttpApplicationState object for this request. This object stores information relevant for the entire ASP.NET application, and it's described in more detail later in this chapter.

- **Cache:** allows storing information for an ASP.NET application. The Cache object is similar to the Application object, but it provides several extra features. For example, information stored in this object can be set to expire in a specific period of time or to exist only as long as a specific file exists.

- **Session:** allows access to the HttpSessionState object for this request. This object stores information solely about the client that made this request. Like HttpApplicationState, this object is also described in more detail later in this chapter.

- **Error:** allows access to an Exception object for an error that occurred during processing of this request.

- **User:** contains the identity of the client that initiated this request, if known.

- **Handler:** allows access to the instance of an HttpHandler class associated with this request. HTTP handlers allow access to the low-level functions of processing a request. Rather than writing code using the Internet Server API (ISAPI), such as an ISAPI extension, you can create a custom HTTP handler instead. Most people won't need to write their own handlers, but ASP.NET provides this relatively low-level option for hard-core .NET developers.

The most important properties of the HttpContext object are also accessible directly through the Page class. The properties that Page exposes include Request, Response, Session, Application, Error, and Cache, each of which is actually a way to access the corresponding property of the HttpRequest object for this request. Since Page is the parent class for every .aspx page, this information is readily accessible to every application, as the examples earlier in this chapter demonstrated.

The Page object provides direct access to the most important properties of HttpContext

ASP.NET Applications: Beyond the Basics

Creating .aspx pages, using controls, defining applications, and exploiting context are fundamental to creating any ASP.NET application. Most applications need more than this, however, including a way to manage state, mechanisms for managing information about their users, and more. The rest of this chapter takes a look at these important areas.

Managing State

Objects in an .aspx page can't maintain their state internally between requests

Every request a client makes to an ASP.NET application causes the objects on the loaded page to be created, used, and then destroyed. This helps in building scalable applications, since no resources are taken up on the server for clients that aren't currently running requests, and load balancing requests across a group of servers also gets easier. This stateless behavior can also make writing those applications more difficult, however. If all of an application's objects forget everything they've been told after every request, the application won't be very intelligent. To make it easier to create smarter software, ASP.NET provides several different ways for an application to maintain state information between client requests. These options divide into two major categories: storing state on the client and storing state on the server.

Storing State on the Client

State can be sent to a client inside a cookie

One way for an ASP.NET application to maintain state between requests from a client is to send that state to the client, then have the client send the state back on its next request. A common way to do this is by using *cookies*. A cookie is a chunk of information that the ASP.NET application sends to the browser, and it can contain anything: a key for a database lookup, a user identity, or something else. Whatever it is, the user's browser automatically provides the cookie on the next request (unless the user has disabled this function), allowing the application to access and use the information the cookie contains.

State can be contained in a query string within a URL

It's also possible to store some simple state in a *query string*, which is text following a "?" at the end of a URL. This information can be expressed as attribute/value pairs, like this:

```
http://www.qwickbank.com/example.aspx?account=492284 &
   type=checking
```

Query strings are only useful for small amounts of state, and they're not at all secure. Still, they're the right answer in some situations, and they're quite commonly used.

As already described, the properties in Web controls are automatically saved by inserting their values into the Web pages sent to the user and then reading those values out again when the page is sent back. What actually happens is that this state information is inserted into one or more hidden fields in the page, then read back from those fields when the page is returned. This approach, referred to as *view state,* offers another way for an application developer to store any other information maintained by a particular page. This mechanism allows an application to store values inside the page sent back to the browser, then have them restored when the user resubmits the page.

Information used by a page can be saved in view state

Storing State on the Server

Storing state on clients is simple, and it's commonly used. Only a relatively small amount of information can be stored, however, and there are other limitations as well. Accordingly, ASP.NET applications often store state on the server.

Information used throughout an application can be saved in the Application object

A limitation of view state, for example, is that it saves information only for a particular page in an ASP.NET application. What if you want to save information used by several pages in the application? To do this, an application can rely on the Application object mentioned earlier. Rather than being sent to the client with each page, information placed in the Application object is maintained on the server and made accessible to all pages in an application. A reference to the Application object from any page in an ASP.NET application will always access the same instance. For example, if an application wishes to record the time at which some event takes place and then let that time be accessed by another page in the same application, it might contain the following line:

```
<% Application("Timestamp") = Now() %>
```

A page that wished to access the value of this variable can reference it directly, as in

```
<% Response.Write (Application("Timestamp")) %>
```

This book hasn't said much about threading in the .NET Framework, but it's important to note that ASP.NET applications are multithreaded. Since there's only one Application object for an entire ASP.NET application, if two different pages running on two different threads write to it simultaneously, problems can occur. Depending on the threading choices an application uses, explicit concurrency controls might be needed to avoid conflicts.

Information used throughout an application can also be stored in the Cache object

Alternatively, the Cache object can be used instead of the Application object. As mentioned earlier, the objects are broadly similar in function. The biggest difference is that the Cache object allows much more control over how long information is held and what causes it to be removed. An application can also ask that it be informed when a particular item is deleted from the Cache object, providing an event handler that runs when the information is deleted.

Load balancing complicates state management

Storing state in either of these objects has a problem, however: Both are physically stored on a single machine. If an ASP.NET application is deployed on several Web servers, with client requests load balanced across those servers, storing state in the Application or Cache objects will be problematic. Each copy of the application will have its own instance of these objects, so the information these instances contain will likely be different. Applications that will be load balanced should be careful about how, or even if, they use these objects.

Information used throughout a single client session can be stored in the Session object

The options just described can be useful ways for an application to store state. Yet none of them addresses the most common state management problem in building ASP.NET applications: maintaining per-client state. Think of a Web application that allows its user to add items to a shopping cart, for example. Given that the objects created by the application are destroyed after every request, how can that information be retained? Every page accessed by that client (and only that client) within an ASP.NET application should have easy access to this per-client state, but nothing described so far provides this. Yet building reasonable applications requires some way to store client-specific information across the life of a client session. In ASP.NET, the Session object provides a way to do this.

Accessing a Session object looks much like accessing the Application object. To store a value, an .aspx page can contain a line such as

```
Session("ItemSelected")= 13
```

To access that value, the page can refer to it like this:

```
Response.Write(Session("ItemSelected"))
```

Even though Session and Application objects are accessed in a similar way, don't be confused. There's only one Application object shared by all pages in an ASP.NET application, while every client has its own Session object. When an application accesses the Session object, it will always get the instance associated with the client that made this request. To figure out which client each request comes from, ASP.NET assigns each client a unique session identifier that gets stored in a cookie. The client then presents this cookie with each request it makes, allowing ASP.NET to identify all requests that come from the same client. Because users can turn off cookies if they wish, ASP.NET is also capable of embedding this identifier in the URL string returned to a user. However it's done, the creator of an ASP.NET application doesn't need to worry about determining which request comes from which user—it's done for him.

One Session object can exist for each active client

But what about load balancing? Suppose an ASP.NET application's Session object is bound to a particular machine, like the Application object. If this application is load balanced across several different machines, only one of those machines will store this object. Requests from a client that get sent to other machines due to load balancing won't be able to access the object's contents, so they won't execute correctly. While it's possible to use the Session object in this way, only relatively simple applications will adopt this approach.

Using the Session object naively can conflict with load balancing

The Session object can work well with load balancing

While the Session object for a particular client can still be stored on just one machine, it can also be stored in a separate Session State Store. If this is done, the contents of the Session object are available to all copies of the application running on all machines in a load-balanced configuration. And because the state is in another process (and perhaps another machine), it can remain available even if the ASP.NET application itself is restarted.

The Session object can store its state in several different ways

The standard Session State Store server provided with version 2.0 of the .NET Framework provides five options:

- **InProc:** The Session object is stored in the same process as the application. This is the default setting, although for the reasons described earlier, it doesn't work well with load-balancing.

- **StateServer:** The Session object's state is stored in another process that can run locally or on another machine.

- **SQLServer:** The Session object's state is stored on disk using SQL Server.

- **Custom:** The Session object's state is stored in a custom data store, such as an Oracle database.

- **Off:** The Session object is disabled.

Any state in the Session object is automatically destroyed when a client hasn't accessed the application for a configurable length of time. Note too that how the Session object's state is stored depends entirely on the contents of an application's Web.config file. No code in the application needs to be modified to change which option is used.

Information about particular users can be maintained using profile properties

Yet another way for an application to store state information on the server, one that's new in ASP.NET 2.0, is using *profile properties*. Profile properties let an application persistently store information about particular users in an ASP.NET-provided database. Whenever a user accesses the application, her information can be accessed via these properties. Users are identified using one of ASP.NET's login mechanisms, described later, and the association between a user and her properties is made automatically—the developer isn't required to do any direct database access. The goal is to provide an easy-to-use mechanism for maintaining information about users across multiple accesses.

Maintaining state is an important and challenging part of building Web applications. As this short summary has described, ASP.NET provides a number of different ways to do it. Which options make sense for a particular application depends on what the application does and how it's used. Even though it would make life simpler, there's no one-size-fits-all solution for state management.

Caching Data

Clients of an ASP.NET application often access the same information. To make that access faster, it's possible to cache repetitively accessed data. Rather than doing the work required to recreate that data each time it's requested, the information can be read quickly from an in-memory cache and returned. To allow this, ASP.NET provides a way to cache the output of a page. (Don't confuse this with the Cache object described earlier, which is a separate idea.)

Output caching allows saving recently accessed results in memory

To use ASP.NET's output caching mechanism, an .aspx page can contain a directive such as

```
<%@ OutputCache Duration="60" VaryByParam="none"%>
```

The duration specifies how long (in seconds) the results of that page can be cached before the information must be recreated. Requests that arrive for the same information within this period will have their responses returned immediately from the cache.

The required VaryByParam attribute is set to none in this example, but if desired, it can be used to control exactly which results are cached. The parameter this attribute refers to can be

Output caching has several options

any named value contained in a query string, which is the text following a "?" on a client request. For example, suppose an .aspx page contained the directive

```
<%@ OutputCache Duration="60" VaryByParam=
  "name" %>
```

Suppose further that this page received two requests with these query strings:

```
http://www.qwickbank.com/page1.aspx?name=Bob

http://www.qwickbank.com/page1.aspx?name=Casey
```

Because output caching was instructed to vary by a parameter called "name," the results of each request would be cached. Requests to this page with names of either Bob or Casey that are received within the 60-second window specified on the Duration attribute will return cached results. Other things, such as the type of browser from which a request originated, can also be used to control exactly which pages are cached. The result is a more responsive application, especially if the same data is accessed over and over.

Authentication and Authorization

Browser applications must be secure

Securing Web applications is incredibly important. A plethora of well-publicized attacks have made even nonprofessionals aware of the dangers of too little security. Really understanding Web security is a large topic, one that's outside the scope of this book, but grasping the basics of authentication and authorization is essential.

ASP.NET provides several options for authenticating users

Authentication, requiring a user to prove his identity, is a fundamental part of securing an ASP.NET application. Although a developer is free to create her own authentication mechanism, ASP.NET applications have several built-in authentication options provided for them. The choices, which build on what IIS provides, include the following:

- **Windows authentication:** Reflecting the IIS choices, there are three options. Basic authentication, simplest of the three, requires a client to send an unencrypted password across the network, which by itself is no one's idea of good security. Digest authentication, the second choice, requires a client to send a hashed version of a password and other information, which provides somewhat better security. The third option, called Integrated Windows Authentication, allows using the authentication protocol available in a Windows domain, such as Kerberos. This choice is quite secure, but it's available only for authenticating users in a Windows domain.

- **Forms authentication:** This option allows an application to display a custom form to acquire user credentials, such as a login name and password, and then to decide whether the user is who he claims to be. It relies on the Secure Sockets Layer (SSL) protocol to ensure that those credentials are encrypted when initially sent across the network.

- **Passport authentication:** Allows using Microsoft's Internet-based Passport service. System.Web.Security contains several classes that allow applications to access Passport and then use the authenticated client identity it provides.

Once a client has been authenticated, the next step is to make an authorization decision, i.e., to determine whether that client is allowed to do what it's requesting. If one of the Windows authentication options is used, a client's attempt to access a particular file such as an .aspx file will be subject to *file authorization*. This means that Windows will automatically check the access control list (ACL) on the file to ensure that the user's request is allowed. With Windows authentication or any of the other authentication options, an approach called *URL authorization* is also available. This option allows fine-grained control over who is allowed to perform what operations against a particular ASP.NET application.

ASP.NET applications can make an authorization decision in different ways

Managing Users: Membership

Web applications often keep information about their users

Many Web applications require users to log in before accessing some or all of what the application provides. Knowing who a user is lets the application provide specific services, such as remembering the user's mailing address, and it can also enforce various business relationships, such as payment of a subscription fee. Doing this requires a way to maintain information about the site's users, commonly called *membership* information, and a mechanism for logging in that uses that information. Version 2.0 of ASP.NET adds support for both of these.

ASP.NET's membership facility allows storing and managing information about an application's users

ASP.NET's membership support allows creating and storing information about users, including names, passwords, and more. This information can be stored in SQL Server (the default) or some other data store, although the details of data access are hidden from the developer. Instead, a Membership class is provided that exposes methods such as CreateUser, DeleteUser, FindUsersByName, GeneratePassword, and more. An ASP.NET application can use these methods to perform typical membership operations without dealing explicitly with the underlying data store.

ASP.NET includes Web controls for creating and managing user login

ASP.NET's membership support can be used together with the forms authentication described earlier, an approach that lets the developer specify in detail exactly what the login process looks like. ASP.NET also includes a set of login controls to help implement membership-based authentication. By default, these controls use the ASP.NET membership system. For example, the CreateUserWizard control collects information from a user such as her user name, password, and e-mail address, then creates an account in the ASP.NET membership system for her. Once this is done, the Login control can be used to let a user log in to an account maintained by the membership system. Other controls are also available, such as a ChangePassword control and a PasswordRecovery control that can let a user have her password

■ Perspective: Packing More Into the System

Providing built-in support for doing common things can make creating applications significantly easier. The designers of ASP.NET 2.0 believe strongly in this approach, as exemplified by the addition of membership facilities and login controls. What were once extras are now a standard part of the platform.

In fact, this approach is a fundamental aspect of Microsoft's business model. ASP.NET and the entire .NET Framework are part of Windows, which means they come at no extra charge. Compare this to competing application platforms, such as Java application servers, where all but the open source options carry four- and five-figure price tags. As Microsoft packs more and more into ASP.NET and the other parts of the .NET Framework, they're increasing the value these technologies provide to customers. The company still gets revenue for these things, of course, but it's part of the price that customers pay for Windows. In future releases, we should expect to see features that we now pay extra for, such as some parts of the integration-oriented BizTalk Server, move into Windows itself. Commoditizing technology appears to be a primary goal for Microsoft.

sent to whatever e-mail address is registered for her account. To secure the interaction with the user's browser, the login controls can be configured to use SSL.

Working with Data: Data Binding
ASP.NET applications frequently need to access data in a database, a file, or someplace else. Like any .NET Framework application, ASP.NET applications can use ADO.NET, System.XML, or other mechanisms to do this. Yet for some very common requirements, such as displaying data to a user and allowing him to update it, using these relatively low-level technologies can entail a significant amount of work. To make these common problems easier to solve, ASP.NET 2.0 includes a set of Web controls for working with data (controls that differ significantly from those in earlier releases). Their goal is to make it as simple

ASP.NET provides Web controls to simplify working with data as possible to implement the most common things that ASP.NET applications do with data.

Data binding allows accessing diverse data and displaying it in various ways

The idea of directly connecting what's displayed by a control with data that lives outside that control, such as data in a database, is referred to as *data binding*. Doing this requires solving two distinct problems: accessing the data, which might be stored in diverse ways, and displaying that data, again in diverse ways. For example, the data an application uses might be contained in SQL Server or some other database, or in an XML file, or someplace else. Similarly, the application might wish to display that data in a table, a list, or some other fashion. Both problems must be addressed for a complete solution, but they're quite distinct. Accordingly, the Web controls provided by ASP.NET for data binding are divided into two categories: data source controls, which know how to access data, and data-bound controls, which know how to display data. Figure 5-6 shows how these two kinds of controls relate to one another.

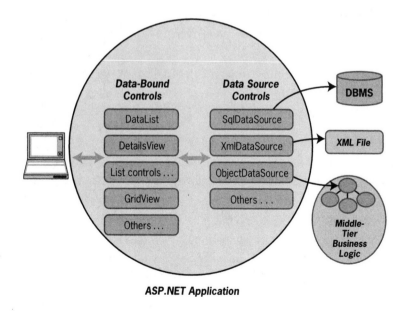

ASP.NET Application

Figure 5-6   **Data-bound controls display data that's accessed via data source controls.**

As the figure illustrates, data source controls connect to actual sources of data. Several different data source controls are provided, each capable of connecting to a particular type of data source. The SqlDataSource control uses ADO.NET to connect to a database, for example, such as SQL Server or Oracle, while the XmlDataSource control knows how to access and work with information stored in an XML file. ASP.NET applications can also

Data source controls know how to access data

What's New in ASP.NET 2.0

As is probably obvious by now, version 2.0 of ASP.NET adds a good deal to this technology. The most important new additions, including support for membership, revamped data binding, and Web Parts, are described in the text. Quite a few other things were also added that are worth mentioning. They include:

- The ability to add on-screen navigation of a Web site using a site-map file and the new TreeView and SiteMapPath controls. It's also possible to automatically display the position of the current page in the page hierarchy using a format like Home > Accounts > Balances. Sometimes called a *breadcrumb*, the goal is to help users navigate the site more effectively.

- A way to define a master page for an application, then have the standard format of that page automatically applied to all pages in this application. A similar concept called *themes* can also be used to give pages and controls a consistent look.

- An option to precompile applications, which avoids the performance hit caused by compiling pages when they're first accessed. This option can also be used to remove all source code from an ASP.NET application, which helps protect the intellectual property of its creators.

- Better tools for managing a Web site created using ASP.NET.

It's fair to say that, of all the changes in version 2.0 of the .NET Framework, the most significant are in ASP.NET. And given the wide use of this technology, these changes are certainly the ones that will affect the most developers.

use business logic implemented in a middle tier, and so the ObjectDataSource control is capable of connecting to data contained in objects within this logic. Other data source controls are also provided, and a developer can create her own if necessary.

Data-bound controls know how to display data

Once data has found its way into a data source control, it can be accessed by any data-bound control. Each data-bound control knows how to render data in a browser using an appropriate HTML format. The DataList control, for example, is capable of displaying data in a customizable table, while the DetailsView control allows examining and updating individual records. Various list controls, such as ListBox, DropDownList, and BulletedList, allow displaying data in the variety of list styles that user interfaces commonly employ, and the GridView control, new in ASP.NET 2.0, provides a powerful way to examine and modify data in a grid format.

ASP.NET 2.0 changes how data binding is done

The goal of all of this technology is to make life as simple as possible for ASP.NET developers who build applications that work with data. Rather than writing detailed code to access, display, and update information, a programmer can just configure the appropriate controls. ASP.NET 2.0 introduced significant changes in this area, and the result should be increased developer productivity.

Customizing User Interfaces: Web Parts

Web Parts allow creating user-customizable interfaces

People like to be in charge. Even with the potentially mundane, such as how an application looks in a Web browser, giving users the ability to customize things makes people happy. Web Parts, a new addition in ASP.NET 2.0, makes this possible. By allowing users to modify the appearance and behavior of a Web page, add new controls, and more, Web Parts let those users change an application's interface to suit them.

Interface customization relies on Web Parts controls

ASP.NET Web Parts is actually just a set of controls. A page that uses these controls can contain one or more *zones*, each of which can contain one or more Web Parts controls. These controls expose actions to a user, such as the ability to change the content the control displays or change the control's position on the screen. Users can also change the pages themselves, including adding new columns with specific Web Parts controls, changing the page's color, and more. This kind of interface customization is commonly referred to as *personalization*.

As usual with ASP.NET, applications that use Web Parts can be created using Visual Studio 2005. Like any other control, a Web Parts control can be dragged and dropped onto a page, then

Standard Web Parts controls are provided for various functions

---

The Role of Windows SharePoint Services

Portal is surely one of the most poorly defined words in software today. To most people, it suggests a way to access information through a common Web-based interface. Microsoft provides a more specific meaning with Windows SharePoint Services, a standard part of the Windows Server operating system. Built on ASP.NET, this technology (commonly called just *SharePoint*) allows creating portal sites that help people collaborate. Microsoft also provides a large set of SharePoint application templates to quickly create sites for employee timesheets and scheduling, expense reimbursement, room reservations, and other purposes.

A key part of a portal is the ability to customize the user interface. Accordingly, SharePoint includes Web Parts much like those in ASP.NET 2.0. Yet ASP.NET and SharePoint are quite different. The goal of ASP.NET is to help developers build all kinds of Web applications, using various data sources and allowing access by all kinds of users. The goal of SharePoint, by contrast, is to make it possible for IT professionals to quickly assemble, deploy, and manage portal applications. Given these distinct goals, the two technologies differ in significant ways. For example, while ASP.NET focuses on the developers who create Web applications, SharePoint also offers options to help administrators deploy and administer sites over a number of machines. ASP.NET takes a more general approach in other ways as well, letting developers choose how to store data, identify users, and more. SharePoint relies on SQL Server for storage, Active Directory for accessing user information, and other standard parts of the Windows environment. While there is some overlap in the two technologies, they nonetheless solve different problems.

customized as needed. More advanced developers can create their own Web Parts controls, all of which inherit from the System.Web.UI.WebControls.WebParts.WebPart class. Wherever the controls come from, a page will always contain one WebPartManager control that's responsible for coordinating the activity of all other Web Parts controls on this page. A page will also commonly contain controls such as CatalogZone, which allows presenting users with a list of Web Parts controls that can be added to this page, and EditorZone, which lets users modify a page's Web Parts controls.

Changes a user makes via Web Parts can be stored persistently

ASP.NET Web Parts also includes its own mechanism for persistently storing the changes a user makes. This allows someone to access the application, modify their interface in any way they like, then have this modified interface presented when they next use this application. This storage mechanism is entirely separate from the profile properties described earlier, as it's intended to be used only by Web Parts controls.

Web Parts allow building a wider range of Web applications

The Web Parts technology is a useful addition to ASP.NET. By letting developers create portal-like applications, it expands the range of problems that the .NET Framework can address. As always, this expansion increases the complexity for developers, but for applications that need it, the capability is essential.

Conclusion

ASP.NET is a very important part of the .NET Framework class library

The types in System.Web.UI—that is, the types that make up ASP.NET—just might be the most important parts of the .NET Framework class library. They're certainly among the most commonly used, as Web applications built on Windows are very popular. As this chapter has described, ASP.NET 2.0 contains significantly more than its predecessors, making it possible for developers to create a wider range of applications. The goal, as always, is to help those developers build software that makes life better for the people who use it.

6

Accessing Data: ADO.NET

Working with data—searching, updating, and processing it—is one of the fundamental tasks of software. Today, much of that data is commonly stored in some kind of database management system (DBMS), usually a relational DBMS. Developers need some way for their applications to access this information. In the .NET Framework, this mechanism is provided by ADO.NET.

ADO.NET provides access to stored data

Like everything else in the .NET Framework class library, ADO.NET is nothing more than a group of types, all of which reside in the System.Data namespace. These types are used by applications that need to work with stored data, and they allow access to that data in various useful ways. The most common need is to work with relational data, such as tables stored in SQL Server or Oracle, and so much of ADO.NET focuses here. Yet data defined using XML gets more important every day, and so ADO.NET's creators also added support for working with XML documents. This chapter takes a look at what

ADO.NET allows access to both relational and XML-defined data

ADO.NET provides for applications built on the .NET Framework.

Using .NET Framework Data Providers

A .NET Framework data provider allows access to stored data in a specific way

An application that uses ADO.NET to access data commonly relies on some *.NET Framework data provider,* software able to access data in a particular way. Figure 6-1 illustrates how clients, .NET Framework data providers, and DBMSs fit together. The client, written as managed code running on the CLR, can use various .NET Framework data providers to access stored data. Each .NET Framework data provider is also written as managed code, but a data provider might also rely on software that doesn't use the .NET Framework to accomplish its task.

■ Perspective: Oh, No, Not Another Data Access Interface!

ODBC, OLE DB, ADO, and more: The list goes on and on. If you've been working in the Microsoft world for a while, you've surely encountered some of these data access technologies. Each of them was at one time presented as the optimal way to access data, especially data in a relational database system. Yet today, each of them is a legacy technology, which means that while new applications shouldn't in general use them, somebody still has to support the old applications that do.

Why does Microsoft do this? Why can't the people in Redmond make up their minds in this terrifically important area? After all, the dominant database model hasn't changed in 20 years—a relation today is pretty much the same as it was then—so why should the way we access relational data be so volatile?

There are many answers. For one thing, the interface between object-oriented software and relational databases is inherently a messy place. With few exceptions, the database people never bought into objects as a core abstraction. There are good reasons for this—objects work much better for creating software than they do for storing data—but the result is a mismatch of models and a plethora of pain. In its attempts to make this difficult interface as useful as possible, Microsoft has taken a few wrong turns.

A more obvious reason for creating new data access interfaces is that the fundamental development technologies on which they depend change over time. For example, ADO.NET's predecessor, ADO, was based on the Component Object Model (COM), while the .NET Framework is not. While .NET Framework applications can use ADO through the Framework's COM interoperability features, this is a suboptimal approach. It makes more sense to offer a data access mechanism built solely with managed code, which is exactly what ADO.NET provides.

Another reason for the instability in data access interfaces is that the problem being addressed changes regularly. A primary goal of ODBC, for instance, was to let applications written in C and C++ issue SQL queries against a database system. These applications were either running on just one system or were spread across two machines in a two-tier client/server configuration. Yet today a very common scenario is a browser or Windows Forms client talking to business logic on a middle-tier server. In this kind of application, it's this middle-tier logic that accesses data and then passes it across a network to the browser. ODBC didn't address this situation at all, since it provided no way to serialize its results for transmission across a network. ADO addressed it in a way that made some sense inside the firewall but didn't work well on the Internet, especially with browsers other than Internet Explorer. ADO.NET, however, was designed with exactly this style of application in mind. And because the older models are still the right approach for some applications, ADO.NET also allows writing code in a more traditional style.

Finally, new people join development teams at Microsoft all the time, and the existing people move on to other groups or other companies. New people bring new ideas, and as ownership of a technology changes, that technology will also change. I don't believe Microsoft is intentionally making developers' lives difficult, but that has sometimes been the result of the technology churn in data access interfaces. Still, ADO.NET is a clean, attractive, and relatively simple technology for today's applications. All historical confusion aside, it's a good fit for the world of the .NET Framework.

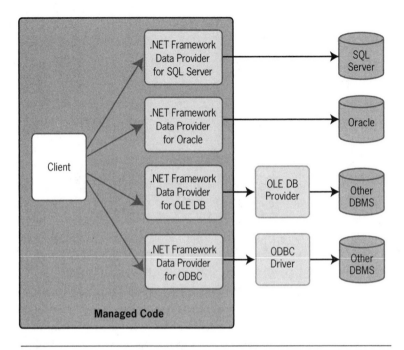

Figure 6-1   Applications using ADO.NET rely on .NET Framework data providers to access information.

As Figure 6-1 shows, ADO.NET version 2.0 includes four .NET Framework data providers:

- **.NET Framework Data Provider for SQL Server:** This data provider allows access to Microsoft's SQL Server 7.0 or later. Access to earlier versions of SQL Server requires using another provider option.

- **.NET Framework Data Provider for Oracle:** This data provider allows access to an Oracle database.

- **.NET Framework Data Provider for OLE DB:** Many pre-.NET applications, such as those built using ActiveX Data Objects (ADO), rely on Object Linking and Embedding for Databases (OLE DB) providers for access to data. This data provider implements a wrapper around any OLE DB provider that lets it be used by .NET Framework applications.

- **.NET Framework Data Provider for ODBC:** Open
  Database Connectivity (ODBC) is another of the
  many data access interfaces Microsoft has provided for
  Windows developers, and applications that use it rely
  on ODBC drivers to get at stored data. Much like the
  .NET Framework Data Provider for OLE DB, this data
  provider implements a wrapper around an ODBC
  driver, allowing managed code to use that driver for
  accessing data.

Each .NET Framework data provider is made visible to a
developer as a group of types, each in its own namespace.
The primary types that implement the SQL provider are
located in the System.Data.SqlClient namespace, for instance,
while those that implement the OLE DB provider are in
System.Data.OleDb. Regardless of which provider a developer
chooses, each one offers an analogous set of classes. Figure 6-2

*Each .NET
Framework data
provider exposes
the same core set
of classes*

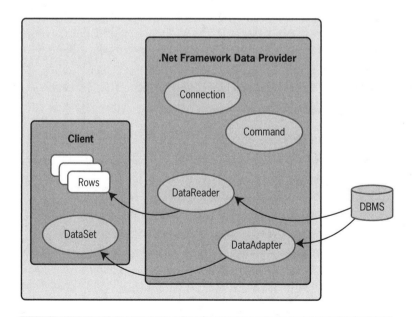

**Figure 6-2   A .NET Framework data provider allows clients to access
data either directly as rows or through a DataSet.**

shows the fundamental kinds of objects supported by any .NET Framework data provider. They are as follows:

- **Connection:** allows establishing and releasing connections. This class can also be used to begin transactions.

- **Command:** allows storing and executing a command, such as a SQL query or stored procedure, and specifying parameters for that command.

- **DataReader:** allows direct, sequential, read-only access to data in a database.

- **DataAdapter:** creates and populates instances of the class DataSet. As described later in this chapter, DataSets allow more flexible access to data than is possible using just a DataReader.

With the exception of DataSet, these names are descriptive—they're not actual class names. There is no DataReader class, for example. Instead, each .NET Framework data provider implements its own version of these classes. The DataReader for the .NET Framework data provider for SQL Server, for example, is implemented by the SqlDataReader class, while that for the .NET Framework data provider for OLE DB is implemented by the OleDbDataReader class.

Clients can access data through a DataReader or by using a DataSet

Using these four kinds of objects, a .NET Framework data provider gives clients two options for accessing data. Both use Connections and Commands to interact with a DBMS, but they differ primarily in how a client can work with the result of a query. As Figure 6-2 shows, a client that needs read-only, one-row-at-a-time access to a query's results can use a DataReader object to read those results. Clients with more complex requirements, such as accessing a query's result in an arbitrary order, filtering that result, sending that result across a network, or modifying data, can use a DataAdapter object to retrieve data wrapped in a DataSet. In both cases, clients use Connection and Command objects in similar ways, so how these objects are used is described next.

Writing Provider-Independent Code: System.Data.Common

Doesn't it seem odd that ADO.NET has different .NET Framework data providers for different DBMSs? After all, one of the reasons for using a common interface such as ADO.NET rather than one provided by a DBMS vendor is to access different vendors' products in a common way. Yet each .NET Framework data provider uses its own specific names for most of the fundamental classes. The result is that clients become wedded to just one .NET Framework data provider.

To address this oddity, ADO.NET version 2.0 includes an extended version of the System.Data.Common namespace. This namespace provides generic versions of the fundamental ADO.NET types, including DbConnection, DbCommand, DbDataReader, and DbDataAdapter. Rather than using the provider-specific incarnations of these types, a developer who needs to create provider-independent code can use these more general options. (In fact, the provider-specific classes for Connection, Command, DataReader, and DataAdapter all now inherit from their generic equivalents in System.Data.Common.) Taking this more general approach constrains an application's ability to exploit DBMS-specific features, but the independence it brings can sometimes outweigh this limitation.

Using Connection and Command Objects

Regardless of whether a DataReader or DataSet is used to access data, an ADO.NET client application relies on a connection to the DBMS. The application can explicitly open a connection by calling the Open method of a Connection object. To open a connection using the .NET Framework data provider for SQL Server, for example, the client invokes this method on an instance of the SqlConnection class. To open a connection to some other data source, the client invokes a similar method on the Connection class provided by whatever .NET Framework data provider it's using. With the .NET Framework data provider for OLE DB, for example, the client calls Open on an instance of the OleDbConnection class. Whatever Connection class is used, the client must first set the

A client uses a Connection object's Open method to open a connection to a DBMS

class's ConnectionString property, indicating which database it's interested in and other information.

A client relies on Command objects to issue queries and perform other DBMS operations

Once a connection exists, a client can issue queries and other commands on it using a Command object. An application can create a Command object by invoking a Connection object's CreateCommand method. Once again, different data providers use different Command object classes. The .NET Framework data provider for SQL Server uses SqlCommand, for example, while the .NET Framework data provider for OLE DB uses OleDbCommand. Whatever Command class is used, all of them allow specifying a SQL query by setting the object's CommandText property.

A Command object provides several options for execut-ing the operation it contains

Once a Command object exists, a client can choose one of several methods this object provides to execute the command it contains. Those methods are as follows:

- **ExecuteReader:** returns a DataReader that can be used to read the results of the query. A DataReader can access the result of a SQL query one row at a time.

- **ExecuteScalar:** returns a single value, such as the result from a SQL SUM function. If the result of the query contains more than one value, this method will return the value in the first column of the first row—everything else will be ignored. The value it returns is of the type System.Object, which means that it can contain a result of any type.

- **ExecuteNonQuery:** returns no data, but instead sends back the number of rows affected by the query. This method is used with commands that don't return results, such as SQL UPDATEs, INSERTs, and DELETEs.

The SqlCommand class provided by the .NET Framework data provider for SQL Server also has another choice:

ExecuteXmlReader. This method returns an XmlReader object that can be used to access XML-formatted data returned by SQL Server. And regardless of which data provider a developer chooses, Command objects can also be used to execute stored procedures and can have parameters whose values are set before the command is executed.

When finished, an ADO.NET client must invoke either the Close or the Dispose method on an in-use Connection object. You can't just forget about the object and rely on garbage collection to shut down the open connection—it won't work. Each connection must be explicitly closed.

Connections must be explicitly closed

Connection objects are also used to start a transaction in the DBMS. If a client is using the .NET Framework data provider for SQL Server, for instance, calling the BeginTransaction method on a SqlConnection object instructs SQL Server to start a new transaction. This method allows the client to specify the transaction's isolation level, offering the usual choices: Serializable, RepeatableRead, ReadCommitted, and a few more. Interestingly, however, although the Connection object is used to start a transaction, it isn't used to end one. Instead, a call to SqlConnection. BeginTransaction returns an instance of the SqlTransaction class, and a client ends the transaction by calling a method in this object rather than in SqlConnection. To commit the work done in the transaction, the client calls SqlTransaction.Commit, while calling SqlTransaction.Rollback instructs the DBMS to abort the transaction, rolling back all changes made to data since the call to SqlConnection.BeginTransaction. The details of how this is done vary slightly across different data providers, but the basics are the same in every case.

Clients can start and end DBMS transactions

Accessing Data with DataReaders

Straightforward read-only access to data relies on DataReader objects. DataReaders are fast, and they don't use much memory, because only one row of data at a time is made accessible

A DataReader object provides fast access to data

(although more may be cached). An application using a DataReader can read a query's results only one row at a time, and can move forward only through those results—no random access is allowed. This is very simple, but it's the right solution for a significant set of applications. Like everything else, data access should be as simple as possible. There's enough inherent complexity in software development without unnecessarily adding more.

A client reads data from a DataReader one row at a time

To read a row, the application calls a DataReader's Read method, which makes the next row from the result of the executed query accessible. (This method returns FALSE when there are no more rows to be read from the result.) Once this has been done, the contents of that row can be accessed in various ways. If you know the types of the columns in the result (which is the usual case since you probably wrote the query), the values from the current row can be read by calling the appropriately typed Get methods (officially called *typed accessor* methods) provided by the DataReader. For example, if a SQL query asks for a list of all employee names and ages, each row in that query's result will contain a string and an integer. To read these, a client application could use the DataReader's GetString and GetInt32 methods, respectively. DataReaders also provide many more Get methods, each capable of reading a particular type of data in a row. It's also possible to access each column of the current row by the column name or position, but using the Get methods is more efficient.

Here's a C# class that illustrates opening a connection, creating a command, and reading the results using a DataReader:

```csharp
using System.Data.SqlClient;
class DataReaderExample
{
  public static void Main()
  {
    SqlConnection Cn = new SqlConnection(
      "Data Source=localhost;" +
      "Integrated Security=SSPI;" +
      "Initial Catalog=example");
    SqlCommand Cmd = Cn.CreateCommand();
```

```
        Cmd.CommandText =
          "SELECT Name, Age FROM Employees";
        Cn.Open();
        SqlDataReader Rdr = Cmd.ExecuteReader();
        while (Rdr.Read())
        {
          System.Console.WriteLine(
            "Name: {0}, Age: {1}",
            Rdr.GetString(0),
            Rdr.GetInt32(1));
        }
        Rdr.Close();
        Cn.Close();
      }
}
```

This example uses the .NET Framework data provider for
SQL Server, so it begins with the appropriate using statement for
this set of classes. Following this is a single class,
DataReaderExample, containing the single method Main. This
method begins by creating a new Connection object, passing in
a very simple connection string. The example then creates a
Command object and sets its CommandText property to contain
a simple SQL query. Next, the Connection object's Open method
is used to open a connection to the database, the command is
executed by a call to ExecuteReader, and a DataReader object is
returned. The result of the query is read using a simple while
loop. Each iteration reads an employee name and age from the
current row in the result using the appropriate Get method.
When there are no more results, first the DataReader and then
the Connection object are closed. And although it's not shown in
this simple example, using a try/ catch block to handle any exceptions that occur is a common thing to do.

Accessing relational data in a DBMS using a DataReader object
is simple and fast. For applications that need nothing more
than sequential access to data or straightforward updates, this
approach is perfect. Not all applications can get by with this
simple mechanism, however. For those that need more,
ADO.NET provides the much more flexible (and much more
complicated) alternative of a DataSet, described next.

*DataReaders are
useful, but they're
not always the best
approach*

ADO.NET and SQL Server 2005

The release of SQL Server 2005 was a big step for Windows-based data management. The first new version of SQL Server in five years, this product added a wide range of new features. One of the most interesting, and perhaps most important, was incorporating the Common Language Runtime (CLR) directly into the DBMS. It's now possible to create stored procedures in C# or Visual Basic (VB) as well as in SQL Server's native T-SQL language. While developers should use this option with care—T-SQL is still a better choice in many cases—it offers a useful alternative in some situations.

SQL Server 2005 includes many other changes, some of which are more directly relevant to ADO.NET. Because version 2.0 of the .NET Framework was designed to work with this new product, ADO.NET's .NET Framework data provider for SQL Server has a number of additions that allow developers to use these new features. Among the most important are the following:

- Support for new SQL Server 2005 data types. This includes large value types that allow creating data values as big as 2^{32} bytes, user-defined types for storing CLR objects and other information, and a new XML data type that allows working with data using the System.Xml types described in Chapter 4.

- The ability for an application to use SQL Server 2005's new database mirroring capability. This allows maintaining a current copy of a database on another machine that can be used if the primary system fails.

- Access to runtime statistics about SQL Server 2005. The information available to an ADO.NET client application includes how many bytes have been sent to and from the DBMS, how many SQL SELECT statements have been executed, how many transactions have been started, and much more.

- Query notifications that let an application be notified when data is changed. For example, an application that caches data retrieved from SQL Server 2005 might use this to know when to refresh its cache.

- Support for SQL Server 2005's notion of snapshot isolation, a new mechanism for reducing the number of locks placed on shared data.

- The ability to change a user's password without administrator intervention, a new option in SQL Server 2005.

- Integration with System.Transactions. As described in Chapter 4, the types in this namespace allow an application to create a transaction that spans multiple resource managers, including SQL Server and others. SQL Server 2005 can work intelligently with System.Transactions, taking control of a transaction when necessary. It can also determine when a transaction must be handed off to the Distributed Transaction Coordinator (DTC), a standard Windows component that handles distributed transactions.

Accessing Data with DataSets

An instance of the class DataSet, contained in the System.Data namespace, is an in-memory cache for data. Most commonly, that data is the set of rows resulting from one or more SQL queries, but it can also include information derived from an XML document or from some other source. Unlike Connection, Command, and DataReader, each of which has a unique class for each .NET Framework data provider, there is only one DataSet class used by all .NET Framework data providers.

A DataSet is an in-memory cache that can store data from various sources

DataSets are very general things, so they're useful in many different situations. For instance, if a client application wishes to examine data in an arbitrary way, such as scrolling back and forth through the rows resulting from a SQL query, a DataReader won't suffice—but a DataSet will. DataSets are also useful for combining data from different data sources, such as two separate queries, or different types of data, such as the result of a query on a relational DBMS and the contents of an XML document. And because DataSets are serializable, they can be used for data that will be sent across a network. In fact, once it's been created, a

DataSets allow much more flexible access to data than is possible with a DataReader

DataSet can be passed around and used independently—it's just a managed object with state and methods like any other.

DataSets also allow updating data

Another important distinction between a DataSet and a DataReader is that DataSets can be used to modify data. Changes made to information stored in a DataSet can be written back to a database. Unlike DataReaders, DataSets aren't purely read-only objects, and so any ADO.NET client that wishes to update data will rely on DataSets.

A DataSet contains DataTables

Figure 6-3 shows a simplified picture of a DataSet. Each DataSet object can contain zero or more DataTable objects, which are instances of the DataTable class defined in System.Data. Each DataTable can contain the result of a query or perhaps something else. A DataSet can also maintain relationships among DataTables using DataRelation objects. For example, a column in one table might contain a foreign key for another table, a relationship that could be modeled by a DataRelation. These relationships can be used to navigate

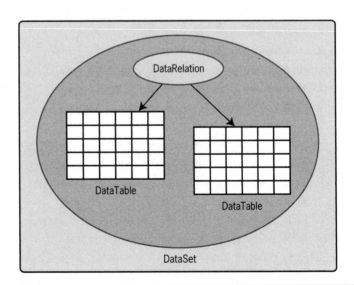

Figure 6-3   A DataSet contains DataTables, and it can have DataRelation objects that describe relationships among those tables.

through the contents of a DataSet. A simple DataSet, one that contains the result of just a single SQL query, might have only one DataTable and no DataRelations. DataSets can be quite complex, however, so an application that needed to maintain the results of several queries in memory could stuff them all into one DataSet, each in its own DataTable.

Each DataSet has a schema. Since DataSets hold tables, this schema describes those tables, including the columns each one contains and the types of those columns. Each DataSet and DataTable also has an ExtendedProperties property that can be used in various ways. For example, the ExtendedProperties value for each DataTable might contain the SQL query that generated the information stored in that table.

A DataSet has a schema

Creating and Using DataSets

As mentioned earlier, DataSet objects can be created using a .NET Framework data provider's DataAdapter object. For example, the .NET Framework data provider for SQL Server offers the class SqlDataAdapter, while the .NET Framework data provider for OLE DB uses OleDbDataAdapter. Whatever data provider is used, all of the specific DataAdapter classes offer a similar set of properties and methods for creating and working with DataSets. Among the most important properties of a DataAdapter are the following:

A DataAdapter object can be used to create a DataSet

- **SelectCommand:** contains a Command object that can be used to populate a DataTable within some DataSet with the results of a query on some database. The Command typically references a SQL SELECT statement.

- **InsertCommand:** contains a Command object used to insert rows added to a DataTable into an underlying database. The Command typically references a SQL INSERT statement.

- **UpdateCommand:** contains a Command object used to update a database based on changes made to a

DataTable. The Command typically references a SQL
UPDATE statement.

- **DeleteCommand:** contains a Command object used to
delete rows in a database based on deletions made to a
DataTable. The Command typically references a SQL
DELETE statement.

*A DataAdapter's Fill
method can be
used to execute a
query and store the
result in a DataSet*

The contents of these properties, which can be explicit SQL
statements or stored procedures, are accessed by various methods provided by the DataAdapter. The most important of these
methods is Fill. As shown in Figure 6-4, this method executes
the command in the DataAdapter's SelectCommand property
and then places the results in a DataTable object inside
whatever DataSet is passed as a parameter on the Fill call.
The connection to the database can be closed once the desired
results are returned, since a DataSet object is completely independent of any connection to any data source.

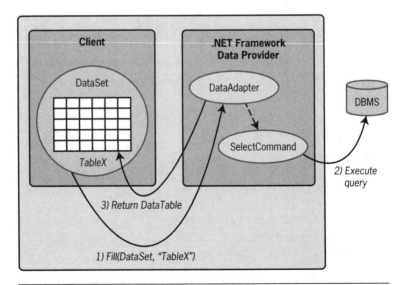

**Figure 6-4   Calling a DataAdapter's Fill method causes the associated
SelectCommand to be executed and the results placed in a DataSet
as a DataTable.**

Here's a C# example that shows how a DataAdapter can be used to add a DataTable containing the results of a query to a DataSet:

```
using System.Data;
using System.Data.SqlClient;
class DataSetExample
{
  public static void Main()
  {
    SqlConnection Cn = new SqlConnection(
      "Data Source=localhost;" +
      "Integrated Security=SSPI;" +
       "Initial Catalog=example");
    SqlCommand Cmd = Cn.CreateCommand();
    Cmd.CommandText =
      "SELECT Name, Age FROM Employees";
    SqlDataAdapter Da = new SqlDataAdapter();
    Da.SelectCommand = Cmd;
    DataSet Ds = new DataSet();
    Cn.Open();
    Da.Fill(Ds, "NamesAndAges");
    Cn.Close();
  }
}
```

This example begins with using statements for the System.Data namespace, home of the DataSet class, and for System.Data.SqlClient, because this example will once again use the .NET Framework data provider for SQL Server. Like the previous example, this class's single method creates Connection and Command objects and then sets the Command object's CommandText property to contain a simple SQL query. The example next creates an instance of the SqlDataAdapter class and sets its SelectCommand property to contain the Command object created earlier. The method then creates a DataSet and opens a connection to the database. Once this connection is open, the method calls the DataAdapter's Fill method, passing in the DataSet in which a new DataTable object should be created and the name that DataTable object should have. Closing the connection, the last step, doesn't affect the DataSet in any way—it never had any idea what connection was used to create the data it contains anyway.

A DataSet can contain results from different queries on different DBMSs

The DataSet created by this simple example contains just one DataTable. To add other DataTables with different contents to this same DataSet, the Fill method could be called again once the SelectCommand property of the DataAdapter had been changed to contain a different query. Alternatively, as shown in Figure 6-5, another DataAdapter could be used on a different data source. In the figure, a single DataSet is being populated with DataTables from two different .NET Framework data providers accessing two different databases. In each case, the same DataSet is passed into a call to the appropriate DataAdapter's Fill method. The result of each call is a DataTable within this DataSet whose contents are the result of running whatever query is represented by the SelectCommand object associated with the DataAdapter.

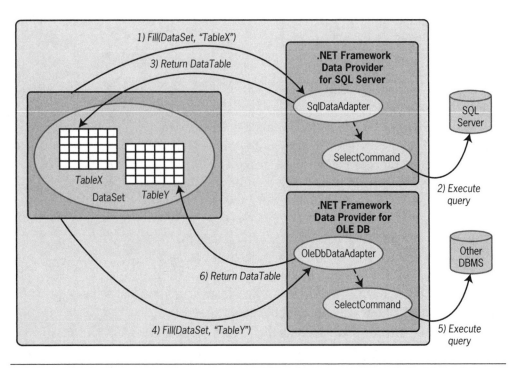

Figure 6-5   A single DataSet can contain DataTables whose contents are derived from different databases.

As mentioned earlier, it's also possible to modify information in a DBMS using a DataSet. Once one or more DataTables have been created in the DataSet, the information in those tables can be changed by the client in various ways, as described later in this section. As shown in Figure 6-6, calling a DataAdapter's Update method will cause the DataAdapter to examine the changes in any DataSet or DataTable passed into this call and then modify the underlying database to reflect those changes. These modifications are made using the commands stored in the DataAdapter's InsertCommand, UpdateCommand, and DeleteCommand properties described earlier. Because these commands can be stored procedures as well as dynamically executed statements, these update operations can be quite efficient.

DataSets can also be used to modify data in a DBMS

Note that there is no way for the DataSet itself to maintain a lock on the underlying data from which its contents were derived. As a result, it's possible that the data in the database has changed since

A DataSet can't itself maintain a lock on data

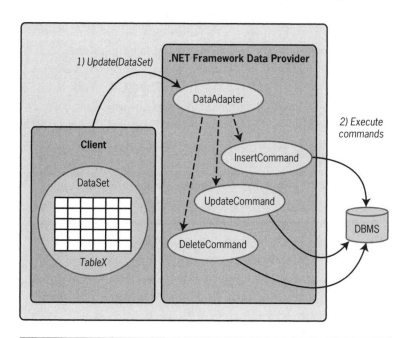

Figure 6-6   Calling a DataAdapter's Update method updates the DBMS to reflect any changes made to a DataSet.

some of its information was copied into the DataSet. Whether updates succeed if the underlying data has changed depends on what commands are placed into the InsertCommand, UpdateCommand, and DeleteCommand properties of the DataAdapter. For example, it's possible to generate those commands automatically using a CommandBuilder object supplied by the .NET Framework class library. If this is done, the automatically generated update commands are designed to fail if any of the affected data has changed since it was originally read. This need not be the case for commands created manually, however—it's up to the developer to decide what's best for each application.

The contents of a DataSet are grouped into collections

Every DataSet has a few collections that logically group some of the DataSet's objects. For example, all of the DataTables in a DataSet belong to the Tables collection. An application can create a freestanding DataTable object, one that's not part of any DataSet, then explicitly add it to some DataSet object[1]. To do this, the application can pass this DataTable object as a parameter on the Add method of the DataSet's Tables collection. Similarly, each DataSet has a Relations collection that contains all of the DataRelation objects in this DataSet, each of which represents a relationship of some kind between two tables. Calling the Add method of a DataSet's Relations collection allows creating a new DataRelation object. The parameters on this call can be used to specify exactly which fields in the two tables are related.

Accessing and Modifying a DataSet's Contents

Applications access a DataSet's contents by examining the DataTables it contains

DataSets exist primarily to let applications read and change the data they contain. That data is grouped into one or more DataTables, as just described, and so access to a DataSet's information is accomplished by accessing these contained objects. Because applications need to work with data in diverse ways, DataTables provide several options for accessing and

---

1. DataTable objects can also be used on their own without belonging to a DataSet. In version 2.0 of ADO.NET, DataTables can even be serialized and passed around independently.

modifying the data they contain. Whatever option is used, two classes are commonly used to work with information in a DataTable:

- **DataRow:** represents a row in a DataTable. Each DataTable has a Rows property that allows access to a collection containing all of that table's DataRows. The data in a DataTable can be accessed by examining its DataRows. In fact, a common way to access a DataTable's information is by directly accessing the Rows property as a two-dimensional array.

- **DataColumn:** represents a column in a DataTable. Each DataTable has a Collections property that allows access to a collection containing all of the table's DataColumns. Rather than defining the table's data, however, this collection defines what columns the table has and what type each column is. In other words, this collection defines the table's schema.

For more complex examinations of data, each DataTable provides a Select method. This method allows an application to describe the data it's interested in and then have that data returned in an array of DataRow objects. Select takes up to three parameters: a filter, a sort order, and a row state. The filter allows specifying a variety of criteria that selected rows must meet, such as "Name='Smith'" or "Age >45." The sort order allows specifying which column the results should be sorted by and whether those results should be sorted in ascending or descending order. Finally, the row state parameter allows returning only records in a specific state, such as those that have been added or those that have not been changed. Whatever criteria are used on the call to Select, the result is an array of DataRows. The application can then access individual elements of this array as needed to work with the data each one contains.

A DataTable's Select method can be used to choose a subset of its data

To add data to a DataTable, an application can create a new DataRow object, populate it, and insert it into the table. To

New rows can be added to a DataTable

What's New in ADO.NET 2.0

Like many other parts of the .NET Framework class library, version 2.0 of ADO.NET provides a number of enhancements. The most important are described in the main text of this chapter, but other significant changes include:

- The ability to make asynchronous (nonblocking) calls using the .NET Framework data provider for SQL Server. This allows an application to issue, say, a long-running query, then do other work while waiting for the result.

- Support for tracing database calls. This ability is available in all of ADO.NET 2.0's .NET Framework data providers, and it makes debugging database applications less painful.

- The addition of DataTableReader, a generic object that can be used with any .NET Framework data provider as a simple way to access information in one or more DataTable objects. A DataTableReader object provides forward-only, read-only access to the data it contains.

- A way for an application to determine which .NET Framework data providers are installed on the system it's running on.

- Performance improvements in a number of areas, such as operations on DataTables.

For anyone familiar with earlier releases of ADO.NET, moving to version 2.0 won't present a steep learning curve—the changes aren't large. Given Microsoft's historical fondness for radical change in Windows data access interfaces, this stability is unquestionably welcome.

create the new DataRow, the application can call a DataTable's NewRow method. Once this DataRow exists, the application can assign values to the fields in the row, then add the row to the table by calling the Add method provided by the DataTable's Rows collection. It's also possible to modify the contents of a DataTable directly by assigning new values to the contents of its DataRows and to delete rows using the Remove method of the Rows collection.

The state of a DataRow changes as that DataRow is modified. The current state is kept in a property of the DataRow called RowState, and several possibilities are defined. Changes made to a DataRow can be made permanent by calling the DataRow.AcceptChanges method for that row, which sets the DataRow's RowState property to Unchanged. To accept all changes made to all DataRows in a DataTable at once, an application can call DataTable.AcceptChanges, while to accept all changes made to all DataRows in all DataTables in a DataSet at once, an application can call DataSet.AcceptChanges. It's also possible to call the RejectChanges method at each of these levels to roll back any modifications that have been made.

Each row in a DataTable keeps track of its state

Using DataSets with XML-Defined Data

Information stored in relational DBMS probably comprises the majority of business data today. Increasingly, though, data defined using XML is also important, and XML's hierarchical approach to describing information will probably matter even more in the future. Recognizing this, the designers of ADO.NET chose to integrate DataSets and XML-defined data in several different ways. This section describes the available choices.

DataSets can be used with XML-defined data

Translating Between DataSets and XML Documents

In the description so far, the contents of a DataTable inside a DataSet have always been generated by a SQL query. It's also possible, however, to create DataTables in a DataSet whose contents come from an XML document. To do this, an application can call a DataSet's ReadXml method, passing as a parameter an indication of where the XML data can be found. The possible sources for this data include a file, a stream, and an XmlReader object. Wherever it comes from, the XML-defined information is read into a DataTable in the DataSet.

An XML document can be read directly into a DataSet

■ Perspective: The Revenge of Hierarchical Data

The relational model has been the dominant approach for storing and working with data for more than 20 years. Older systems that organized data hierarchically, such as IBM's IMS, were shoved aside by the more flexible notion of putting everything into tables. Today, relations rule.

Yet the idea of hierarchical data refuses to die. The object database crowd attempted to revive this notion, reasoning that since objects in software were commonly organized into a tree, organizing data the same way could give better performance and a better match between code and data. This insight was correct, but since the information in most databases is shared by multiple applications, no single hierarchy worked well for all of them. The more general relational approach was still better in most cases.

XML is the latest technology to exploit the utility of hierarchical data. Unlike the object database people, XML proponents didn't try to displace the entrenched relational world. Instead, they attempted to work with it, a strategy that's proven much more successful. The truth is that some kinds of information really are better modeled as a tree than as a table. And given XML's tremendous value as a common interchange format among applications, software to work with XML documents is required anyway. Since XML is going to be around, merging the hierarchical structure it uses with relational data access is a very good idea.

Microsoft got XML religion some years ago. One way the company expressed its newfound faith was by combining the groups in Redmond responsible for relational data access and those responsible for XML data access. ADO.NET was one major result of this religious conversion, as were the features in the System.Xml namespace described in Chapter 4. Each has a streaming API—DataReader and XmlReader, respectively—along with a navigational API—DataSet (which has at least some navigational characteristics) and XmlDocument. More important, the .NET Framework's integration of these two models, described later in this chapter, can allow the same data to be accessed as either a relational table or an XML hierarchy.

Relational dominance notwithstanding, there's still a place for trees. XML, the modern expression of hierarchical data, is the latest technology to remind us of this fact.

There's an obvious problem here. Both XML and the relational model have the notion of schemas for describing data. Yet the two technologies view this notion in very different ways. An XML schema defines a hierarchy using the XML Schema definition (XSD) language. The relational model defines a schema as a set of tables, each having a particular group of columns in a particular order. DataSets and the DataTables they contain are firmly in the relational camp. When an XML document is loaded into a DataSet, what should the schema of the resulting table look like?

Like most questions, the answer to this one is: It depends. The DataSet.ReadXml method allows passing an XmlReadMode parameter to control how the XML document's schema is mapped into the schema for the DataTable in which that document's information will be stored. One option is to tell the DataSet to read an XSD schema that appears in the XML document being read, while another instructs the DataSet to infer a relational schema from the XML schema.

A schema for a DataSet can be automatically created from an XML document

Mapping the hierarchical form of an XML document into the tables contained in a DataSet can be a nontrivial undertaking. In particular, the rules for inferring a relational schema are not especially simple. Some parts are easy, though. For instance, all columns have the type String, since if no XSD schema is available a DataSet has no way to identify any other types. Mapping the document's hierarchy into tables is more interesting. When inferring a relational schema, a DataSet assumes that an XML element with attributes should become a table, with the attributes and the element value represented as columns in that table. Similarly, an element with child elements will also become a table containing some number of values.

Mapping between a hierarchical XML document and a relational DataSet can get complicated

Figure 6-7 shows how the simple XML document we saw in Chapter 4 might be mapped into a DataSet if it were read with DataSet.ReadXml. The <employee> elements are placed into a single DataTable named *employee*, with the information in

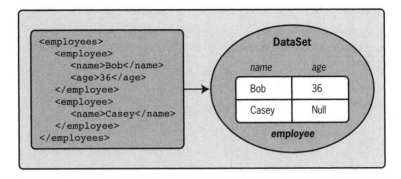

Figure 6-7   A DataSet can infer a relational schema from an XML document read with DataSet.ReadXml.

each of the child elements mapped into a row in that table. Notice that because there's no age present for Casey that value is of the type null (or more exactly, the type DBNull defined in the System namespace).

A DataSet can also explicitly read an XSD schema

While this simple example worked fine, inferring a relational schema from an XML document is in general likely to produce a less attractive result than creating one directly from an XSD schema. When possible, then, it's better to tell the DataSet to read an XML document's schema. Also, if an XML document is being read into a DataSet that contains data and already has a schema, the ReadXml method can be instructed just to use the DataSet's existing schema. Note too that it's possible to read an XML schema explicitly from a stream, a file, or somewhere else into a DataSet by calling the DataSet's ReadXmlSchema method.

Any DataSet's contents can be serialized as an XML document

Once an XML document has been loaded into a DataSet, the data it contains can be treated just like any other data in any other DataSet—there's nothing special about it. And just as an application can populate a DataSet from an XML document, so too it's possible to write out a DataSet's contents as an XML document. In other words, the contents of any DataSet can be serialized as XML, whether or not its data originally came from an XML document. A primary choice for doing this is the DataSet's WriteXml method. This method writes the DataSet's contents as an XML document to a stream, an XmlWriter, or some other destination. A parameter on this method can be used to control whether an XSD schema is written with the data. If desired, a developer can specify how columns are mapped to XML and control other options in the transformation from table to hierarchy.

One common reason for serializing a DataSet as an XML document is to allow the information it contains to be sent to a browser. Similarly, an XML document received from a browser can be read into a DataSet and then used to update a DBMS or in some other way. It's also worth noting that because DataSets are serializable, they can be passed as parameters by applications that use .NET Remoting[2]. Data wrapped in XML can be applied in many contexts, and so being able to easily serialize a DataSet into this format is quite useful.

Synchronizing a DataSet and an XML Document

Reading an XML document into a DataSet converts the information it contains into a set of tables. Similarly, writing the contents of a DataSet as an XML document converts the information in that DataSet into a hierarchical form. Being able to translate data between tables and trees is certainly a useful thing. Yet sometimes you'd like the ability to treat the same data as either relational tables or an XML tree at the same time. Rather than converting between the two formats, a transformation that can lose information, you'd like to maintain the flexibility to view the same data in either form depending on your requirements. ADO.NET allows this by synchronizing a DataSet with an instance of a class called XmlDataDocument.

A DataSet can be synchronized with an XmlDataDocument object

---

2. ADO.NET 2.0 allows DataSets and DataTables to be serialized into a binary representation as well as XML. This allows faster data transfer when .NET Remoting is used to move these serialized objects.

Relational data can now be accessed with tools such as XPath

Figure 6-8 shows how this looks. By having the data available in a DataSet, it can be accessed using standard operations such as DataTable.Select. Yet having the same data available in an XmlDataDocument allows running XPath queries on the data, performing XSLT transforms, and doing other kinds of hierarchically oriented access. XmlDataDocument inherits from XmlDocument, a class described in Chapter 4 that implements the standard navigational API for XML, the Document Object Model (DOM). Since it derives from XmlDocument, XmlDataDocument also allows its contents to be accessed using this navigational interface. Along with this, however, XmlDataDocument also allows its user to work simultaneously with the data it contains as a DataSet.

To view an existing XmlDataDocument's information as a DataSet, an application can simply access the

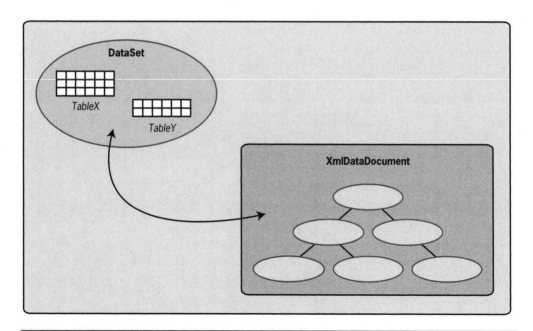

Figure 6-8   Synchronizing a DataSet with an XmlDataDocument allows an application to view the same data either relationally or hierarchically.

▪ Perspective: The Object/Relational Mapping Morass

Most applications use objects, and most data is stored in relations. Translating between these two distinct abstractions is challenging. Like it or not, this reality isn't going to change anytime soon.

Many, many attempts have been made to make the object/relational mapping easier. In the Java world alone, a range of technologies is available for doing this. Enterprise JavaBeans (EJB) has offered various versions of entity beans, for example, all of which tried to automate the process of reading an object's state from a relational DBMS and storing it back into that DBMS. Java Data Objects (JDO) addresses this problem in a slightly different way, as does the open source technology Hibernate. Each of these technologies has pros and cons, and each has fans and detractors.

Yet while the Java community has attempted to address this problem in a variety of ways, the .NET world has largely relied on the simpler approach offered by ADO.NET. Hibernate is now available for .NET Framework applications in a version known as NHibernate, but Microsoft itself hasn't provided any standard approach comparable to, say, EJB's entity beans. In late 2005, however, the people in Redmond went public with the *Language Integrated Query* project. Commonly referred to as *LINQ*, it offers an interesting new approach to integrating objects with data. Rather than focus solely on the problem of mapping between objects and relations, LINQ actually adds extensions to CLR-based languages such as C# and VB that allow querying various kinds of data. (This is why the technology is called "language integrated query.") LINQ queries can be performed against relational tables, XML documents, and other kinds of information. A primary goal is to make translating between the abstractions used by objects and those used by data as natural as possible for developers.

LINQ isn't included in version 2.0 of the .NET Framework. In fact, by the time you read this, its name may well have changed, since "LINQ" is just a code name. Whatever it's called, this technology certainly holds promise as an interesting approach for dealing with the challenge of translating between objects and the data they use.

XmlDataDocument's DataSet property. The result is a DataSet object containing the XmlDataDocument's information in a relational form. There are also other ways to create a synchronized DataSet/XmlDataDocument pair. One choice is to create an instance of an XmlDataDocument and pass in a DataSet on the new operation. This will create an XmlDataDocument that provides a hierarchical view of whatever data is in that DataSet. Another option is to create a DataSet containing only relational schema information rather than data, then pass this DataSet on the new operation that creates an XmlDataDocument. An XML document can now be loaded into the XmlDataDocument using its Load method, and the data in that document will be both loaded as an XML hierarchy and mapped to tables using the DataSet's existing schema. However it's done, the ability to use the same data either hierarchically or relationally is an interesting idea, one that's quite useful for some kinds of applications.

Conclusion

ADO.NET is an important part of the .NET Framework class library

The need to work with data is fundamental to software. Accordingly, the mechanisms used to do this are an important part of a developer's world, and so ADO.NET is used by a large percentage of .NET Framework applications. It's fair to say that the types comprising ADO.NET are among the most important soldiers in the army of support provided by the .NET Framework class library.

7

Building Distributed Applications

Allowing communication between software running on separate computers is an essential part of modern software. Different distributed applications have different requirements, however, and so various technologies have been created to do this. This chapter describes the three most important approaches to building distributed applications that the .NET Framework provides: ASP.NET Web Services, .NET Remoting, and Enterprise Services.

Distributed applications are fundamental to modern software

ASP.NET Web Services: System.Web.Services

In the last ten years, nothing has had a bigger impact on software development than the World Wide Web. Browser-based applications became the norm as the world adopted this new environment. Yet the Web has also affected applications that don't use browsers through the advent of Web services. Defined by a group of related specifications, Web services provide a way

Web services let diverse software interact over the Web

for any kind of software to interact with any other kind of software using standard communication protocols.

ASP.NET Web Services allow .NET Framework applications to use this style of communication. Commonly known as ASMX, after the file extension it uses, this technology provides a straightforward way for developers to create applications that expose and invoke Web services. Given this, understanding ASMX first requires a grasp of Web services basics, described next.

Web Services Fundamentals

Web services rely on XML, WSDL, and SOAP

The core technologies of Web services can be broken down into three separate areas, each addressing a particular aspect of the problem. Those areas are:

- *Describing information sent over the network.* Invoking a remote operation commonly involves passing in infor- mation and getting back some kind of result. With Web services, this information is described using *XML*, today's lingua franca for describing data.

- *Defining Web service capabilities.* Some mechanism must exist to allow the provider of a Web service to specify the technical details of exactly what services are offered. As with other types of services, it makes sense to group related operations into interfaces, then provide some way to describe each of those operations. For Web services, this can be done using the *Web Services Description Language (WSDL),* commonly pronounced "wizdel." Each WSDL-defined interface contains one or more operations, and WSDL itself is defined using XML.

- *Accessing Web services.* Once an interface has been defined, clients must use some protocol to invoke the operations in that interface. Although WSDL explicitly allows specifying different protocols for invoking the operations in an interface, the standard choice is *SOAP*. This universally supported protocol provides a way to identify which operation to invoke, convey that operation's inputs as XML-defined data, and return any outputs, also as XML-defined data. SOAP defines only a simple envelope for conveying this information, one that can be carried in various ways. For example, SOAP calls can be carried on the Hypertext Transfer Protocol (HTTP), directly over TCP, or in other ways.

Several other Web services technologies have also been defined. To locate services, for example, developers and applications can potentially rely on *Universal Description, Discovery, and Integration (UDDI)*. Using UDDI, providers of Web services can advertise their offerings in a standard way, allowing clients to learn what services each provider offers and letting creators of client software learn what they need to know to build those clients. UDDI is an interesting idea, but the technology isn't widely used today. Still, Microsoft includes support in Windows for creating a UDDI registry, and developers who create .NET Framework applications can use this or other UDDI implementations if they wish.

UDDI lets developers and software find services

A number of extensions to SOAP have also been defined. Known collectively as the WS-* specifications, each defines how to solve a particular kind of communication problem. The WS-Security specification, for instance, lays the groundwork for secure SOAP-based communication, while WS-AtomicTransaction addresses the challenge of achieving distributed transactions via SOAP. An extension to ASP.NET Web Services known as *Web Services Enhancements (WSE)* provides an implementation of WS-Security and a few other WS-* specifications. A more complete implementation of these specifications (and much more) is contained in Windows Communication Foundation (WCF), described briefly at the end of this chapter.

The WS- specs add extensions to SOAP for security and more*

All of these technologies have broad vendor support

Each of these technologies was created by groups of vendors and users working together. XML, for instance, was created by a large group working under the auspices of the World Wide Web Consortium (W3C), while WSDL was created primarily by Microsoft and IBM. SOAP comes from a group somewhere in between in size, with Microsoft, IBM, DevelopMentor, and several others playing a role. The key point to notice about the origin of each Web services technology is that none of them is a single-vendor solution. Because of this broad support, Web services based on XML, WSDL, and SOAP can be used across virtually all platforms, languages, and object models.

■ Perspective: Creating Common Connections: Why COM and CORBA Couldn't

Wouldn't it be nice if all kinds of software on all kinds of systems could snap together like Legos? The technical problems that stand in the way of this goal aren't really all that hard. What has stopped us in the past is will: Users have had it, but vendors haven't. And in this case, vendors rule.

Microsoft, for example, was quite successful in creating snap-together software for Windows platforms. The Component Object Model (COM) made this possible even for software running on different machines. But other major vendors never seriously supported COM, and one could debate whether Microsoft ever really wanted them to. Similarly, the Object Management Group's (OMG) CORBA was intended to connect all kinds of applications on all kinds of systems. Two problems doomed the OMG's efforts, though. First, their standards weren't complete enough, so organizations were all but forced to stick with a single CORBA vendor to make their systems communicate. And second, Microsoft didn't support CORBA.

Today, however, a technology exists with both the right technical merits and, more important, complete vendor agreement. That technology, of course, is Web services. SOAP and its fellow travelers have emerged as the standard mechanism that all software can use to expose its services to the outside world. The decades-long battle over what protocol should be used to connect applications is over: SOAP has won.

ASP.NET Web Services Applications: Basics

Any application that communicates via Web services must expose one or more interface definitions expressed in WSDL, and it must also allow the operations in those interfaces to be invoked using SOAP. A technology that allows creating these applications should make doing these things as natural as possible for developers. Achieving this is a primary goal of ASP.NET Web Services.

ASP.NET Web Services allows creating applications that communicate through Web services

As with most distributed computing technologies, ASP.NET Web Services distinguish between clients and servers. Creating a basic server, the first thing that most developers do, is simple. Because it's part of ASP.NET, the ASP.NET Web Services technology relies on pages to implement services. As shown in Figure 7-1, the files containing those pages have an .asmx extension (rather than the .aspx extension used by browser-oriented ASP.NET applications), and they don't contain any HTML. Apart from an occasional directive, they're just code. No HTML is required because a Web service is accessed by software, not by people, so it doesn't

ASP.NET Web Services applications use .asmx pages

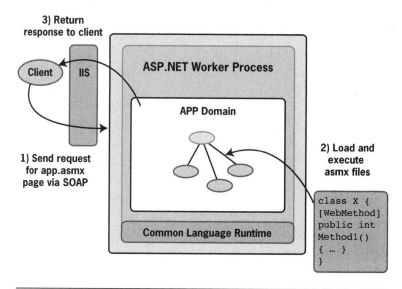

Figure 7-1   An ASP.NET Web services application is built using .asmx pages, which produce managed objects when they're accessed.

display a user interface. Ultimately, of course, there is often some human being whose request triggered the Web service, but the interface that person uses to accomplish this is outside the scope of the Web service itself. Web services don't define GUIs, and so .asmx pages don't contain HTML.

Still, the process of accessing an .asmx page is similar to what happens when an .aspx page is accessed. A client makes a request for the page via SOAP (step 1). Note that, unlike an .aspx page, the client for an .asmx page is generally an application rather than a vanilla Web browser. The named file is loaded into an app domain in the ASP.NET worker process[1], then executed (step 2). As with an .aspx page, everything in the .asmx file becomes a managed object—it's a .NET Framework application like any other. The result of executing the page is then returned to the client, again via SOAP (step 3).

The WebMethod attribute is used to expose a method in a class as a Web service

To expose a method contained in an .asmx file as a Web service, all that's required is to insert the attribute WebMethod in front of the method declaration. When the file is compiled, this attribute will be stored in the metadata of the resulting assembly, like all attributes. Its presence signals to the ASP.NET infrastructure that this method should be made accessible as a Web service. To give you a sense of how simple this is to do, think back to the Compute class used in Chapter 4's language examples. An .asmx file that exposed the C# version of that class's two methods as Web services might look like this:

```
<%@ WebService Language="c#" Class="Compute" %>
using System.Web.Services;
public class Compute
{
    [WebMethod]
    public int Factorial(int f)
    {
        int i;
        int result = 1;
```

___

1. It's also possible to run ASP.NET Web Services applications in other processes—using IIS isn't strictly required.

```
        for (i=2; i<=f; i++)
            result = result * i;
        return result;
    }
    [WebMethod]
    public double SquareRoot(double s)
    {
        return System.Math.Sqrt(s);
    }
}
```

The file's contents begin with a WebService directive. Similar in form to the Page directive shown in Chapter 5, this line indicates that the Web service specified in this .asmx page is written in C# and defines a class named Compute. Next appears a using statement for the namespace System.Web.Services, followed by the definition of the Compute class. This class is virtually identical to what was shown in Chapter 4. For simplicity, this version doesn't use an interface, although that's not an important distinction here. What is important is the presence of the WebMethod attribute before both of the class's methods. This attribute is defined in System.Web.Services, hence the using statement that precedes this class, and it's the only addition required to expose these methods as Web services. (Note, however, that only public methods can be marked with the WebMethod attribute.)

Version 2.0 of ASP.NET Web Services also allows applying the WebMethod attribute to methods defined in an interface, then implementing that interface with a class as usual. This option clearly separates the definition of the operations this service exposes, commonly known as its *contract*, from the implementation of those operations. Whichever option is chosen, ASP.NET automatically generates a WSDL interface expressing the contract in a form that can be read by any Web services client on any system.

Methods marked with the Web-Method attribute can also appear in interfaces

Web services applications are deployed as ASP.NET applications, just like applications built using .aspx pages. As with .aspx pages, an .asmx page is compiled when it is first accessed

Web services applications are ASP.NET applications, too

by a client. The resulting assembly is stored on disk and then reused until the .asmx page that produced it is modified. Changing this page results in an automatic recompile the next time the page is accessed.

ASP.NET allows accessing an .asmx page from a browser

When an .asmx page is accessed through a browser, ASP.NET uses reflection to learn what Web services it exposes. ASP.NET uses this knowledge to create a Web page that allows learning about these services. The Web page provides a way to invoke the services, examples of what calls to these services look like on the wire, and even a full WSDL definition of the Web services defined in this .asmx page. In reality, of course, the clients for Web services will usually be software other than a browser, but it's still nice to have this Web page generated for you, as it provides an easy way to verify that your methods are available.

ASP.NET Web Services applications can use the code-behind option

Like browser-focused ASP.NET applications, ASP.NET applications that provide Web services can also use a code-behind option. In this case, the .asmx file contains just the WebService directive with a reference to the assembly that contains the class. The actual code for that class is in a separate file, just as with browser-accessible ASP.NET applications.

ASP.NET Web Services clients depend on proxies

Servers are useless without clients. To create a client capable of invoking the Web services in some server, a developer must first create a proxy class that exposes the same methods. This proxy can be created in Visual Studio by adding something called a *Web reference* to a project or by specifying an .asmx file or a WSDL file. Given this information, Visual Studio will extract the information it needs to build a proxy for the desired Web service. It's also possible to create a proxy manually using wsdl.exe, a command-line tool that reads in a WSDL file and produces a proxy in the desired programming language. Once this proxy exists, the client can create an instance of that class and call its methods just like any other class. The proxy will forward each call to the destination Web service, that method will execute, and any results will be returned though the proxy.

It's also possible to invoke a Web service asynchronously. Rather than make the call and then block waiting for a response, a client can call the Web service and go about its business. When it gets the chance, the client can check to see what results, if any, the call has returned. To do this, the client uses two methods provided by the proxy along with the normal synchronous method for each Web service it supports. The first of these begins the call, passing in any parameters, and then returns control to the client. The second ends the call, returning any results that have come back. Other options are also possible, allowing the client to avoid repeatedly checking for the call to be completed.

Web services can be called asynchronously

ASP.NET Web Services Applications: Beyond the Basics

Building straightforward Web services such as those just shown could hardly be simpler. Adding one attribute isn't much work, and building a client proxy is also dead easy. But then, the methods in this example's Compute class don't do much either. Web services methods that do real work commonly require a bit more complexity than what's been shown so far. This section describes some of the options ASP.NET Web Services provides for creating more powerful and more useful Web services.

For example, what if an ASP.NET Web Services application needs to maintain state about its client between requests? Just as with the .aspx pages of a browser application, object instances defined via an .asmx page are created, used, and then destroyed for each request. Without some outside help, a Web services application can't store any in-memory information between requests. Fortunately, this outside help is available in the form of the standard objects provided by ASP.NET for this purpose. If a class that includes Web services methods inherits from System.Web.Services.WebService, for example, code in that class can access the Session object, the Application object, and others described in Chapter 5. These objects are also available via a static property called HttpContext.Current. However

ASP.NET Web Services applications can use built-in objects to manage their state

they're accessed, a Web services application can use these objects to maintain state about its clients, access the User object to learn who the client is, and use other services provided by these objects.

Using the Session object requires specifying the EnableSession parameter

To use the Session object, although not the others, a method within this class must also specify the EnableSession parameter in its WebMethod attribute. For example, if the Factorial method in the Compute class shown earlier were to do this, its declaration would look like this:

```
[WebMethod(EnableSession=true)]
public int Factorial(int f)
{ ... }
```

ASP.NET Web Services applications can also use transactions

Here's another concern: What if a method exposed as a Web service needs to group the work it does into a transaction? If the method uses ADO.NET to access a DBMS, it can certainly use the services of the Connection and Transaction objects, described in Chapter 6, to demarcate transaction boundaries, just like any other ADO.NET client. But suppose the method needs to create a transaction that spans multiple DBMSs or includes work done by other components? In the .NET Framework, these services are provided by the classes in System.EnterpriseServices, as described later in this chapter. To access these services, a method exposed as a Web service can use another parameter of the WebMethod attribute called TransactionOption. If a method to transfer money between two bank accounts were exposed as a Web service, for example, that method might be declared like this:

```
[WebMethod(TransactionOption=
    TransactionOption.Required)]
public bool MoveMoney(int fromAccount,
    int toAccount, decimal amount)
{ ... }
```

Transactions don't span SOAP calls

When the method executes, it will automatically run within a transaction managed by code in System.EnterpriseServices. It's important to note that this transaction includes only the work done by the MoveMoney method, which might, say, add to one account and subtract from another. It does not involve the client, whose only role is to call MoveMoney. Addressing the challenge of transactions that span SOAP calls is beyond the scope of ASP.NET Web services.

Another issue that might confront the creator of a Web services method is how to deal with SOAP headers. A SOAP message can include various headers, and each of those headers can have a mustUnderstand attribute. Given that SOAP headers are allowed to contain virtually anything, ASP.NET provides quite generic support for working with them. The foundation of that support is the SoapHeader class, contained in the namespace System. Web.Services.Protocols. This class defines common properties found in a SOAP header, including a MustUnderstand property to contain the value of a header's mustUnderstand attribute. By inheriting from this class, a developer can more easily create a class that reflects the specifics of a particular SOAP header.

ASP.NET Web Services supports processing SOAP headers

One more concern stems from every Web service's dependence on XML, the representation for all information sent and received via SOAP. This information, including method names and more, will belong to a default XML namespace unless an explicit alternative is provided. It's a good idea to provide this alternative since XML namespaces are used to differentiate between information carried by different services. The WebService attribute, defined in System.Web.Services, can be applied to the class, with the attribute's Namespace parameter used to specify the XML namespace. For example, if the Compute class shown earlier were provided by the fictitious QwickBank, its declaration might look like this:

An ASP.NET Web Services application can define its own namespace

```
[WebService(Namespace=
    "http://www.qwickbank.com/mathinfo")]
public class Compute
{ . . . }
```

■ Perspective: The Short Happy Life of .NET My Services

Perhaps the most controversial part of the original .NET technology family was .NET My Services. The codename for this technology was Hailstorm, and it was a well-chosen name: The proposal brought down a storm of criticism on Microsoft.

The idea of .NET My Services was certainly interesting: provide a set of Web services to applications over the Internet that allowed access to useful information. Among the proposed services were network storage of personal calendars and contact lists, a generalized alert service, a user presence service that could determine where to send those alerts, and several more. The goal was to help developers build a new kind of application using .NET My Services as a platform. For example, an application might detect an upcoming meeting on your calendar, use your contact list to discover how to get in touch with all of the participants, then use the alert and presence services to send all of them a meeting reminder wherever they might be via whatever device was appropriate. It was a creative idea, one that had the potential for significant value.

Yet .NET My Services never made it out of beta. For one thing, Microsoft found it challenging to excite potential customers about what this out-of-the-ordinary idea could do for them. Even more problematic, however, were the security and privacy concerns this technology raised. Many people were unsettled by the prospect of storing their personal information on Microsoft-owned servers accessible via the Internet. As a result, Microsoft largely wrote off its investment in creating this technology.

But still, the question remains: Was .NET My Services a good idea? In many ways, I'd argue that the answer is yes. Being able to access useful information from anywhere in the world, especially if that access is only by a controlled set of authorized applications, is a powerful thing. The security and privacy issues this raises can't be minimized, yet neither can the potential benefits. While it might be from some other company and it will certainly be under a different name, I wouldn't be surprised to see something much like .NET My Services rise again. You can't keep a good idea down.

ASP.NET Web Services was Microsoft's first serious attempt to implement this new technology family. Since its original design, Microsoft and the industry as a whole have learned more about how best to use Web services. Accordingly, there are aspects of ASP.NET Web Services, such as its orientation toward a remote procedure call (RPC) model, that don't necessarily reflect current thinking. Still, this technology has become a very popular approach for creating applications that communicate using SOAP. ASP.NET Web Services conforms to the Web Services Interoperability (WS-I) Organization's Basic Profile 1.1, and this ability to interoperate with software written on non-Microsoft platforms is a huge plus. It's probably fair to say that ASP.NET Web Services is the most important option in version 2.0 of the .NET Framework for creating distributed applications.

.NET Remoting: System.Runtime.Remoting

Given that Web services provide a quite general mechanism for communication between software on different machines, a simpleminded view might suggest that Web services are all that's required. After all, this technology can be used on both intranets and the Internet, and it potentially allows the client and server to be written using software from different vendors. Effective distributed computing requires more than just Web services, however. To see why, think about some of the limitations of standard Web services. For one thing, an explicit goal of Web services is to allow communication between different vendor implementations. Yet doing this isn't free. Mapping from the CLR's type system into the one defined by XML can be problematic, and depending on how it's done, this translation might lose some information. If both parties in the communication are built using the same technology, such as the .NET Framework, there's no reason to pay this price. Because using the .NET Framework at each end is a common scenario, some option that allows transmitting the complete set of CLR types must exist.

Web services are necessary but not sufficient

Serializing data into XML isn't always the best choice

Another problem is that the XML-based serialization used in Web services is not very efficient. We may have to live with this for Internet-based communication, since XML and SOAP are becoming the world's common mechanisms for exchanging information. Yet for communication inside a firewall, such as on a corporate intranet, there's no need to use a relatively inefficient XML-based format for data. Instead, a faster binary representation can be used.

It's sometimes useful for the same object instance to handle multiple calls

Still another issue is how an object's lifetime is handled. In ASP.NET Web Services, every client call results in a new instance of the target class being created and then destroyed when the call returns. But for some kinds of applications, allowing the same instance to handle multiple calls from the same or different clients is very useful. This kind of behavior isn't what ASP.NET Web Services is designed to do.

.NET Remoting focuses on communication between CLR-based applications

.NET Remoting addresses these concerns. While it is possible to expose SOAP-based Web services using .NET Remoting, it's typical to use this part of the class library when both ends of the communication are using the .NET Framework. Whether they're communicating across an intranet or over the Internet through firewalls, the communicating systems will then have the same type system, a common set of available communication protocols, and even the same implementation of those protocols.

.NET Remoting supports both synchronous and asynchronous communication

As you might expect, .NET Remoting provides traditional RPC functionality, allowing a client to invoke a method in a remote object and have some result returned. It can also be used for asynchronous (nonblocking) calls, however, as well as one-way calls that have no result. The mission of .NET Remoting is to make all of these interactions as simple yet as flexible as possible.

An Overview of the Remoting Process

.NET Remoting is used for communication between different app domains

Although the word *remoting* implies communication between different machines, it's used a bit more broadly in the .NET Framework. Here, remoting refers to any communication between objects in different application domains, whether those app domains are on the same machine or on machines

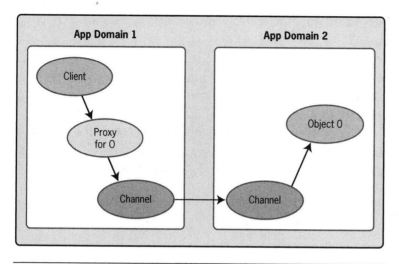

Figure 7-2   Calls to remote objects rely on a proxy object in the calling app domain and channel objects in both app domains.

connected by a network. Figure 7-2 shows a very high-level view of the major components of the remoting process.

When a client calls a method on an object in another app domain, that call is first handled by a *proxy* object running in the client's app domain. The proxy represents the remote object in the client's app domain, allowing the client to behave as if that object were running locally. The CLR automatically creates a proxy by using reflection to access the metadata of the remote object being accessed. (Note what this implies: The assembly containing the remote object's classes and/or interfaces must be available on the client's machine.)

Clients rely on proxy objects

A proxy eventually hands a call's information to a *channel* object. The channel object is responsible for using some appropriate mechanism, such as a TCP connection, to convey the client's request to the remote app domain. Once the request arrives in that app domain, a channel object running there locates the object for which this call is destined, perhaps creating it if the object isn't already running. The call is then passed to

Communication is handled by channel objects

the object, which executes it and passes any results back through the same path.

.NET Remoting provides many opportunities for customization

At a high level, the process is simple. In fact, however, there's much more going on than this initial description shows. It's possible, for instance, to insert code that intercepts and customizes the in-progress call at several points in the path between caller and object. In fact, the details of .NET Remoting can get fairly involved—remote access is never simple to implement well—but thankfully, most of the complexity can remain invisible to developers.

Passing Information to Remote Objects

Values passed between app domains must be marshaled and unmarshaled

Calling a method in an object is straightforward when both the client and the object are in the same app domain. Parameters of value types such as integers are passed by value, which means that their contents are simply copied from client to object. Parameters of reference types, such as classes, are passed by reference, which means that a reference to the instance itself is passed—no separate copy is made. Calling a method in an object gets more complicated when the two are in different app domains, however, and so .NET Remoting must address these complications. For one thing, accessing a remote object's properties or fields requires some way to transfer information across an app domain boundary. The process of packaging values for transfer to another app domain is called *marshaling*, and there are several options for how it gets done.

Marshal by value passes the value itself to another app domain

One option is *marshal by value (MBV)*. As the name suggests, transferring an instance of some type using this option copies its value to the remote app domain. For this to work, a user-defined type must be serializable, that is, its definition must be marked with the Serializable attribute. When an instance of that type is passed as a parameter in a remote call, the object's state is automatically serialized and passed to the remote app domain. Once it arrives, a new instance of that type is created and initialized using the serialized state of the original. (Note that the code for the type isn't passed, however, which means that for types such as classes, an assembly containing the MSIL for that type must exist on whatever machine the object's state is passed to.) An MBV object should usually be reasonably simple, or the cost of serializing and transferring the entire object to the remote app domain will be very high.

It's also possible to pass an instance of a reference type across an app domain boundary by reference. This option, called *marshal by reference (MBR)*, is possible only with reference types that inherit from MarshalByRefObject, a class contained in the System namespace. When an MBR object is passed across an app domain boundary, only a reference to the object is passed. This reference, which is more complex than the one used to refer to the object in its own app domain, is used to construct a proxy back to the original object in its home app domain. When code in the remote app domain references this object, such as by calling one of its methods, those references are actually sent back to the original instance of this object. Passing MBR objects as parameters makes sense in cases where the overhead of accessing the object remotely is less than the cost of making a copy of the object.

Marshal by reference passes only a reference to another app domain

Figure 7-3 illustrates the difference between MBV and MBR objects. When object X, an MBV object in app domain 1, is passed to app domain 2 as a parameter on a call to object O, a copy of X is created in the remote app domain. Passing object Y, however, does not result in a copy of Y being created in app domain 2 because Y is an MBR object. Instead, a proxy to Y is created, and all accesses to object Y are sent back to the instance of Y in app domain 1. (Although it's not shown in the picture, communication from Y's proxy back to Y itself relies on channels, just as described earlier.)

Finally, if a user-defined type isn't serializable and doesn't inherit from MarshalByRefObject, it is neither an MBV nor an

Not all types can be marshaled

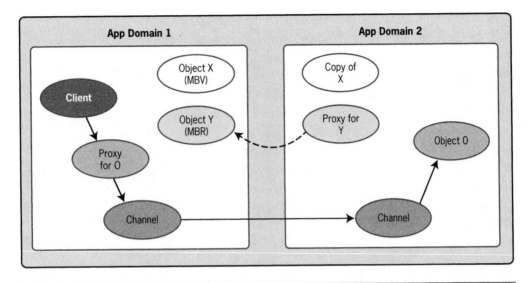

Figure 7-3   Marshal by value objects are copied when passed across an app domain boundary, while marshal by reference objects have a proxy created for them in the remote app domain.

MBR object. In this case, instances of that type can't be marshaled across an app domain boundary at all. In other words, any instance of this type can be used only within the app domain in which it is created.

Choosing a Channel

.NET Remoting provides a TCP channel, an HTTP channel, and an IPC channel

Applications using .NET Remoting ultimately rely on channels to convey calls and responses between app domains. Three standard channels are provided: a *TCP channel*, an *HTTP channel*, and an interprocess communication option called the *IPC channel*. It's also possible to build custom channels when necessary. While not especially simple to create, a custom channel might provide special security services, use a nonstandard protocol, or perform some other function in a unique way. It's safe to assume, however, that most applications will work happily with one of the three choices built into the .NET Framework.

The TCP channel is the best choice for fast machine-to-machine communication. By default, it serializes and deserializes a call's parameters using the binary formatter described in Chapter 4, although the SOAP formatter (which was also described in Chapter 4) can be used instead. Once the parameters have been serialized, they're transmitted directly in TCP packets. In version 2.0 of the .NET Framework, the TCP channel can also provide authentication and data encryption if required.

The TCP channel sends binary information directly over TCP

The second option, the HTTP channel, uses the SOAP formatter by default to serialize and deserialize a call's parameters. Rather than sending those parameters directly over TCP, they're sent as SOAP requests and responses embedded in HTTP. It's also possible to use the binary formatter with the HTTP channel, which can be useful for communication through firewalls. The binary formatter is more efficient than the SOAP formatter, so if the .NET Framework is on both sides of the communication, this option makes sense. For applications that need distributed security, the HTTP channel can use the security options provided by Internet Information Services (IIS). In this case, one possibility is to use the Secure Sockets Layer (SLL) protocol with HTTP, an option sometimes referred to as HTTPS.

The HTTP channel sends SOAP envelopes over HTTP

The third choice, the IPC channel, is new in version 2.0 of the .NET Framework. Rather than allowing communication between applications on different machines, the IPC channel is intended for communication between applications in different processes on the same machine. It uses named pipes, a standard Windows mechanism for interprocess communication.

The IPC channel allows communication between app domains on a single machine

Deciding which channel to use depends on your goals. If the communication is cross-machine and entirely within an organization's intranet—if no firewalls will be traversed—use the fast and simple TCP channel. If a cross-machine communication must go through firewalls, however, as do most packets sent on the Internet, use the HTTP channel. Although it's a bit less efficient, riding on HTTP means passing through port 80, the only port that virtually all firewalls leave open. Also, if the goal is to

Which channel is best depends on the situation

provide a standard Web service whose clients might not be based on the .NET Framework, the HTTP channel is the only .NET Remoting option you can use. (It's worth pointing out that ASP.NET Web Services is typically a better choice in this situation, however, since unlike .NET Remoting, it's designed to interoperate with non-Microsoft platforms). And for communication between processes on the same machine, the IPC channel is the obvious choice.

It's also possible for a single application to use different kinds of channels simultaneously. This allows clients to communicate with remote objects using the mechanism that's most appropriate for each one. A client, for instance, might use the more efficient TCP channel to talk to an object inside the firewall while also invoking methods in an object across the Internet via the HTTP channel.

Performance: What's the Fastest Choice?

Given that the .NET Framework offers several choices for creating distributed applications, it's natural to wonder which ones offer the best performance. Before answering the question, it's important to emphasize that relatively few applications require the highest performance possible. Other considerations, such as interoperability with other technologies, are often more important. Still, it's useful to know which choices are fastest.

Of the three main choices the .NET Framework offers, Enterprise Services and .NET Remoting using binary encoding over a TCP channel are fastest. This shouldn't be surprising. Enterprise Services relies on the efficient and highly tuned Distributed COM (DCOM) protocol, and using Remoting's binary-over-TCP option clearly minimizes overhead (although Enterprise Services–based applications will scale better). ASP.NET Web Services is a significantly slower option, as is the seldom-used SOAP option in .NET Remoting. All three technologies have their place, however, since each addresses a somewhat different set of problems.

For a more detailed look at the relative performance of these three technologies in the .NET Framework 2.0, see the paper by Ingo Rammer and Richard Turner at http://msdn.microsoft.com/library/default.asp?url=/library/en-us/dnwebsrv/html/asmxremotesperf.asp.

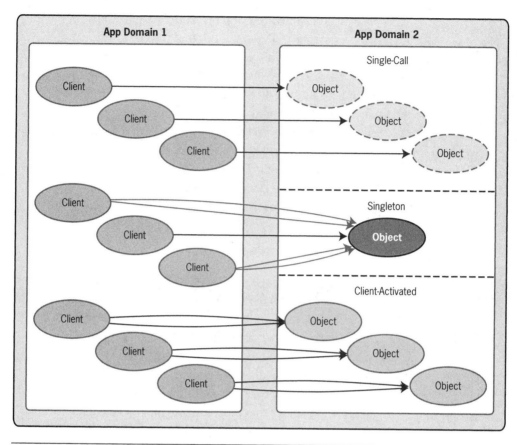

Figure 7-4   Objects accessed via .NET Remoting can be single-call, singleton, or client-activated.

Creating and Destroying Remote Objects

One of the most challenging issues in designing a remoting technology is determining what options to support for creating remote objects, referred to as *activation*. .NET Remoting provides three options, each of which is illustrated in Figure 7-4.

.NET Remoting provides three styles of activation for remote objects

- **Single-call objects:** A new instance of the class is created for each call from each client and then is destroyed (that is, made available for garbage collection) when the call ends.

- **Singleton objects:** Only one instance of the class is created on a given machine, and that same instance handles all calls made by all clients to that class on this machine.

- **Client-activated objects:** A separate instance of the class is created for each client that wishes to use it and then is destroyed only when that client is finished with it.

Regardless of which option is chosen, the server will create each new object on its own thread. Importantly, any object that will be accessed from outside its app domain must be an MBR object, which means that the class must inherit from MarshalByRefObject. These similarities notwithstanding, however, each of these options varies in who creates the object, how the object is destroyed, as well as in other ways. Accordingly, each is worthy of its own short discussion.

Single-Call Objects

A new single-call object is created for each call and then is destroyed when the call ends

As the name suggests, single-call objects exist only for the life of one method call from one client. A new instance is created for each new call, and that instance is destroyed when the call ends. This model, which is also how ASP.NET and ASP.NET Web Services applications work, means that the object can't maintain any internal state between method calls since a new instance is created for each call. It works well with a load-balanced set of server machines, however, where each request might be handled by a different machine. Since the object stores no in-memory state, using different machines for a sequence of requests is not a problem.

Single-call objects must be registered with the .NET Remoting infrastructure

To expose a single-call object to clients in other app domains, a server must register the object's type with the .NET Remoting infrastructure. There are two ways for servers to do this. One possibility is to perform the registration explicitly by calling methods provided by classes in System.Runtime.Remoting and its subordinate namespaces. For example, a server process can specify a channel that clients can use to access the single-call object by calling the RegisterChannel method of the ChannelServices class, found in the namespace System.Runtime.Remoting.Channels. Next, the server can call the RegisterWellKnownServiceType method of the RemotingConfiguration class, contained in System.Runtime.Remoting. The server specifies several things on this call, including the type being registered, the mode (which in this case is SingleCall), and the URL at which this object can be found.

A second (and usually better) way for a server to register a single-call type is to specify the desired options in a configuration file and then tell the remoting infrastructure to read this file by passing the file's name as a parameter on a call to RemotingConfiguration's Configure method. This allows changing details of the exposed type, such as the URL at which it can be found, without recompiling the server code. However it's done, registering a type doesn't actually create an instance of that type. No running instance is created until it's absolutely necessary, as described later in this section.

Once a server is running and has registered an appropriate type for a single-call object, a client can invoke methods on that object. A client has two choices for how it does this. The first lets the client use the standard new operator provided by CLR-based languages such as C# and Visual Basic (VB). With this option, the client application first tells the .NET Framework's remoting infrastructure various things, such as what channel to use, the type of the remote object, and a URL at which that object can be found. As with the server, this can be done either by using explicit calls or by referencing a configuration file. Note that to access a remote object, the client must know the URL at which it can be found (there's no built-in support for using a directory service such as Active Directory to learn this information). Alternatively, rather than explicitly passing the remoting infrastructure the information required to access the remote object, a client can specify this information in a configuration file, just like the server. Whichever approach a developer chooses, the client code can now create instances of the remote object using the new operator.

A client can use the new operator to access a single-call object

A client can also use Activator. GetObject to access a single-call object

If a developer is willing to forgo the relative convenience of using the standard new operator, she can use another approach for accessing a remote single-call object. Rather than setting up the configuration information and then calling new, a client can instead call the Activator class's GetObject method. The parameters to this call include the type of the object to be accessed and the URL at which the object can be found. Instead of specifying these separately, as in the previous case, they're passed directly on this call.

In either case, the server actually creates the single-call object

Whichever choice is used, however, neither one actually creates an instance of the remote object. Instead, single-call objects are server-activated, which means that the server creates an instance of the object only when a method call actually arrives. And because they're single-call objects, the object is destroyed after the call completes.

Singleton Objects

One singleton object handles all client requests for a particular class

Like single-call objects, singleton objects are activated by the server. Accordingly, the steps required for the server to register and the client to access a singleton object are similar to those just described for a single-call object. The only difference is that the server specifies a mode of Singleton instead of SingleCall on its call to RemotingConfiguration.RegisterWell KnownServiceType or in the configuration file. On the client, the code is exactly the same as with single-call objects.

Singleton objects can maintain state between calls, unlike single-call objects

The behavior of the object is not the same, however. Unlike a single-call object, which gets destroyed after each method call, a singleton object stays active until its (configurable) lifetime expires. Since a singleton object isn't destroyed between calls, it can maintain state internally. Yet because the same instance is accessed by all clients that use this singleton, that state is potentially accessible by any of these clients.

If another client makes a call on a singleton class after the running instance of that class has died, a new instance will be created. This new instance will handle all calls from all clients until its lifetime expires. Note, however, that for a singleton object accessible at a given URL, there is never more than one instance of the class active at any time.

Client-Activated Objects

Even though a client can use the new operator to "create" an instance of a single-call or singleton object, the server doesn't really create this instance until the first method call from the client arrives. This is why these two choices are called *server-activated:* The server is in charge of determining when activation occurs. *Client-activated* objects, by contrast, are explicitly created when the client requests it. The server still does the actual creation, of course, since that's where the object is running—the name is something of a misnomer. Still, the distinction between client-activated objects and the two types of server-activated objects is significant. The most important difference is that with client-activated objects, each client gets its own object instance, and each object can maintain internal state specific to its client between method calls—the object isn't destroyed after each call. Instead, as described later in this section, each client-activated object has a lease that determines when the object is destroyed.

Each client gets its own instance of a client-activated object

Just as with the first two types of remotely accessible objects, the server must register the type before the client can access it. As before, this can be done either through explicit calls or via a configuration file. To create the object, the client can also make explicit calls, much like the previous cases, or rely on a configuration file. In either case, the client can use either the new operator or make an explicit call to the CreateInstance method provided by the Activator class. (GetObject can't be used with client-activated objects.) Both of these directly contact the server, which then creates an instance of the specified client-activated type. All calls made by the client to this object will be handled by this instance, and each client that creates a client-activated object of this type will have its own instance.

A client can create a client-activated object using the new operator or Activator. CreateInstance

One problem remains: When is a client-activated object destroyed? With single-call and singleton objects, the server decides when to destroy the object. With client-activated objects, however, the server can't destroy the object until it knows the client is finished using it. Theoretically, the client could tell the server when it's done with the object, but what happens if the client fails unexpectedly, or just forgets to do this? The server could wind up with objects that no longer have clients yet will never be destroyed.

A client-activated object is destroyed when its lease expires

To avoid this problem, each client-activated object has a lease assigned to it[2]. The lease controls how long an object can remain in existence. A client can set an object's lease time when that object is created, or an administrator can control default lease times. Optionally, each method call from a client can reset the lease timer to zero. If an object's lease time elapses, the lease manager in the app domain that contains this object contacts any *sponsors* of the object. If any of these sponsors wishes to renew the lease, the object's lifetime is extended. If not, the object can be marked for garbage collection. Clients can also explicitly extend the lease of an object or even set it to infinity, ensuring that the server won't destroy it prematurely.

.NET Remoting provides a diverse group of options

Remotely activating and accessing objects is inherently nontrivial. Is it better to provide many options, running the risk of making the technology too complex to use? Or should the design stay simple, supporting only the most common scenarios? .NET Remoting aims for a middle ground, offering built-in services for common situations while still allowing enough complexity to address more advanced applications. Pleasing everybody is hard, but .NET Remoting offers enough choice to please at least most of the people most of the time.

---

2. In fact, leasing is used to control the lifetime of all remotely accessed MBR objects, including those passed as parameters.

■ Perspective: Why Are There Two Separate SOAP Implementations in the .NET Framework?

.NET Remoting can use the SOAP Formatter to handle SOAP messages. ASP.NET Web Services also uses SOAP, although it provides its own code for this. On the face of it, this makes no sense. Why include two completely separate implementations of the same technology in the .NET Framework class library?

The short answer is: different groups, different goals. Recall that the goal of .NET Remoting is to communicate effectively across a network when both client and server are built on the .NET Framework. SOAP is used primarily because, when mapped to HTTP, it allows this communication to pass through firewalls. In ASP.NET, on the other hand, the goal is to interoperate with any other implementation of SOAP, not just with the .NET Framework. SOAP is used both because it can pass through firewalls and because it's supported by many vendors.

A primary result of these distinct goals is different approaches to mapping serialized CLR types into XML. .NET Remoting uses the SOAP formatter, which allows everything that can be expressed by a CLR-based application to be passed across the network, including private data members and more. ASP.NET's SOAP implementation is not so committed to full-fidelity transfer of CLR types. Instead, it strives to produce a purely standard XML representation in everything it transmits, so it uses the XmlSerializer class to serialize and deserialize information. Sending a serialized type across ASP.NET's SOAP implementation won't send any private data members, for example, since XML has no notion of private members. The XmlSerializer emphasizes faithfulness to XML's XSD type system, while the SOAP formatter used in .NET Remoting emphasizes faithfulness to the CLR types.

Where .NET Remoting targets the homogeneous case, ASP.NET's Web services are optimized for heterogeneity. Given the complexities engendered by different type systems and different vendors, the need for multiple implementations of the same thing shouldn't be so surprising.

Enterprise Services: System.EnterpriseServices

The types in System.EnterpriseServices allow access to COM+ services

Modern multitier applications often locate the bulk of their business logic in the middle tier. Much of the time, writing this logic with a technology such as ASP.NET is perfectly adequate. In some cases, however, especially for applications that need to be very scalable and require features such as distributed transactions, more is required. Prior to .NET, the Microsoft technology that provided these services was known as COM+. With the advent of the .NET Framework, those services are still available to CLR-based applications. In fact, the services themselves haven't changed much at all, but two things about them have: how they're accessed and what they're called. Now known as Enterprise Services, all of the traditional COM+ services for building robust, scalable applications are usable by applications written on the .NET Framework.

What Enterprise Services Provides

Classes that use Enterprise Services are known as serviced components

For a class to use Enterprise Services, that class must inherit from EnterpriseServices.ServicedComponent. Because of this, a class using these services is referred to as a *serviced component*. Serviced components have access to the full range of what Enterprise Services provides, including the following:

- Support for (possibly distributed) transactions

- Just-in-time activation (JITA), which optimizes server resources by allowing objects to exist only when they're needed

- Object pooling, which allows instances of a class to be pooled and reused rather than being destroyed and recreated

- Role-based authorization services that allow Enterprise Services to verify a client's role and then grant services only to clients in specific roles

One of the innovations brought by COM+ (or more correctly, by Microsoft Transaction Server, the original incarnation of this technology) was the ability to control what services a component received by setting attributes in a configuration file. In the .NET Framework, however, attributes are supported directly. Every assembly can have extra metadata represented as attributes, and attribute values can be set in the source code of a CLR-based application. This built-in support for attributes matches well with how COM+ provides its services, and so an Enterprise Services developer specifies what services should be used by including attributes directly in his code. And because it's sometimes useful to be able to change a component's attributes after the assembly that contains it has been installed, it's still possible to set or modify a deployed component's attributes if desired.

Serviced components use attributes to specify what services an application needs

Here's a simple VB.NET class that shows how attributes can be used to control the use of Enterprise Services transactions:

```vbnet
<Transaction(TransactionOption.Required)> _
    Public Class BankAccount
        Inherits ServicedComponent
    <AutoComplete()> _
    Public Sub Deposit(Account As Integer, _
                        Amount As Decimal)
        ' Add Amount to Account
    End Sub
    <AutoComplete()> _
    Public Sub Withdrawal(Account As Integer, _
                        Amount As Decimal)
        ' Subtract Amount from Account
    End Sub
End Class
```

This class, called BankAccount, inherits from Serviced Component, as is required for any class that wishes to use Enterprise Services. The class definition is also preceded with an attribute indicating that this class uses the Required setting for transactions. This means that whenever a client calls one of the class's methods, Enterprise Services will automatically wrap the work done by that method in the all-or-nothing embrace of a transaction.

■ Perspective: System.EnterpriseServices vs. System. Transactions

In Enterprise Services and its predecessors, support for transactions is bundled together with other services, such as just-in-time activation and role-based authorization. In fact, ending an Enterprise Services transaction also requires destroying any in-memory objects that were participating in that transaction. The people who designed this technology were smart guys, and so there's a good argument for grouping these behaviors together. That argument goes like this: Objects that use transactions, especially the more complex distributed transactions that Enterprise Services make possible, are typically part of an application's middle-tier business logic. This code needs to scale, and forcing transactional objects to be stateless (that is, to not maintain any in-memory state between transactions) is a great way to do this. Prohibiting objects from retaining state across a transaction boundary also eliminates the possibility of the object's in-memory state not matching the state stored in, say, a database involved in the transaction if an abort occurs that the object never learns about (which is possible). Since the primary purpose of Enterprise Services is to support scalable, transactional business logic in a middle tier, coupling transactions with instance management and other services makes perfect sense.

Yet separating the ability to control transactions from these other services would allow developers more flexibility and more choice. Requiring objects to be stateless just to use distributed transactions can seem a little extreme. Accordingly, System.Transactions doesn't impose this requirement. Instead, this new addition in version 2.0 of the .NET Framework is focused strictly on transactions, imposing no other requirements on an application.

It's important to understand, though, that the increased flexibility provided by System.Transactions also makes it easier for developers (not you, of course, but *other* developers) to do dumb things, such as allowing an object's in-memory state to differ from what's in the database after a transaction has aborted. Enterprise Services and its predecessors are like controlling parents. They know what's best for you—stateless objects for transactional middle-tier logic—and so they make you do the right thing. Used intelligently, System.Transactions allows the exact same behavior, but you're no longer forced into it. Instead, Microsoft has decided that you're now a mature, grown-up developer. Doing the right thing is left up to you.

The two methods in this simple class, Deposit and Withdrawal, each begin with the AutoComplete attribute (and since this is just an example, the code for these methods is omitted). This attribute indicates that if the method returns an exception, the serviced component will vote to abort the transaction of which it's a part. If the method completes normally, however, this component will vote to commit the transaction to which it belongs. Note that different attributes are applied at different levels. The Transaction attribute, for example, can be applied only to a class—it can't be set per method—while AutoComplete can be applied only on a per-method basis. If the developer of this application wished to add a method to check the balance, she might well choose to put this method in some other class. Adding it to the BankAccount class would require the method to use a transaction, which isn't generally necessary for this kind of simple read operation.

Attributes can be used to specify a class's transactional requirements

Many other attributes are available for controlling aspects of a serviced component's behavior. For example, the JustInTime- Activation attribute allows turning just-in-time activation on and off (although this feature is automatically turned on for classes that use transactions), while the ObjectPooling attribute controls whether pooling is used and, if it is, how large the pool will be. Other available attributes set application-wide options such as the name of the application.

Attributes can also be used to specify the use of other services

Enterprise Services and COM+

Unlike most of the .NET Framework, the code that provides COM+ services was not rewritten as managed code. Instead, the classes in System.EnterpriseServices provide a wrapper around the existing implementation that allows managed objects access to these services. In spite of this, serviced components are able to use those services without leaving

COM+ has not been completely rewritten as managed code

What's Next: Windows Communication Foundation

In some ways, all of the technologies described in this chapter do the same thing: Let developers build distributed applications. Each one addresses this problem in a slightly different way, and so each has strengths and weaknesses for a particular situation. Still, why have three similar solutions for what is really the same problem? The Microsoft people who control these technologies asked themselves the same question. The answer they came up with was Windows Communication Foundation (WCF).

Part of the WinFX technology suite, WCF effectively combines the functionality of ASP.NET Web Services, .NET Remoting, and Enterprise Services. It also provides a way to use queued messaging via Microsoft Message Queuing (MSMQ), along with a number of other features. Once WCF is available, applications that would have been built on ASP.NET Web Services, .NET Remoting, or Enterprise Services will instead largely be built on this new foundation.

Designed from the start for a world of interoperable Web services, WCF's core protocol is SOAP, although it supports an optimized binary protocol for WCF-only communication as well. WCF implements a full set of the WS-* specifications, allowing secure, reliable, and transactional communication using Web services. WCF also provides a variety of activation options, as in .NET Remoting, allows controlling transactions and other behavior using attributes, as in Enterprise Services, and more. A primary goal of WCF is to support the creation of service-oriented applications, the building blocks of service-oriented architecture (SOA).

While WCF provides the services of the various communication technologies that preceded it, it doesn't provide the same programming interfaces. Except for SOAP, it also doesn't provide the same protocols. A WCF application won't interoperate with a .NET Remoting application, for instance, and porting code from any earlier technologies to WCF will require at least some effort. Applications built using ASP.NET Web services will interoperate with WCF, however, and they'll also be easiest to port to this new foundation. Prior to WCF's release, it makes sense to create applications that use ASP.NET Web Services whenever possible.

WCF represents a big step forward for .NET developers. By rationalizing Microsoft's technologies for creating distributed applications, it lowers the bar for creating modern software. In the very complex world that confronts developers today, this certainly counts as progress.

the managed environment. As Figure 7-5 shows, key COM+ services such as transactions are provided using context information maintained by COM+ itself in unmanaged code. When this context is accessed, such as when a serviced component votes to commit or abort a transaction, that request flows across the boundary between managed and unmanaged code. Interactions among serviced components, however, remain completely within the managed environment provided by the

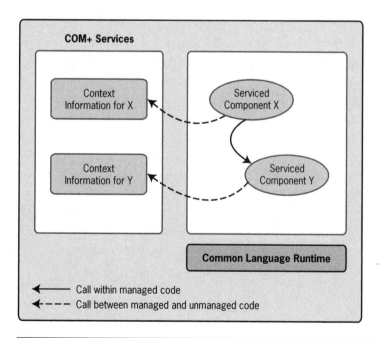

Figure 7-5   COM+ maintains context information for serviced components, allowing it to provide services across the managed/unmanaged boundary.

CLR. Since crossing into unmanaged code incurs a slight performance penalty, this ability to remain almost entirely within the managed space is a good thing.

An important part of standard COM+ is an interface called IObjectContext that contains fundamental methods for components to use. Perhaps the most important of these are SetComplete and SetAbort, the two methods that allow a component to explicitly cast its vote in a transaction. In Enterprise Services, these same methods are available through a class called ContextUtil. If a transactional method wishes to control its commitment behavior directly, it can do so by calling these methods.

The methods in the traditional COM+ IObjectContext interface are still available

Enterprise Services also has a few more artifacts of its foundation in unmanaged code. For example, when a serviced component is accessed remotely, that access relies on DCOM rather than on .NET Remoting. Similarly, serviced components must have entries in the Windows registry, like traditional COM+ components but unlike other .NET classes. These entries can be created and updated automatically by the Enterprise Services infrastructure—there's no need to create them manually—but requiring them at all betrays this technology's COM foundations.

Remote access to serviced components is via DCOM

Enterprise Services is an important part of the .NET Framework. While it's used by only a minority of applications, the services it provides significantly simplify the lives of the people who create those applications. And while its implementation as a veneer on the old COM+ introduces some messiness, this technology nevertheless succeeds in bringing these essential services into the .NET world.

Enterprise Services is essential to the .NET environment

Final Thoughts

Since its initial release in 2002, the .NET Framework has been used in thousands of applications with millions of users. Its success took a while, in part because .NET was launched during the worst IT recession in history, but surveys today suggest that the bulk of enterprise software development is divided more or less evenly between .NET and the Java environment. Competition is a good thing, and both camps continue to produce interesting new ideas.

The .NET Framework is a successful technology

Yet nobody would claim that today's technologies represent the last word in software development. Innovations keep appearing from Microsoft and others. Some of these ideas succeed, while others fail utterly. Yet whatever the fate of individual innovations, moving forward into the unknown space of new technology is guaranteed to remain the mainstay of software. The best is yet to come.

New ideas are the lifeblood of software

About the Author

David Chappell is Principal of Chappell & Associates in San Francisco, California. Through his speaking, writing, and consulting he helps information technology professionals around the world understand, use, and make better decisions about enterprise software.

David has been the keynote speaker for dozens of events and conferences in the U.S., Europe, Asia, and Latin America. His popular seminars have been attended by tens of thousands of developers, architects, and decision makers in 40 countries. He has also spoken at many universities, including the National University of Singapore, Moscow State University, and Sweden's Uppsala University.

David's books on enterprise software technologies have been published in ten languages and used in courses at MIT, ETH Zurich, and other educational institutions. He has been a columnist for several publications, and more than 100 of his articles have appeared in print. In his consulting practice, David has helped Hewlett-Packard, IBM, Microsoft, Stanford University, Target Corporation, and others adopt new technologies, create business plans, market new products, and train their sales staffs.

David's comments have appeared in the *New York Times*, on CNN.com, and in many other publications. Earlier in his career, David wrote networking software for supercomputers, chaired a U.S. national standardization group, and played keyboards on National Public Radio with the Peabody-award-winning Children's Radio Theater. David holds a B.S. in economics and an M.S. in computer science, both from the University of Wisconsin-Madison.

Index

BOOKS ONLINE

ENABLED

THIS BOOK IS SAFARI ENABLED

INCLUDES FREE 45-DAY ACCESS TO THE ONLINE EDITION

The Safari® Enabled icon on the cover of your favorite technology book means the book is available through Safari Bookshelf. When you buy this book, you get free access to the online edition for 45 days.

Safari Bookshelf is an electronic reference library that lets you easily search thousands of technical books, find code samples, download chapters, and access technical information whenever and wherever you need it.

TO GAIN 45-DAY SAFARI ENABLED ACCESS TO THIS BOOK:

- Go to **http://www.awprofessional.com/safarienabled**

- Complete the brief registration form

- Enter the coupon code found in the front of this book on the "Copyright" page

Addison
Wesley